DISTANT READINGS OF DISCIPLINARITY

WRITING RESEARCH, PEDAGOGY, AND POLICY

Elizabeth Wardle, Director of the Howe Center for Writing
Excellence at Miami University, Series Editor

DISTANT READINGS OF DISCIPLINARITY

Knowing and Doing in Composition/Rhetoric Dissertations

BENJAMIN MILLER

UTAH STATE UNIVERSITY PRESS
Logan

© 2022 by University Press of Colorado

Published by Utah State University Press
An imprint of University Press of Colorado
1624 Market Street, Suite 226
PMB 39883
Denver, Colorado 80202-1559

 The University Press of Colorado is a proud member of
the Association of University Presses.

The University Press of Colorado is a cooperative publishing enterprise supported, in part, by Adams State University, Colorado State University, Fort Lewis College, Metropolitan State University of Denver, University of Alaska Fairbanks, University of Colorado, University of Denver, University of Northern Colorado, University of Wyoming, Utah State University, and Western Colorado University.

∞ This paper meets the requirements of the ANSI/NISO Z39.48-1992 (Permanence of Paper).

ISBN: 978-1-64642-321-7 (paperback)
ISBN: 978-1-64642-322-4 (ebook)
https://doi.org/10.7330/9781646423224

Library of Congress Cataloging-in-Publication Data

Names: Miller, Benjamin (Poet), author.
Title: Distant readings of disciplinarity : knowing and doing in composition/rhetoric dissertations / Benjamin Miller.
Description: Logan : Utah State University Press, [2022] | Includes bibliographical references and index.
Identifiers: LCCN 2022040377 (print) | LCCN 2022040378 (ebook) | ISBN 9781646423217 (paperback) | ISBN 9781646423224 (epub)
Subjects: LCSH: Composition (Language arts)—Study and teaching (Higher) | Academic writing—Study and teaching (Higher) | English language—Rhetoric—Study and teaching (Higher) | Dissertations, Academic—Authorship—Research. | Online data processing—Authorship—Research. | Big data. | Research—Methodology—Data processing.
Classification: LCC PE1404 .M55 2022 (print) | LCC PE1404 (ebook) | DDC 808/.0420711—dc23/eng/20220920
LC record available at https://lccn.loc.gov/2022040377
LC ebook record available at https://lccn.loc.gov/2022040378

The University Press of Colorado gratefully acknowledges the support of the University of Pittsburgh toward this publication.

Cover image by Alissa DeBerry/Unsplash

CONTENTS

FOREWORD

Elizabeth Wardle

Roger & Joyce Howe Distinguished Professor of
Written Communication, Miami University

When I first proposed the creation of this book series Writing Research, Policy, and Pedagogy in 2016, I imagined that it would publish empirical research about writing, broadly conceived, and provide a much-needed outlet for writing studies research. This vision skirted some of the bigger conceptual and philosophical questions that these goals raised: what is "writing studies" and what is the "research" that moves forward the work of our field—and what "work" are we seeking to move forward?

These are the questions that Ben Miller raises and helps to answer in this beautiful, careful, and rigorous monograph. He asks what it is that our field is credentialing its members to do and what methods enable us to do that. To answer these questions, he builds a "macroscope through which to see" the larger disciplinary system, beyond our limited individual "direct experience" (10–11). His analysis seeks to move beyond his own "anecdotal readings" and instead draws on "large-scale data and metadata" compiled from the field's doctoral dissertations (16). Drawing on this data, he seeks to offer a "series of maps" of the broader landscape of our field (20). Rather than get bogged down in subjective questions about whether we are a field and what we should and should not name or do, Miller attempts to rigorously document "what has been present in the recent past" (21). What he offers provides a foundation that enables us to "make informed decisions—about curriculum, about research agendas, about how we represent the field to newcomers" (21).

Miller's work provides a way for us to understand not only a textbook definition of "research" but also what engaging in research looks like for new scholars in our field—what methods they use and how and how often. His analysis also illustrates *why* research is *used* in the work of new scholars: to theorize writing and language, to inform teaching practices, and (in most cases) both.

Miller's book is an important one for our field, whatever we may call that field and whatever our personal understanding of "research" may be. As we seek to influence the larger world(s) with which we engage, Miller helps us understand the various ways we can do and have done this.

I cannot imagine a better book to announce the move of the Writing Research, Policy, and Pedagogy book series to Utah State University Press.

ACKNOWLEDGMENTS

The book was made possible by generous funding from the University of Pittsburgh, including through the Richard D. and Mary Jane Edwards Endowed Publication Fund; the City University of New York; and an Emergent Research/er award from the Conference on College Composition and Communication. Big-data-sized thanks to ProQuest Dissertations and Theses (PQDT) for granting access to the dissertations analyzed here, and especially to Austin Maclean at PQDT for continuing to support my work throughout the long journey from my initial queries to final publication.

Many thanks go to the team at Utah State University Press/University Press of Colorado who brought this book to shelves, including my profound gratitude to Rachael Levay for encouraging me and this book from my first blind query through trickling chapters and on to final revisions, and for carrying the review process on swift wings. Thanks, too, to the two anonymous reviewers, whose kind words came as light in a dark moment, and whose advice for revision was both clear and clearly beneficial.

Thank you to the National Council of Teachers of English (NCTE) and the editors and reviewers of the NCTE journal *College Composition and Communication*, including Kathleen Blake Yancey, who first published an earlier version of chapter 3 in the September 2014 issue (66.1) under the title "Mapping the Methods of Composition/Rhetoric Dissertations: 'A Landscape Plotted and Pieced.'"

I owe a debt of gratitude to those who shepherded this project in its earliest stages at the City University of New York (CUNY) Graduate Center. Thanks to George Otte, whose insights into and questions about the visualized data shaped my sense of what topic modeling could show. Thanks to Mark McBeth, whose advice on time, workflow, and playful seriousness has sustained me for years. Thanks, especially, to Sondra Perl, for whom a single sentence truly cannot suffice. Your careful attention to both systematic analysis and phenomenological uniqueness modeled for me the breadth of commitments that one person—and how much more so, one field—can contain; your active listening throughout my graduate career pushed me to find the heart of still-inchoate intuitions;

your "Guidelines for Composing" continue to get me writing even (or especially) when I feel overwhelmed by competing possibilities. Thank you! Micki Kaufman provided essential guidance and code when I was just starting out with data visualization and corpus analytics: thank you, Micki. Thank you to all the faculty and students in the Interactive Technology and Pedagogy programs, and what was then called the Instructional Technology Fellowship, for giving me the confidence to keep exploring new tools until I find the right one for the job; particular shout-outs go to Steve Brier, Matt Gold, Kimon Keramidas, and Joe Ugoretz. Amanda Licastro, my collaborator and companion on so many academic quests: even though you weren't along for this one, our concurrent conversations have continued to inspire and energize me. Thank you!

At Pitt, Jean Ferguson Carr and Annette Vee have been incredible all-around mentors, reading numerous drafts and returning spot-on comments, steering the composition ship while offering steady companionship, and helping me find the balance between "what is done" and what is "done." Jean, thanks for sharing the wisdom of your years as a book series editor to help me better see my rhetorical situation. Annette, thanks for telling me directly what I needed to hear, whether that was a firm deadline or affirming my direction. The rest of my colleagues, too, are ever a delight and a wonder and a tremendously supportive group to be around. Particular thanks to Khirsten Scott for challenging me to think more deeply about the stakes and consequences of disciplinary and departmental identities. Thanks to Tyler Bickford for probing questions on how words are assigned to topics. Thanks to Alison Langmead for healthy doses of skepticism and equally healthy doses of good cheer. Thanks to Matt Lavin, Scott Weingart, Lou Maraj, Oriana Gatta, Elizabeth Pitts, and Annette (again!) for sharing workspace and time with me: you steadied me onward with your momentum.

I count myself incredibly lucky to be part of a near-daily virtual writing group of faculty from across the disciplines: Gemma Marolda, Marcy Pierson, Rika Asai, and Young Ji Lee. Just when trips to the coffeeshop became a health risk, you zoomed in to keep me honest about starting that pomodoro timer and accounting for my time. I could not have finished this book without you. Thanks as well, therefore, to Moriah Kirdy and Jean Grace at the William S. Dietrich II Institute for Writing Excellence, who arranged the faculty workshop through which we met.

Many, many thanks to S. L. Nelson and Andrew Thurman for taking on the coding of dissertation abstracts with me; you directly helped to build this macroscope. What fingerprints remain on the glass I apologize for. Thanks as well to Alyssa Hernandez, Emma Wolinsky, Janetta

Brundage, Michelle Hillock, Yuanton Rachel Li, and Michael Barmada for your efforts to pin down departmental and program affiliations of RCWS graduates, and to the Office of Undergraduate Research and the English department for sponsoring your time. It was not upon us to finish the task, but you made a great deal of progress when I could not, and I am grateful for every step you took forward.

Thanks, too, to my English department chairs while I was writing, Gayle Rogers and Don Bialostosky, for being reliable advocates for and sounding boards about the department's digital research futures. I appreciate the clarity you've striven to give me and hope this book returns the favor with clarity about composition's pursuits and how our program fits into the larger field.

Within that larger field, I gratefully acknowledge the pathbreaking inspiration of scholars of computers and writing, such as Derek Mueller, Collin Brooke, Jim Ridolfo, Bill Hart-Davidson, Dànielle Nicole DeVoss, Ben McCorkle, Jason Palmieri, Doug Eyman, and Cheryl Ball, who not only made it possible for me to justify this ambitious digital research project but were kind enough to bat around ideas with me at conferences and after speaking gigs. Thank you all!

I do not know how I would have finished writing without Spotify, especially once all the CD playing devices in my home passed into obsolescence. Though I cannot name every artist on every playlist here, I am grateful for their music; and, because I sometimes do take listening recommendations from acknowledgment sections, I'll mention that The Oh Hellos, Snarky Puppy, and Darlingside were in especially high rotation as this manuscript came together.

Thanks to my parents, Marc Miller and Judith Miller-Greenberg, my stepparents, Martin Greenberg and Rebekah Alpert Miller, and my parents-in-law, Michele and Allen Morrison, for listening when I tried to explain what I meant by "composition/rhetoric"; it may have felt sometimes like I would never finish this book, but you had the grace never to say so and to reassure me instead of the opposite.

Thanks to my children, Nathan and Aaron, who keep me on my toes and bring me back to the here and now when I start to zoom out too far. And my eternal gratitude to my wife, Sara Morrison, who puts up with my late nights, who spent extra time solo-parenting so that I could finish chapters and make presentations, and whose influence on my attitudes toward disciplinarity and research is immeasurable. It's not enough to say I love you. But it's a start.

DISTANT READINGS OF DISCIPLINARITY

OPENING

My son and I like to play with Legos. New sets often come with pieces wrapped off into several plastic packages, sealed up separately within the one box. I used to think these were meant to make it easier to find what you're looking for, to follow the instructions to build the set. But often it's turned out that the piece we actually need is in the other bag: we have to cut across what seemed like natural divisions to assemble the structure, machine, or character we're working to build. The separations, then, aren't as intentional, or as optimal, as they seem at first: maybe the pieces are where they are simply because of where they were made, which assembly line produced them, or maybe they were sealed off from new pieces just because the space was already filled. So we've learned to take out all the pieces, spread them across the floor or the table, and sort them—sometimes by color, sometimes by shape or size. We take stock of all that we have, and when we figure out what we need, it's that much easier to find.

Academia isn't made of plastic bricks, but it sometimes feels like all the pieces that are meant to interact and intersect are instead wrapped up in separate bubbles. Even within the supposedly single discipline of rhetoric, composition, and writing studies, you can feel the multiple packages crinkling in all those commas. Every graduate program aims to give its students enough of what the field has produced before them to make something new—to build structures of ideas, operational pedagogies, a professional, scholarly ethos. But which pieces of the past our graduate professors have on-hand to impart depends, in part, on where they "came up," on their own past graduate instruction. Which departments they land in depends, in part, on what faculty lines were open and which were already filled. Until we take the time to open up and sort through all the pieces of the discipline, to cut open the received packaging, it's hard for a graduate program, student, or advisor to be intentional about what pieces to choose. And that limits what we're able to build.

In this book, I spread out and sort through the components of graduate research in rhetoric, composition, and writing studies as it has emerged from many different packages.

https://doi.org/10.7330/9781646423224.c000

1

DISCIPLINARY ANXIETY AND THE COMPOSITION OF COMPOSITION

From the start, then, this field has been marked by its multimodality and use of starting points from a variety of disciplines, all marshalled to investigate a unique and pressing set of problems.

But what are the criteria by which a field may be judged a functioning discipline? The question is an important and tough one to answer.

—Janice Lauer, "Composition Studies: Dappled Discipline"

Determining who "we" are is no easy matter, but what "we" do may be one means of getting closer to that end.

—Brad Lucas, *Histories of Research in Composition and Rhetoric*

To declare oneself *a compositionist*, as I learned to do in grad school, is to risk a blank stare. The term shares something, I suppose, with *contortionist*, and maybe aptly so: it takes a few steps of untwisting to recover its origins in the act of *composing*, and I've never heard anyone talk about an intermediary of composition*ism* that might make it feel more natural. But more than that, the terms of the field it refers to—call it composition/rhetoric for the moment—are mostly not well known outside the field.

One reason, surely, is that what compositionists study—to keep it simple, we might call it writing—already seems familiar to nonspecialists. People write in nearly every profession; children learn to write in elementary school (or sometimes before), and, in short, writing is everywhere. It may not occur to some people that one *could* specialize in studying it, or, if they stopped to think about it, that some specialist somewhere would be able to say more about how it works in their life without actually living their life. (Indeed, not everyone who *does* specialize in composition/rhetoric would agree it could do that.) It's easy to see the need for, say, trained medical experts, and thus to attend to those

https://doi.org/10.7330/9781646423224.c001

experts, and thereby to pick up some medical language for use when interacting with (or avoiding) medical doctors. It's harder, I imagine, to see the need for trained composition experts, and that makes trained compositionists harder to see.

But another reason, I think, is that the nature of the training, and the terms with which to describe it, are themselves subject to rather a lot of debate, apprehension, and misapprehension.

Consider these three recent encounters.

Scene One. I greet a senior member of the literature faculty in the hall, and he asks what I am working on. I describe this book—a study of dissertations, to better understand my field's disciplinary parts and proportions, and possibly some central hub connecting its expanding spokes—and his curiosity is piqued. "And what *are* the lines of theoretical inquiry in your field?" he asks. It feels to me, in the moment, that *theoretical inquiry* is for him synonymous with *inquiry*, and this surprises me. While I am able to point to rhetorics of power or the role of digital media in identity formation, I sense I am leaving more out than in with such a description. How does theoretical inquiry encompass, or not, writing program assessment, or longitudinal studies of students and their writing across and outside of coursework? Is statistical analysis of a textual corpus a theoretical inquiry? Does it matter if it's not?

Scene Two. In students' weekly posts in the online discussion forum for my graduate seminar in composition studies, one question has been surfacing under various guises: how to apply the scholarship I've assigned to their teaching, which is then mostly of first-year writing, plus a few professional communication courses. Finally, after a week of readings about genre and activity theory, the frustration seems to reach a head. When I ask what they're thinking about, one student sums up why the readings don't feel meaningful to them: "What does this actually give us that we didn't have before? How useful is it to a student writing an essay or brainstorming or analyzing texts?" Though I do see connections to their teaching, especially for thinking about what motivates an audience to read on, or how writing "moves" circulate and change (and thus how brainstorming writers need to apply them in flexible ways), I can also see how the moves in these theory texts feel mismatched and unmotivating for this audience. But if these graduate students training as compositionists (if that's the right word) aren't part of the target audience, who is?

Scene Three. After an English department meeting, I am talking with a colleague, a fellow member of the graduate composition faculty, about programmatic identity. She asks, "What would you say is the big idea that drives our program? Not a work-in-progress, not a particular publication, but an idea we put out in the world?" When I hesitate, trying to encompass the wide range of projects I've seen from faculty and students, she continues: "See, and if *we* can't say that, what do people come here for?" I want to say: with all the MFAs in our student and faculty ranks, maybe it's not a big idea, but a little one: the idea that the wording of things matters, that we move in lots of different directions but always with an eye on writing *as writing*, as rhythmic and sonic and worth attending to, even at the sentence level. But that doesn't address her larger point: left only with words and sentences, without articulating our separately written sentences together (whether they add up into a poem or a paragraph, and so on into larger structures and socializations), how can we support each other, let alone our students? And even if I've come to that conclusion, privately, she's right that we haven't had a programmatic conversation about it. It's implicit, tacit, assumed, and for all I know assumed differently by each of us.

Each of these encounters highlights the challenge of explaining to the world, or even to ourselves, what it means to be "in composition." But it's less that the field has nothing to say, and more that we have too much to say; it's hard to synthesize simply. Taken together, they raise questions about identifying an academic field through research method or research focus, and even whether research is where we should locate identity at all. They also point to the importance of shared referents: without common language to talk about goals, our multiple goals feel atomized, rather than engaged in a push and pull for an overall direction. It's possible to form a complex whole out of many moving parts (even when some parts are moving in opposite directions), but it's difficult to see that whole from inside of it.

Discussions trying to encompass the big picture—to explain composition/rhetoric as a *discipline*—have often presented newcomers with either overly simple or overly chaotic understandings of "what counts." For example, to declare composition *A Teaching Subject* (Harris 1997) elides the work of researchers who study literacies and literate practices beyond the classroom, not to mention theorists and historians of such practices; to say, on the other hand, that it is a "dappled discipline" (in Janice Lauer's oft-quoted phrase), that is, to say it has many variations and influences, but to then stop there, doesn't tell anyone *how* it varies, or in what proportions.

How, then, do we talk about what's being credentialed by the PhD in composition/rhetoric? It's important that we're able to do so: the uncertainty has contributed to difficulty communicating the value of the field to stakeholders within the academy and without—and writing, being ubiquitous, has quite a few stakeholders willing to claim authority over it. It has also engendered concern about mismatches between graduate preparation and post-graduate responsibilities, whether in faculty positions or elsewhere.

The field *has* long been marked by a multitude of methods and interlocking purposes, as Lauer noted back in 1984. It partakes of not just humanities approaches but social scientific ones, too, with data drawn from interviews and surveys alongside historical and philosophical arguments, corpus analytics in large-scale collections jostling against small-scale case studies of individuals. And these areas of study aren't always cleanly separable. But rather than see this shifting of modes as a mark of shiftiness, I would suggest (like Lauer) that they mark us as open, welcoming the influx of a lot of currents. That does pose a challenge at times, to be sure. In order not to be buffeted by the waves, we need to put them into circulation: an ecosystem of complementary exchanges, rather than a single settled currency. And that requires some degree of familiarity with methods beyond those that any of us, individually, will use.

In order to improve our sense of what counts, we need to know what has counted—at a larger scale than direct experiences "inside" the swirl of the field can afford. In this book, I use algorithmic visualization of disciplinary metadata to better equip us to articulate how work done locally fits into larger contexts. Such visualization work, repeated over time and with varying datasets, can bridge across scales, advancing or expanding our sense of what a comp/rhet degree entails, and enabling more fruitful collaborations and thus more wide-reaching conclusions.

WHAT'S IN A NAME?

For now, we don't even agree on what the field itself should be called. The journal *enculturation* dedicated a double issue in 2003 (http://enculturation.net/5_2/) to "the relationship between rhetoric and composition," which engendered a series of meditations on rhetoric/composition (and rhet/comp); composition/rhetoric (and comp/rhet); rhetoric and composition studies; composition studies; composition-rhetoric; composition and rhetoric studies; writing; literacy studies; composition, literacy, and culture; and more. Around the same time, Charles Bazerman (2002) was making "The Case for *Writing Studies* as a Major Discipline" (emphasis added) alongside Susan Miller's (2002) separate argument for "Writing Studies as a Mode of Inquiry," both in the collection *Rhetoric and Composition as Intellectual Work.* As the shifts even within conversations and collections suggest, while some authors insist on distinctions among these terms (Sharon Crowley's [2003] *enculturation* article was titled "Composition Is Not Rhetoric," for example) or express preferences for one formulation or another (e.g., Cynthia Haynes [2003] meditated on the appropriateness of the slash, versus the hyphen or "and," in signaling both closeness and division), in many cases it seems clear that they are talking about the same basic areas of study, with the many terms not necessarily signaling different perspectives, or at least not consistently signaling the *same* different perspectives. For instance, some advocate for *writing studies* as a broad umbrella term, to signal that it's not just student writing in first-year composition courses that are being studied, while others resist the same term as too restrictive, directing attention only to alphabetic texts.

And the naming question hasn't been resolved, nearly twenty years later. A footnote disclaiming the use of multiple terms is a recurring feature of books in the field, including in the recent collection *Composition, Rhetoric & Disciplinarity*, in which, despite the book's title, the editors offer numerous points in favor of "Writing Studies" (Malenczyk et al. 2018, 4) before acknowledging that "throughout the book, chapter authors refer to the discipline in a range of ways: as Rhetoric and Composition, as Writing Studies, as Writing and Rhetoric" (that last a new one compared to my earlier list). They "felt these differences in nomenclature reflected the current state of the discipline, and so didn't attempt to regularize" them (2018, 11, fn1).

In this book I, too, will shift among these names for what I will also sometimes call, simply, "the field." In part, this serves purely to provide sonic variety—and I will often need to refer to the field as a whole, so there would otherwise be quite a lot of repetition. Beyond that end, I'm somewhat taken with Brad Lucas's argument that the fluidity of names for the field is metonymic to fluid and hybrid identities claimed by its members, which he suggested they (we) may adopt for pragmatic reasons—for example, to negotiate shifting cultural values or institutional positions (2002, 1–2). (That includes, I would add, to address confused responses when people don't recognize a descriptive term you start with, such as *compositionist*—or, for that matter, *rhetorician*. In such circumstances, taking a flexible stance on labels can give one a better chance at a strong second impression.)

But the term for the field I come back to most often is *RCWS*, an abbreviation that conveniently points to not one but two prominent organizational designations: "Rhetoric, Composition, and Writing

Studies," which is a forum (major division) of the Modern Language Association (MLA), and "Rhetoric and Composition/Writing Studies," a recognized field of study in the federal Survey of Earned Doctorates (SED). As Louise Wetherbee Phelps and John M. Ackerman (2010) have noted, the linking of *rhetoric* with *composition* in one phrase is probably "the most distinctive to the field and . . . the least likely to produce confusion with other disciplines" (190). Adding *writing studies*, though they did not put it in these terms, has the benefit of improving search engine optimization: whichever combination of terms are searched, there's a good chance RCWS (in either expanded form) has at least one.

That RCWS is included in the SED at all is the result of extended efforts by the Consortium of Doctoral Programs in Rhetoric and Composition (hereafter "the Consortium"), through their Visibility Project (Phelps and Ackerman 2010, 194, 199); data under that label goes back only to 2012. The MLA forum structure is even more recent: recognition of rhetoric, composition, and writing studies as a major area was still being contested in 2013 ("Draft Proposal, 11 September 2013: An Open Discussion of MLA Forum Structure" n.d.). Phelps and Ackerman's account makes clear that the process of attaining this recognition was far more complicated than simply asking to be included: codes in the SED, it turns out, are dependent on another list of disciplines, the Classification of Instructional Programs (CIP), a list whose instructional focus in turn inflects how disciplinary self-definitions in published scholarship are interpreted and valued (or not). Moreover, the CIP's oversight within the National Center for Education Statistics also means that stakeholders outside the field can decide (and did), independent of the Consortium's wishes or requests, to add "Creative Writing" as a subfield of "Rhetoric and Composition/Writing Studies" (Phelps and Ackerman 2010, 199) or to reject their proposed "literacy and language studies" as an alternate term for "rhetoric and composition" (200). Still, RCWS is a useful umbrella, even without attempting to annex creative writing, and its adoption in the SED makes it particularly apt for thinking about doctoral education, as I will throughout this book, in the fields and subfields of rhetoric, composition, and writing studies—however you imagine nesting them.

THE LOCAL IS NOT THE ONLY CONTEXT THAT MATTERS

One of my core goals in writing this book is to help build a macroscope through which to see the system out beyond any one of our local eddies, and thereby to help readers build what Derek Mueller (2017) calls a "network sense" of doctoral training in RCWS: "incomplete but nevertheless vital glimpses of an interconnected disciplinary domain focused on relationships that define and cohere widespread scholarly activity" (3). Ordinarily, our experience of these domains is limited to direct experience: people we interact with, texts we read, conference sessions we attend, classes we take or teach. But left as the *only* way we experience the discipline, those direct experiences are varied enough to also lead to a highly varied sense of what the discipline seeks to do and how it works.

Cindy Johanek (2000), in *Composing Research*, called out the way highly localized storytelling—anecdote—had, between the 1980s and the turn of the century, become the dominant form of evidence used in a wide range of composition studies journals. One outcome, she wrote, of "the rapid rise of anecdotal evidence, story-telling, and qualitative research" outside of a shared research agenda is to have "multiplied the ways in which the field can define itself" (21). In effect, by focusing on only local experience as a way of understanding writing studies, the field had by that time largely reduced a shared network sense of what everyone else was doing.

Resistance to scalable sources of evidence may explain the sustained anxiety around disciplinary status in RCWS—a longstanding pattern of worrying about whether it is a "real" discipline, usually framed as a question of whether it has a collectively shared research paradigm (in the sense of Thomas Kuhn). Richard Haswell, in a much-cited 2005 article with the provocative title "NCTE/CCCC's War on Scholarship," analyzed journal articles to demonstrate that "for the past two decades, the two organizations have substantially withdrawn their sponsorship of one kind of scholarship," scholarship that he called "RAD: replicable, aggregable, and data supported" (198). Throwing a gauntlet to the field, he wrote,

> What happens when a professional organization is at war with its own scholarship? What happens when the flagstaff organizations of a disciplinary field stop publishing systematically produced knowledge? The answers to these questions are not known because nothing like these events has happened in the history of academic disciplines. (Haswell 2005, 220)

In other words, Haswell claimed, "systematically produced knowledge" is part and parcel of disciplinarity in the academy:[1] without it, composition is not a discipline, no matter how many graduate students or tenured professors.

Similarly, Kurt Spellmeyer argued in 2003 that "comp, in spite of its expressions of contentment, is still not much of a discipline" (84). To become one would, for Spellmeyer, require two things: first, "an adequate *systemic* understanding of how [its] knowledge fit within a larger constellation of knowledges, some rising in value and influence, some declining, some moving to the center, and some moving to the periphery" (85, italics in original); the second, dependent on the first and a sign of its success, is that "the work we do [would] ever travel[] outside of the field" (84). Without being able to articulate to the outside world the nature of what Comp/Rhet's researchers, scholars, and practitioners know and do, the field renders itself irrelevant, if not invisible, to the rest of academia.

Spellmeyer and Haswell are far from the first to shed ink on the question of rhetoric and composition's disciplinarity, and they weren't the last. (Nor will I be.) Writing scholars have struggled in professional publications to articulate a disciplinary core since at least the mid-1980s, when two major studies of composition's collective efforts appeared in consecutive years, reaching opposite conclusions about the field's trajectory: George Hillocks's *Research on Written Composition: New Directions for Teaching* (1986) and Stephen North's *The Making of Knowledge in Composition: Portrait of an Emerging Field* (1987).

Calling his work a "meta-analysis," a term signaling a social-scientific perspective, Hillocks (with the help of a team of graduate students) aimed to aggregate the findings of empirical studies of writing process and writing pedagogy, to gain predictive power through increased sample size. Despite the absence of a grand unified model of how writing works and how we know it, he insisted, "Systematic and thorough reviews of research can help us to identify variables which might prove significant" (Hillocks 1986, 97)—and while "such variables can never be completely controlled, . . . the more teachers involved, the more reliable will be the generalizations emerging from the research" (99). At the core of Hillocks's study was the assumption that the research being done in composition could (and should) be compiled and aggregated, with homogeneity of findings across multiple contexts the measure of a given conclusion's strength. And, given the findings, he was hopeful: "We have a body of knowledge about the composing process which suggests something about teaching and which raises very interesting questions for further research," he declared in his introduction (xvi). "The climate for improving the teaching of writing has never been better. In short, although many problems remain, we have reason for optimism" (xvi–xvii). For Hillocks, then, the field's central concerns were clear, and they were twofold: gaining "knowledge about the composing process" and, by virtue of that knowledge, "improving the teaching of writing."

North was less sanguine on both the clarity of those goals and the prospects of achieving them. In *The Making of Knowledge in Composition* (1987), he called into question both the aggregability of research in the field and the centrality of teaching in that research. Motivated by a student's failure on their doctoral oral exams to produce a synthetic view of composition's knowledge-base (iv), North drew on his own experience and reading to survey the "modes of inquiry" by which knowledge is produced in the field (1), and thus "to provide that image of the whole" for himself (5). Working in this way, he located eight such modes of inquiry, clustered into three major "methodological communities":

- *Practitioners*, concerned with what works in classrooms on a day-by-day basis, sharing ideas mostly through storytelling (what North calls "lore" [23]);

- *Scholars* (historians, philosophers, and critics), working dialectically, primarily from texts, drawing on humanistic traditions; and

- *Researchers* (experimentalists, clinicians, formalists, ethnographers), working primarily from empirical observation, drawing on social-scientific traditions.

Each community, North claimed, held to an epistemology that was fundamentally at odds with those of the other two. Rather than working together toward a composite understanding of how writing "works," then, North saw these groups as talking past each other, at best, and at worst, competing unproductively for status (321 ff).

He concluded on a note of dire prophecy:

> If Composition is working its way toward becoming a discipline in any usual sense of that word, it is taking the long way around.
>
>   It might not be too much to claim, in fact, that for all the rhetoric about unity in pursuit of one or another goal, Composition as a knowledge-making society is gradually pulling itself apart. Not branching out or expanding, . . . but fragmenting: gathering into communities or clusters of communities among which relations are becoming increasingly tenuous. . . .
>
>   It is not difficult to envision what will happen if, as is most likely, these forces continue to operate unopposed in Composition. Quite simply, the field, however flimsily coherent now, will lose any autonomous identity altogether. (North 1987, 364–65)

More than three decades later, it seems clear that this dissolution has not come to pass: with over ninety doctoral programs identifying with rhetoric and composition ("Members" n.d.; Ridolfo n.d.), dozens of long-running academic journals,[2] and yearly attendance at the annual Conference on College Composition and Communication (CCCC) in the thousands, RCWS seems alive and well—if still actively debating the nature of its disciplinary status and direction.

How has this happened? Has composition/rhetoric overcome the methodological conflicts North identified by settling on one dominant mode of knowledge-making? Have we instead somehow attained an "inter-methodological peace" (North 1987, 369) based on the mutual understanding North hoped his book would help achieve? Or have we simply fragmented without noticing it, retreating into adjacent but separate rooms at shared conferences, maintaining several conversations that never meet?

Johanek, writing in 2000, seemed to suggest it's been more the latter, expressing with some dismay that "if it is possible for a field to become 'more preparadigmatic' as time goes on, composition seems to have done so" (22). Quoting Robert Connors's 1983 diagnosis that "as a research discipline we tend to flail about" (Connors 1983, 10, qtd. in Johanek 2000, 26), she voiced the hope that if we strive "to listen to each other and to create an inclusive research paradigm," it would "help[] us (at the very least) flail about less often and (even more importantly) understand why we flail about at all and (most importantly) help[] us find new ways to appreciate and engage in not just the kinds of research we like but also the kinds of research we need" (Johanek 2000, 26). In that sense, she was trying to push the field back from separate rooms into a shared space, centered on mutual understanding of disparate research methods—to foster the "inter-methodological peace" North had envisioned.

A similar motivation may be behind a recent effort to establish widely shared research-based claims in *Naming What We Know: Threshold Concepts of Writing Studies* (hereafter NWWK), edited by Linda Adler-Kassner and Elizabeth Wardle (2015). The NWWK project invited twenty-nine leading scholars to participate in an extended conversation on a wiki, with the aim of determining what declarative statements of transformative knowledge they could agree on. All together they proposed fifty-one statements, edited them extensively, and put into the book thirty-seven "final-for-now definitions of some of what our field knows" (Adler-Kassner and Wardle 2015, 3–4). The list draws on a broad understanding of "research," incorporating the conclusions of not only observational studies (undergirding concepts such as "Writing is informed by prior experience" and "Habituated practice can lead to entrenchment") but also philosophical reasoning (as in "Writing addresses, invokes, and/or creates audiences"; "Writing enacts and creates identities and ideologies"; "Writing involves making ethical choices," and many more) and reflections on writerly practice and lived experience ("Failure can be an important part of writing development";

"Writing involves the negotiation of language differences"), including teacherly experience (which seems to underlie, e.g., the threshold concept that "Text is an object outside of oneself that can be improved and developed"). Despite this variety, and despite the hedges of "final-*for-now*" and "*some* of what the field knows" quoted above, the book's reception seems to have involved some misapprehensions that empirical studies were privileged above other forms of knowledge-making (Sánchez 2018, 118) and that the very act of compiling a shared knowledge-base was dangerous: a "sedimentation of ways of thinking into norms" that would "foreclose too quickly on how our understanding of writing may change and develop over time" (Alexander and Rhodes, in Wardle et al. 2020, 20–21). In other words, NWWK's effort to bring people into the same room was met, in some quarters, with pushback—and, especially, pushback against methods that aim to systematically document writing practices.

The irony is that only a small part of NWWK derives from empirical evidence; much of it is, instead, based on reasoned (and therefore disputable) argument, in keeping with its framing through *threshold concepts*, characterized as both "transformative" and "troublesome" or "counterintuitive" to those not yet involved in the relevant communities of practice (Adler-Kassner and Wardle 2015, 2). In other words, then, the problem of methodological mistrust is at heart a problem of misrecognition. After North's *Making of Knowledge in Composition*, as Mueller (2017) points out, while "scholars have continued to produce discipliniographies,[3] or accounts of the field, . . . such accounts have resorted in large measure to localized cases" (8). It's as if decades of preference for direct, personal experience as the grounds for claims had made it difficult even for people steeped in the field to comfortably describe what others in RCWS do or how. "What we know" depends a lot on where we're looking from.

This problem of misrecognition compounds significantly when extended beyond one collection to the rapid flow of new growth, new studies, new arguments, new perspectives: there is simply no way to read it all, let alone to read all the precedent literature that engendered it, and so it's easy to get the wrong impression about what's out there. Mueller's proposed method of dealing with this "reading problem" (Mueller 2017, 7), which I take up and run with in this book, is what he calls—combining Franco Moretti's "distant reading" and Heather Love's "thin description"—a *distant/thin methodology* for disciplinary inquiry (Mueller 2017, 25–31), centered on the development of visual models built from databases to find patterns at scale (68). Framed in opposition to Geertzian "thick description," which builds from direct observation of scenes and extended narratives of events, and to New Critical "close reading," which examines single texts in isolation from others, a distant/thin approach compresses large quantities of source materials to data *about* the materials—that is, *metadata*—so they can be summarized and described succinctly: so they can be, in a word, abstracted.

Visual models, that is, function much like abstracts appended to articles: they simplify in order to amplify, and give us some indication of what to look for if and when we read on more closely (Mueller 2012, 197–98). And like any data graph, each abstracted visualization of disciplinary metadata enables us to see a great deal of information at a glance and therefore can often reveal or suggest systemic patterns that are not easily discernable at more fine-grained levels of detail. In short, visualizing metadata enables new metacognition.

DISCIPLINARY DESCRIPTORS

In one way, these techniques are thoroughly modern in that they are built on digital tools for compiling and analyzing large swaths of data (see, e.g., Lang and Baehr 2012; Ridolfo and Hart-Davidson 2015; Johnson 2015); in my particular case, the visualizations and accompanying statistics in this book were programmed in the R language (R Core Team, n.d.), and my code is available for inspection or modification on GitHub.[4] In another way, though, the core idea is actually an old one, making a bit of a comeback in the last few years. Concluding their write-up of the 2007 *Rhetoric Review* survey of doctoral programs in rhetoric and composition (still the most recently published, as of this writing), Brown, Enos, Reamer, and Thompson (2008) called for further large-scale research into graduate student identity and training. Noting the "many impediments to gathering accurate data in a timely fashion" through surveys, they nevertheless "strongly encourage everyone to *engage directly with data*" (339, emphasis added) when and where it can be found. Doing so from as broadly cumulative a perspective as possible, they argue, "will allow for our disciplinary identity to emerge" (339).

In writing about disciplinary identity, rather than rely on my own anec- dotal readings, in this book I draw on the large-scale data and metadata of a core knowledge-making genre in our field: doctoral dissertations.

As a measure of "disciplinary identity," dissertations have much to rec- ommend them: as Todd Taylor (2003) argued (citing Joseph Moxley), dissertation authorship affords a more democratic view of the field's membership than articles or books: whereas "it is estimated that about 10 percent of the professionals in any field are responsible for publishing about 90 percent of the journal articles and book titles" (Taylor 2003, 143), nearly everyone pursuing a career in the field writes a dissertation.[5] Moreover, a journal article is a momentary intervention in a particular argument, whereas a dissertation—given its role in academic hiring, especially at research-focused institutions—is a statement of how one wants to be seen, as what kind of scholar.

What's more, as Rosanne Carlo and Theresa Enos (2011) have found, the subjects of dissertations tend to be predictive of future changes in graduate core curricula: comparing areas of specialization between the 2000 and 2008 *Rhetoric Review* surveys of graduate programs with a follow-up survey in 2011 focused on core course revisions, Carlo and Enos found that "core curricula change is first displayed in the work of graduate student dissertations as they anticipate the flow and direction of the field" (2011, 210). Thus, to the extent that "graduate core curricula give a clear indication of the trends in our field and shape our disciplinary identity" because "curricula reveal the knowledge(s) we value" (2011, 210), dissertations even more so can help us anticipate the revisions and reshapings of that disciplinary identity if we observe shifts in dissertation practices over time.

Although dissertations, being a training genre—with real constraints on graduate students' time—do not encompass the full scope of what is possible in RCWS research, I see their constraints and status as learning instruments as a point in their advantage. By definition, dissertations are written by committed scholars who have sought out training in the discipline and sustained effort over a length of time (now averaging over 5 years). Conference presentations, though perhaps the more common form of disciplinary contribution—many people will present multiple times per year—do not require the same sustained engagement. For good or for ill, dissertations serve a gatekeeping function: before it can pass, a dissertation must be approved by a team of established scholars who recognize its work as being relevant to—and advancing the knowledge of—"the field," as locally construed.

The dataset I'm using can't capture everything about the field; nothing could. It's limited to one slice of time, 2001–2015, and my source of full-text dissertations, the ProQuest Dissertations and Theses database (PQDT), is fairly US-centric (though not exclusively so). In addition, it cannot show what (and, especially, who) is missing. Of particular note are the many students who intended to complete dissertations but did not; the scholarship they would have produced is not represented in the data I have to write about. And, as Xiaoming Li and Christine Pearson Casanave (2008) point out, doctoral student attrition is high, and likely to be especially so "for the so-called marginal groups: non-native speakers of English, the 1.5 generation of immigrant students, minority students, and other non-traditional students" (3), making the absence even more hard felt: we might have expected these students to take the field in directions not anticipated by more "traditional" voices. The metadata I received also did not include demographic information about the writers that were included, and in this study I did not undertake the formidable task of adding a layer to the data that would make an analysis by race or language background possible.

But one advantage of a programmed, database-driven method is that the data can be updated later, whether with additional documents or with additional attributes on which to filter or construct a new view. Mueller (2017), arguing for methods that go beyond anecdote, points out that a distant/thin approach does not replace but rather coordinates more local accounts of the field with each other, "re-associating them with the other perspectives on the ongoing, ever-shifting terrain" of the discipline (22). This is necessary "because the discipline is sufficiently complex that no one vantage point can claim an omnipotent, ascendant view of its totality" (22). But neither can any one distant/thin reading claim such a view; each new model is only an approximation, rather than an absolute truth, which is ultimately unreachable. In that sense, as Mueller puts it (citing Gregory Ulmer's *Heuretics*), "The visual models are not proofs, finally, but provocations; not closures, but openings; not conclusions or satisfying reductions, but *clearings* for rethinking disciplinary formations—they stand as invitations to invention, to wonder, as catalysts for what Ulmer described as 'theoretical curiosity'" (Mueller 2017, 4, emphasis in original).

IF THE TRUTH IS UNKNOWABLE, WHAT'S THE POINT?

By now, some readers may be wondering what's at stake in constructing such openings and vistas of network sense. Why do we need to rethink disciplinary formations? And haven't we tried enough times already? After all, the field has now produced so many articles and chapters and collections debating what composition is that even the backlash has a long history. As far back as 1993, Russell Durst was complaining that we'd spent "an inordinate amount of time defining the field, cataloging it, classifying it, and critiquing it" (qtd. in North 1997, 196). Why, the argument goes, should we care whether composition is a discipline?

Aren't we beyond the need for some shared paradigm? Doesn't post-modernism teach us that everything is radically fragmented anyway?

For example, Stephen North (1997)—in a dramatic turnabout from his earlier book—has urged composition researchers to give up the search for "some (imagined) cumulative disciplinary effort," which he refers to as the "founding Myth of Paradigm Hope" (195): a myth that compositionists invoke, he claimed, so as to summon or create an illusory collective body. Instead, he called for a proliferation of place-based studies of writing in practice, predicting with apparent enthusiasm, or at least relief, that "we will have more research more accessible more quickly, but it will also be both far less transportable and—though the term may seem unpleasant—far more disposable" (205).

Along those lines, Thomas Kent (2002) directly contradicted the findings and assumptions of Hillocks's meta-analysis: under the heading "*Writing Cannot Be Taught*," Kent argued that "if writing cannot be reduced to a process or system because of its open-ended and contingent nature"—a postmodernist premise he had spent the previous several pages defending, albeit one dependent on emphasizing *a* singular process over a plural set of process*es*—"then nothing exists to teach as a body-of-knowledge" (149).

Echoing North, David Smit (2011) called on the profession "to capitalize on the fact that it is now localized, historicized, and contingent, both theoretically and pedagogically" (230) by openly declaring that we don't—and can't—know anything cumulative or transferable about writing. Metaphorically speaking, says Smit, "there is no such thing as 'tree-ness'; there are only particular trees" (230).

Tempting though these isolationist positions might be, it remains the case that an oak is more like a pine than a porcupine. That is, despite infinite local variation, too-close attention to local details can mask larger patterns and trends—and ignorance of those patterns, to extend Spellmeyer's (2003) argument above, could have serious local consequences if it leaves us no way to argue for the value of our work.

Without a sense of what people do and have done in RCWS, even avowed members of the field may have trouble justifying the research agendas that so many graduate institutions require. Kristen Kennedy (2008) worried that graduate training in composition/rhetoric has been fairly consistently divorced from the work that most graduates will undertake (mostly teaching of undergraduates, especially in two-year colleges), and that, forced to choose between her research interests and her teaching interests, she chose teaching. But, she asked, doesn't the need to make such a choice signal a problem with the field's research agendas, which often center on arcane matters of self-definition *and repeated naming of crises* (without action to resolve them)? Invoking John Trimbur's lament about the field's "painful self-consciousness" and "nearly narcissistic fascination with self-scrutiny," Kennedy writes:

> Those lines, coupled with a reading of the fall 2003 special topics issue of *Enculturation,* nearly drew me over the edge. The questions debated by contributors: Do I teach rhetoric? Or composition? Or is it rhetoric-composition? To some, these questions are still of great importance, and ruminating on whether to use the dash or the hyphen and what that means served as the theme for a series of lively, engaging, and myopic articles that all tried to answer whether rhetoric—as art and theory—has lost its connection to composition—as craft and skill. Why, I thought, is this question still important? And perhaps more telling, why wasn't this question important to me anymore? (Kennedy 2008, 528)

In response, I would concede that the names of the field aren't especially important; it's one reason I've chosen to vary them throughout this book. But the substance behind the names is very much related to the question of how we frame graduate curricula, because it speaks to the question of what we expect PhDs in composition to *do*—which, in line with Kennedy's larger argument, has a lot to do with the conversations and interconnections among teaching, teaching-related research, and research unrelated to teaching.

Jillian Skeffington (2011) has argued that the mismatch Kennedy points to is largely a function of most rhet/comp programs' position within departments of English: the research backgrounds of program-founding faculty, and the research interests of other faculty in those departments making decisions about hiring, tenure, and promotion, tended more toward theory than toward pedagogy (62–63). With these programs now more established, we have an opportunity to decide, program by program, whether we are happy with the status quo or want to change it. As Rita Malenczyk et al. (2018) write in the introduction to their collection *Composition, Rhetoric & Disciplinarity,* one benefit of embracing disciplinarity would be "the opportunity to be intentional in our actions" (7), rather than accept our assumptions as commonplace and leaving them unexamined. To establish disciplinarity, though, requires a sense of the broader landscape of both teaching and research. This book offers one series of maps, constructed from one approach to that landscape, through the lens of what graduate students have researched.

A MORE CAPACIOUS DISCIPLINARITY

What North (1997) most criticizes in the "invocation" of paradigm hope is the Mosaic voice decrying composition research as bad science in need of reform (195)—a voice he identifies first in Braddock, Lloyd-Jones, and Schoer (1963), but which is just as surely visible in his own *Making of Knowledge in Composition* (1987). Unlike those earlier efforts to map the field, which tried to pin down and purify the field into a single shared direction, recent calls to examine the discipline are trying to pull multiple things in, and hold them up to the light—to celebrate diversity even as we look for common ground.

This more recent movement shows that "paradigm hope" never really disappeared, despite North and Smit and Kent, but rather evolved, and, if anything, seems to be experiencing a recent surge. Following on *Naming What We Know* (NWWK) (Adler-Kassner and Wardle 2015), we've seen several books in rapid succession aimed at building a shared language for articulating difference in pursuit of mutual goals: *Network Sense* in 2017; *Composition, Rhetoric & Disciplinarity* in 2018; and *(Re)Considering What We Know* in 2019, which acknowledges critiques of NWWK but then pushes forward to explore "*Learning Thresholds in Writing, Composition, Rhetoric, and Literacy*"—the new volume's subtitle, now adding a wider array of disciplinary labels to the earlier "writing studies." What all these books suggest is that what we know influences us, wherever we know it from, and it would be good for us to notice it.

I am issuing no jeremiads. Rather than bemoan something missing or worrisome or impure, in the pages that follow I aim to document what has been present in the recent past. Only with this shared broader context can we begin to make informed decisions—about curriculum, about research agendas, about how we represent the field to newcomers—in our own local contexts. And if we can better understand what we already have, we may find we already have what we thought we would need.

The question of whether Comp/Rhet has achieved "disciplinary status," as it has sometimes been framed, seems to assume there's some critical point at which a field achieves a sort of academic apotheosis, like a nuclear reaction becoming self-sustaining: it wasn't a discipline, and then it was, and is. But disciplines, like genres, are more varied and less cleanly bounded.

Writing in *Composition, Rhetoric, and Disciplinarity*, Gwendolynne Reid and Carolyn R. Miller (2018) advocate for an open approach to classification, "organized around socially perceived similarities based in multiple shared traits, with no rules defining membership and no single feature necessarily shared by all members" (89). Closed categories, they argue, "may lead to counterproductive debates over the criteria for inclusion and exclusion"—for example, how much teaching, versus theory, versus empirical research, should be required. By contrast, the lens of open classification allows us to instead think of disciplines "as continually emergent intellectual categories of networked interests, goals, and practices" (89), with "the scope and relations between research areas . . . historically contingent, [and] with divisions more provisional than 'real'" (91). Similarly, Elizabeth Wardle and Doug Downs (2018), in the same volume, suggest that disciplines are best understood as *radial categories*—George Lakoff's Wittgensteinian term for groups whose "membership is determined by closeness to or difference from" some underlying prototype: birds, say, or dogs, which vary widely in size, coloration, and behavior, but are recognizable nonetheless. As Wardle and Downs put it, this lens means "that it is fairly easy to establish participation in a discipline but more difficult to map its boundaries. A sociolinguist may clearly be a linguist but also look a lot like a sociologist or an anthropologist" (2018, 113).

In other words, *it's not just okay to have different members of the same discipline doing different kinds of work; it's the normal, expected state of affairs.* Sometimes these different strands of work will align in their goals, while at other times shared practices will pursue different interests, but so long as we can read across the strands, we'll continue to be able to knit them together in response to both familiar and new contexts.

At the same time, Wardle and Downs are not ready to shed all semblance of common ground. Drawing on the work of social theorist Andrew Abbott, they suggest that while disciplinary boundaries are permeable and shifting (and, especially, expanding), such boundaries "define what it is permissible *not* to know" (Abbott qtd. in Wardle and Downs 2018, 114, emphasis added): they set an outer limit of expectation. In other words, "disciplines specify not what one is *allowed* to read, but the bare minimum one *must* read for disciplinary participation" (Wardle and Downs 2018, 115, emphasis in original).

All the attempts to locate those boundaries, therefore, or to identify the prototype(s) at the heart of the radial category called rhetoric and composition/writing studies, are less about policing others against going too far and more about orienting ourselves toward one other. Robert Connors (1997), in the introduction of *Composition-Rhetoric: Backgrounds, Theory, and Pedagogy*, described his project as trying "to build a fire around which we can sit and discover that we do know the same stories, and dance the same dances. Historians," he went on, "may not be the shamans of the field, but we are the storytellers, spinning the fabric that will, we hope, knit together the separate, private stories of the researchers, the theorists, the teachers in classrooms" (18). To say we have a discipline is a way of saying that we are not laboring alone, that we matter to each other. Even if we're doing very different things, we can still be doing them together . . . or not. What's at stake is solidarity.

I would add to Connors that to effectively spin this fabric, which is to say, this disciplinary network, takes more than storytelling, important as histories are. We also need to know the present,[6] and to do so broadly we need ongoing access to data. As I have argued elsewhere, following Johanek (2000), "If we take seriously the value of individual, contextualized experience, we should also value the contextualizing power of large-scale, aggregate experience" (Miller and Licastro 2021, 7).

Thus, North's (1997) attempted absolution of the field's "paradigm guilt" hasn't taken hold in all quarters. Writing in the same collection as Smit (2011), Kristine Hansen (2011) prominently positions the ongoing quest for disciplinarity in her title, "Are We There Yet? The Making of a Discipline in Composition." The fact that her answer remains that "we haven't arrived yet" (237) doesn't undermine the element of hope in the word "yet," or in her concluding call to "conduct more and better research to build a stronger body of knowledge" (260). But we also need to build an index to that body of knowledge, lest it sit inert.

WHERE WE'VE BEEN, WHERE WE ARE, WHERE WE'RE GOING

I began this introduction by suggesting that even those who identify with rhetoric, composition, and writing studies don't know, necessarily, what it means to study rhetoric, composition, and writing. The chapters that follow bring the field closer to that knowledge, based on what a broad swath of scholars identifying with the field have recently decided should "count."

In chapter 2, "So What's Your Dissertation About? Subject Expertise in the Aggregate," I challenge the dueling hypotheses that graduate students in the field are either wasting their talent by being forced to apply their work to students and classrooms, or wasting their time by developing theories that do *not* hew closely to pedagogical applications. Using topic modeling to identify strands of discourse running through the collection of documents, I find that neither claim really has the full support of the evidence: a cluster of topics theorizing writing and language does form the biggest single cluster, but that cluster accounts for only a quarter of the corpus. Teaching-related topics form a content cluster of almost the same size, but it's less widely distributed than theory, suggesting that it's not simply forming the final chapter of all or even most dissertations. At the same time, close to 90% of dissertations include at least a little attention to both theory and applications.

Chapter 3, "How Do You Know? Unevenly Distributed Dappling in Dissertation Methods," takes up the question of whether research methods can serve as a unifying principle for the field: that is, if we are not all focused on the same content areas (as I show in chapter two), do we share frameworks for inquiry, kinds of evidence, or ways of evaluating that evidence? This question—which arguably could be traced to *The Making of Knowledge in Composition* (1987)—has often been framed as a distinction between humanistic, text-based approaches (the group North called "Scholars") and social-scientific, empiricist methods ("Researchers"). While North claimed that these two camps were by and large opposed or in competition, later scholars (e.g., Johanek 2000; Hesse 2018) have generally argued that RCWS necessarily draws on both social-scientific and humanistic approaches to research.

My analysis affirms, but complicates, this split: graduate student training, at least as reflected in dissertation projects, is greatly skewed toward "Scholar" approaches, and even within empiricist "Researcher" approaches, the phenomenological (presumed-unique, i.e., nonaggregable) methods of ethnography and case-study greatly outnumber more aggregable methods such as discourse analysis or survey. At the same time, while this pattern may hold at the majority of graduate programs, the data visualization makes clear that there are indeed locations where data-driven and aggregable methods are more common, and that a smaller number of dissertations engage in these methods even at more humanistically focused institutions.

The two chapters just described demonstrate the capacity of a distant-thin approach to intervene in longstanding debates in the field. Contradictory claims about the state of research can persist, unresolved, when they are based only in direct and local observations; while such perspectives are an important source of ethos and authority, they are also, by necessity, limited in scope. Moving to a more distant approach, and thereby incorporating more data, can surface not only large trends but also the less common areas of concern that could otherwise be hidden by the majority.

The analyses in chapters two and three are based on a set of dissertations known to have been completed within the Consortium of Doctoral Programs in Rhetoric and Composition, roughly 1,700 dissertations over fifteen years. But in the same time span, another ~1,900 dissertations were also submitted and tagged "Language, Rhetoric and Composition" in the ProQuest database by students in other programs, such as communication, education, history, and political science. What, if anything, is different about the kinds of training and focus developed in RCWS PhD programs?

In chapter 4, "But Doesn't Everyone Know about Writing? Distinguishing RCWS from Allied Fields," I highlight the combinations of topic and method that mark a dissertation as more likely to be from an RCWS program. From this angle, it becomes clear that a focus on pedagogy, collaboration, and even rhetoric is only modestly predictive of work in the field: these subject areas are roughly as common outside the consortium as within it. Narrative descriptions, too, are broadly acceptable within the academic genre of the dissertation across the programs in the dataset. Seen from departments outside the consortium, more distinctive topical features of RCWS graduate-level research include what I call a "move to the meta," a tendency to shift attention from individual writers to structural forces and systems, or from the thing studied to how we study things; this manifests in differential treatments of literacy, of rhetorical analysis, and of disciplinarity. Looking at aggregate methods, there are again more similarities than differences between RCWS and non-RCWS dissertations, with "scholar" approaches much more common than others; however, aggregable "Researcher" methods, such as Discourse Analysis and Experimental/Quasiexperimental studies, are significantly more likely to occur in departments not affiliated with RCWS. This pattern extends the one Haswell observed in journal articles and sharpens the contrast of aggregable versus nonaggregable program focus I discuss in chapter 3.

Though I have so far presented the fifteen years of these dissertations as a single object of study, changes and fluctuations are visible even within this span, such as increased attention to embodied rhetorics and collaboration, with a corresponding increase in the use of rhetorical-analytical methods. Chapter 5, "A Map Is Not a Manifesto," centers the ways that the data remains in motion, exposing the granularity (and the surprises) afforded by data-driven analysis. In so doing, I end with two important arguments about discipliniographic studies such as this one.

First, we don't need the field to be just one thing: we just need to be able to find our way. In a complex and dynamic landscape, large-scale mapmaking can enable "productive intersections for collaborative dialogue," as Whitney Douglas et al. (2018, 239) argued recently, even or especially when we feel like we "each [hold] pieces of a map of Rhetoric and Composition," but we cannot "see how they coalesce[] into a whole" (229). In other words, while analysis of metadata cannot promise to perfectly define the present state of a discipline, nor predict its future, it does offer a widely integrated view as opposed to a purely anecdotal one. What's more, the patterns we abstract from distant reading enable us to better contextualize the local findings of more traditional reading: they can corroborate—and sometimes challenge—what we have learned to expect through more direct, personal experience.

Second, maps like those in this book are not intended to be drawn only once. The disciplinary terrain is in constant flux, as individuals and departments negotiate their ways through overlapping and diverging interests. But to say that these maps of the field are impermanent does not erase their value. On the contrary, a core strength of an algorithmic approach is that we can repeat the experiment with different starting values. Thus, even if our answers aren't true for all time, they are at least demonstrable, updateable, and comparable to similar studies.

To make a map, then, is not to put up fences and raise the stakes but rather to record positions as they were at a moment in historic, moving time. And in comparing the present to the past, we clarify—for ourselves and for others—the choices we make going forward.

2

SO WHAT'S YOUR DISSERTATION ABOUT?

Subject Expertise in the Aggregate

> *Distant reading and thin description provide a necessary precondition to respect differences and find shared terms in the midst of intellectual diversity.*
>
> —Derek Mueller, *Network Sense*

The capaciousness of writing studies may seem a given to some readers. After all, writing itself is capacious: we write across disciplines, outside the academy as well as in; we write for writing's own sake and in pursuit of other ends. To study writing, we would have to follow writing everywhere it goes—which is to say, everywhere. Nevertheless, even when people agree that this *should* be how it works, among the many in-field laments about the state of research in composition/rhetoric is the feeling that writing studies as a discipline imposes too many constraints on the subjects that are authorized for study.

To take one representative example,[1] Karen Kopelson's (2008) article "Sp(l)itting Images or, Back to the Future of (Rhetoric and?) Composition" is interested in combatting an "entrenched" focus on the split between theory and practice in some "corners of the discipline," a split which she sees as instilling a "resultant pedagogical imperative" that "holds sway" over graduate students, with the result that "the conversation remains stalled" (Kopelson 2008, 752). After surveying graduate students and faculty, she comes away with what she sees as a "disturbing truth":

> that at least some young scholars are entering the field—are often beginning their dissertations— . . . *feeling preemptively constrained by what they perceive as a still primary focus on classroom-based inquiry.* They are joining the rhetoric and composition professional community with a sense of apprehension about a disciplinary future they fear is not "very bright." (Kopelson 2008, 758, emphasis added)

Sidney Dobrin (2011), similarly, surveyed "the past twenty-four years of scholarship in composition studies" and concluded that it "largely

https://doi.org/10.7330/9781646423274.c002

served to institutionalize the inflated claims that classroom-based research counts as the primary form of disciplinary knowledge and to marginalize theory except as a way to explain or support what happens in the classroom" (8). Summarizing the thrust of his proposals in *Postcomposition* (2011), he argued that "writing theory must move beyond composition studies' *neurosis of pedagogy*, must escape the shackles of classrooms, students, and management" (28, emphasis added).

. Yet only a few years before, David Smit (2004), in *The End of Composition Studies*, was asserting very nearly the opposite: that "composition studies needs to go back to basic questions" and "its primary reason for being—the teaching of writing" (2). From Smit's perspective, what's caused the conversation to stall is a *lack* of constraint in research, not an overabundance of it: the fact that "the past forty years have seen research and scholarship in the field proliferate in so many different directions" (2), "much of it only tangentially related to the teaching of writing per se" (6). It's easy to see the theory/practice split that Kopelson (2008) laments in Smit's (2004) summary of his book's argument—and also in Dobrin's (2011) insistence that applied theory is a *shackled* theory, not really theory at all. What's less clear is how these authors, reading across the field's scholarship, come away with such opposing visions of what's actually being produced in the name of writing research.

I'd like to suggest that central to the problem is the restricted vantage points from which they are looking out. In this, the authors cited above are not alone. Observers understandably tend to generalize from what they've been able to see and read themselves, directly, and there are sometimes good reasons to prefer a local view: it affords a certain kind of ethos and authority. But it also means the perspectives are necessarily limited in scope, making it quite possible to accurately describe two different tendencies that hold in separate parts of the field. While there is no place to stand from which we are not implicated by our own subjectivities, there are still steps we can take—and, I would argue, often should take—to consciously *expand* our default perspectives, so as to push *in the direction* of objectivity.[2]

To her credit, Kopelson (2008) conducted a survey to try to ground her claims in concrete evidence beyond anecdote; however, the survey was distributed only "at two large and long-established doctoral programs in rhetoric and composition" (753), so her claims about the state of graduate research in rhetoric and composition ultimately still rest on a small sample size. She reports neither the number of possible respondents, nor the rate of response, making it hard to know for sure how many people's direct experiences she's reporting on. To be fair, she does quote ten different students, in a small article; but consider, as a rough estimate of the possible grad-student cohort at the time, a five-year span centered on 2008 (the year the article came out): in that window, according to my dataset, the Consortium of Doctoral Programs in Rhetoric and Composition produced at least 650 PhDs.[3] Potentially, then, 98.5% of grad-student perspectives were not accounted for in the survey.

I don't mean to attack these authors or to suggest that there's little value in talking to a small number of people; on the contrary, there are clear benefits in the ability to follow up with additional questions or in limiting the locale of inquiry so as to have greater knowledge of its context. And Kopelson's (2008) argument that "at least some" students feel disinvited from pursuing theory, or compelled to always tie theory to practice, is affirmatively grounded in the experiences of those students she quotes.

What I am saying, though, is that findings with one small group, rather than being conclusive for the state of the field as a whole, instead raise a set of questions that can be investigated at a larger scale: *How often **do** doctoral dissertations in RCWS engage with practical applications, such as pedagogy or administration?* And conversely, *how often do they engage in theory? Are those things ultimately separate, or do they co-occur?* In this chapter, I include that line of inquiry in the course of a broader investigation, an attempt to characterize the range of subjects taken up by dissertation writers in the field.

As with so many binaries, the competition between teaching and theory may well be false: after all, that's what Gary Olson (2002) argued in "The Death of Composition as an Intellectual Discipline," a death he foresaw happening only if one or the other "side" were to "win" permanently over the other. Likewise, Jillian Skeffington, after tracing a decades-long "habit of framing major questions in the discipline in terms of these relationships," that is, "in terms of a pull between either theory and practice or rhetoric and composition," has urged us to "move beyond the perpetual expression of binaries, at least in the discussion of doctoral education, because questions of theory and practice alone do not define us as a discipline" (Skeffington 2011, 56). It's hard to disagree: real life is always more complex. Whether we recognize the mutual needs of theory and practice, or the institutional pressures favoring rhetoric or composition as the terms of identification, it's clear that RCWS is richer for its diversity of influences and source material.

Even so, I believe there still remains some value in investigating the sizes of the circles overlapping in the Venn diagram, because they have implications for pedagogical *and* theoretical inquiry, and for the health of the conversation between people reading and acting and interacting across the length of the spectrum. We cannot properly calibrate our sense of balance and understanding if we continually feel beset by overwhelming pressure from some opposing force. A broad-based, data-supported network sense[4] of how things stand will help.

FROM SUBJECTS TO TOPICS: WHY AUTHOR-SUPPLIED METADATA IS NOT ENOUGH

To better trace the many roads taken toward a PhD, I draw here on a corpus of 3,647 dissertations in the PQDT database marked by authors as working within the subject "Language, Rhetoric and Composition."[5] In this chapter, I will focus on a subcorpus of 1,684 documents that I could confirm were completed in a program affiliated with rhetoric, composition, and writing studies.[6]

I argued earlier that improved analysis of metadata should lead to improved metacognition. One might hope that the converse is also true: that, when asked to be metacognitive about their dissertations, which they know better than anyone, newly minted PhDs would supply high-quality metadata in the form of keywords and subject tags we could then simply aggregate. The reality is somewhat more complicated. Although every dissertation in PQDT is indeed labeled with author-supplied content keywords, these turn out to be of limited use for finding commonalities and trends. Of 3,436 keywords attached to 1,684 dissertations, on average each appeared no more than twice, and the median frequency with which they occurred was one—suggesting that these terms likely refer to specific features of each project, rather than any larger disciplinary inquiries to which those projects might belong. Even the top 3 keywords, occurring respectively 273, 196, and 147 times, are simply "rhetoric," "composition," and "writing": names of the field whose content we're trying to unpack. (And note that even the most common of these labels is attached to only 16% of the documents.) In other words, as far as the author-supplied keywords are concerned, there is essentially no overarching disciplinary project: just about everyone is doing their own new thing, on their own new terms.

To help counter this lack of overlap, which we might think of as a kind of folksonomic diffusion,[7] ProQuest also employs a taxonomy of fixed-vocabulary subject terms: for these terms, that is, they limit the freedom of authors to choose their own descriptors, and instead force them to choose from a preexisting list. The fixed vocabulary does improve matters somewhat: the top terms in RCWS from 2001–2015 include broad-yet-informative indicators such as Women's Studies (108 dissertations); Education, Technology of (79); and Education, Curriculum and Instruction (64). But they also include a lot of broad-yet-vague terms such as Education, Language and Literature (263) and Education, Higher (164); the latter, for example, includes dissertations ranging from ethnographic classroom studies to historical analyses of institutional archives to theoretical arguments about the nature of civil discourse. What's more, it's not always clear that the terms' meanings are consistently inferred by the graduating PhDs selecting them—a problem not made easier when the terms associated with particular subject codes change over time, as when 0681: Language, Rhetoric and Composition becomes 0681: Language and Literature: Rhetoric. These shifts, across which PQDT did not document the before/after names or the years in which they changed (S. Johgart and A. Hinkle), also confound efforts to quantitatively compare subject frequency over time. (The numeric codes were included with data I received for 2011–2015, but not for 2001–2010.)

Luckily, we are not dependent on author-supplied metadata, because algorithmic approaches exist for inferring topics from the full text of the corpus. (That is, from roughly 881,025 pages for my full corpus, and 388,884 pages in the subcorpus from confirmed Rhet-Comp programs.) In the following pages, I describe the primary methods I used to investigate the dissertations' contents—including a form of text mining known as *topic modeling*—and these methods' advantages and limitations with regard to the analysis of dissertations as data. Readers already familiar with topic modeling may wish to skip to the final paragraphs of the current section, where I outline the specific analyses and questions that make up the bulk of the chapter.

The simplest form of *text mining* would be to ask the computer to count the number of times each word occurs and see what words occur most frequently. However, basic text mining leads to problems for interpretation in that simple counts of word frequency cannot distinguish multiple meanings of the same grapheme: "program" could refer to a department, a curriculum, a piece of computer code, or a booklet distributed at the theater, each with very different implications for the focus of the texts that contain these words. Straightforward word-counting cannot account for the semantic differences between these various identical *tokens*—individual appearances of the same sequence of characters—and the underlying word *types* of which the tokens are merely instances.

Topic modeling, the primary technique I draw on for the remainder of this chapter, is a family of approaches that attempts to get around this semantic difficulty. Several excellent explanations of the underlying mathematics are widely available,[8] so I will here limit myself to a representative overview aimed at humanists. Based on the work of Blei et al. (2003) and introduced to composition by Clancy Ratliff and Jonathan Goodwin's online analysis of journal articles (Ratliff 2013), a topic model identifies clusters of words that tend to co-occur within documents, and in what proportions those clusters combine to form both individual documents and a large corpus.

Suppose, for example, that you had the following three dissertations:

A. In five classrooms: a descriptive study of "before writing teaching practices" in encouraging college writers to write

B. Inside the teaching machine: the United States public research university, surplus value, and the political economy of globalization

C. Entering the fray: the slogan's place in Bolshevik organizational communication

Through an iterative process of sampling,[9] the computer determines that A and B share one set of words, while B and C share a different set of words (figure 2.1).

In this case, the bin of words at the left seems to contain a list of words—a topic—related to classroom writing practices, while the bin at the right seems to be about power relations among social classes. Note that the word "class" appears in both of these topic bins, but with different definitions implied based on the associated words. By considering words in relation, rather than individually, a topic model is able to more sensitively detect meanings and usages—even without taking into account the syntactical context, which would add a considerable layer of complexity.

Though by no means infallible, topic modeling has a history of success in identifying semantic themes and subjects at a level of scale larger than any individual researcher could read. In particular, topic modeling has recently been applied to several large disciplinary corpora as a way of discerning trendlines in areas of concern within literary studies (Goldstone and Underwood 2014), philosophy of science (Malaterre, Chartier, and Pulizzotto 2019), classics (Mimno 2012), and history of biology (Peirson et al. 2017). Applying the same technique to Composition and Rhetoric, as I do in this chapter, will contribute to our understanding of both our own field and how it aligns with or differs from others. It will also ground that understanding in a revisitable set of data and procedures, making it "replicable, aggregable, and data-supported"

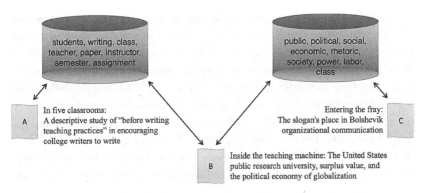

Figure 2.1. *Illustration of words affiliating into topics, and topics associating with texts.*

(Haswell 2005)—if not entirely free of subjectivity, because nothing is. My ability to interpret the topics *as* topics is dependent on having at least some familiarity with the range of possibilities within the field, even as the data-driven approach encourages the possibility of surprises. As I have argued elsewhere, "data doesn't speak for itself, but must be spoken *into* and *from,* based on deep disciplinary knowledge" (Miller and Licastro 2021, 8).

It is also worth noting in figure 2.1 that dissertation B contains words from both topics. This is a significant feature of topic modeling: it assumes that any given text[10] is composed of multiple interacting and potentially overlapping component parts;[11] the goal is to infer these parts, and their proportions, from an observed sample of the text. As Andrew Goldstone and Ted Underwood (2014) put it,

> If each article were about a single topic, we would only need to sort the articles into categories. But in reality, *any article participates in multiple thematic and rhetorical patterns* (4, emphasis added).

What is true for articles is, of course, especially true for dissertations, which not only vary thematically and rhetorically within each chapter but which can and often do include several different approaches or subjects from one chapter to another. (This variation stems from several overlapping needs and goals. In addition to a graduate program's incentive to send alumni into the world with wide-reaching expertise, the research itself may well benefit from triangulation, a desire to examine one's subject from more than one angle. The dissertation writers themselves may also wish to avoid feelings of one-note-ness as a matter of writerly self-efficacy: in prose as in poetry, tensions among multiple threads can produce useful energy that drives the writing forward.)

These distant readings, it is important to note, depend on close reading: the computer can find correlated lists of words, but finding names for such lists is generally up to the human researcher: the algorithm doesn't know what writing or rhetoric is, other than a recurring string of letters. One key interpretive task, therefore, is to assign labels to the topics that emerge from the algorithm, an iterative process that draws on existing familiarity with at least some of the possibilities—in this case, broad exposure to the discipline. To develop the labels I use in the sections that follow, rather than rely on the most probable words alone, I inspected the abstracts and author-supplied metadata for dissertations with high levels of each topic. To help counterbalance the prominence of words common across the full range of topics, which do not help distinguish one topic from another, I also tested a measure of terms' relative specificity to each topic: TF-ITF (term frequency * inverse topic frequency).

A more detailed discussion of model selection and text preprocessing steps is reserved for appendix A, and the TF-ITF algorithm I used is described in appendix B. For now, suffice it to say that I trained the model on the broader set of 3,647 full-text dissertations, to facilitate comparisons across disciplinary boundaries in chapter four, but in this chapter I will discuss the proportions and ranks of the inferred topics as limited to the 1,684-document confirmed-RCWS subset. As in most topic modeling analyses in the humanities, I used the open-source MAchine Learning for LanguagE Toolkit, or MALLET (McCallum 2002) to perform the training. I performed subsequent data analysis using custom scripts in R (R Core Team, n.d.; RStudio Team 2019). Because I am interested in discerning the common lines of inquiry in RCWS, only the most prominent topics, and their terms, are discussed in detail below; the full list of topics and the terms associated with them will appear in appendix C.

Some degree of researcher bias is unavoidable, but to minimize the degree to which the labels I use reflect my own subjectivity, I report not only my assigned labels for topics but also the terms associated with them; and I will discuss the ways the topics relate to one another, hopefully clarifying and triangulating the algorithmic signals I am interpreting.

In the remainder of this chapter, I will (1) discuss the top three and top ten most frequently occurring topics in the aggregate corpus, and their implications for what is and isn't an "allowed" research area in the field: for example, whether there is an "imperative" to include or to exclude

pedagogy; (2) examine what it means to have multiple topics represented within individual documents, through a middle-distance reading
of representative examples; (3) consider a different measurement of
topic prominence, what I call the *topical reach* across documents, as a
further measure of what topics have been considered sufficient and/or
necessary by a broad array of dissertation committees; and (4) explore
clusters of similar or related topics, and the combined proportions (by
aggregate frequency and reach) of such clusters within the corpus, as
an indicator of the field's stable areas of focus—and the limits of such
throughlines. That is, I will first establish what single topics look like in
this model; then examine single dissertations; then look across dissertations; and finally, survey the full array of topics.

Taken together, these analyses extend our view of the field's graduate research agendas beyond individual anecdotes, past surveys of a few
schools, and toward a more complete representation of the areas into
which dissertation work is driving composition, rhetoric, and writing
studies. The resulting map of concerns will help graduate researchers
and their advisors to calibrate (and, I suspect, broaden) their sense
of what is possible, what is common, and what is rare or even novel in
PhD-level studies. More than that, by identifying clusters of topics using
a deep search of full text, this distant reading approach also surfaces
shared lines of inquiry that might not turn up in library searches of only
the most prominent keywords—lines of inquiry that can then be better
brought into conversation and collaboration.

WEIGHTS AND MEASURES: WHAT ARE
GRAD STUDENTS WRITING ABOUT?

In this first analytical section, I want to zoom in on a small number of
topics in the model, showing the keywords and dissertations that are
more associated with those topics than others, as a way of clarifying what
it means to say that these terms represent "topics" at all. I'll start by
describing the individual topics that account for the greatest numbers of
tokens (words) in the aggregated RCWS corpus. These topics, in other
words, answer the question: if we were to pour out the content-bearing
words of all these 1,684 dissertations and sort them into piles of related
ideas, what would the largest word-hoards be about?

At first blush, no one topic dominates the field. The top 10 most
prominent topics, presented in table 2.1 and table 2.2, each represent
only 3–6% of the words in the corpus. (This overall contribution for
each topic is provided in the second column of each row of each table.

The tables' third and fourth columns provide two ways of labeling the topics: first, an algorithmically generated list of twenty keywords strongly associated with that topic, as described in appendix B; second, an interpretive label that I added for ease of discussing what subject matter the topic seems to signal, using the process described above. The titles of the top three such dissertations are provided in the final column of the table, along with the percentage of the text within those dissertations that the model associates with the topic in that row.)

Despite their small absolute size, the top three topics (table 2.1) showcase in a nutshell the wide range of subjects that "count" in composition/rhetoric. It includes both descriptions of classroom writing pedagogy (what I've labeled Scenes of Teaching) and more theoretical discussions of how power circulates through discourse more broadly (labeled Rhetorics of Power, Conflict, and Politics). As single topics, teaching does edge out the rhetoric topic, but only barely; the difference is less than one percentage point of the words in the corpus. Narrowly ahead of them both is a topic I've called Disciplinary Formations, a meta-disciplinary exploration of, well, what counts in composition/ rhetoric. This potentially adds evidence to Kathleen Blake Yancey's (2018, 23) claim in *Composition, Rhetoric, & Disciplinarity* that we are now having a "disciplinary turn"—a development some have lamented as navel-gazing or careerist, as discussed in chapter 1, but which Yancey celebrates as "rejuvenat[ing]," with the potential to "organize the field and . . . set the agenda for forward progress" (2018, 31). Note that the top keywords for this top-ranked topic include both *pedagogy* and *theory*, both *composition* and *rhetoric* (along with *writing*): further evidence that these binaries and tensions have continued to structure the discussions of disciplinarity. Taken together, though, this combination of top topics suggests that the binaries are not collapsing one way or the other: as a discipline, both theory and pedagogy are well represented.

The titles, moreover, seem to conflict with the claim that theory is disallowed outside of the classroom: though some "critical discourse analysis" is, indeed, brought to bear on the "power and accommodation" in "a university ESL classroom," discourse is also analyzed in the context of global political arenas such as "Sulh and Sadat's peacemaking rhetoric," as well as in more abstractly dialectical terms ("Habermas' theory of communicative action," for example, or "an expanded theory of rhetoric" for "transforming social conflict"). Similarly, the analysis of composition's disciplinary history is cast, in part, through the lens of ideology.

This balancing continues throughout the ten top topics as ranked by portion of the corpus, the rest of which appear in table 2.2. In keeping

Table 2.1. The top 3 topics in the confirmed-RCWS corpus, as measured by aggregate percentage of tokens, span the purported theory-practice divide. N = 1,684 dissertations.

Topic rank	% of RCWS corpus	Most topic-specific keywords (TF-ITF)	Assigned label (topic #)	Top titles (% of diss. text from this topic)
1	6.6	writing composition pedagogy students teachers teaching english writers classroom disciplinary pedagogical textbooks rhetoric academic writer pedagogies discipline theory write compositionists	Disciplinary Formations (T32)	Reflecting a history, charting a future: A rhetorical analysis of composition anthologies (60%) One of ours: James McCrimmon and composition studies (60%) Constructing composition: History, disciplinarity, and ideology (57%)
2	6.1	students student class classroom writing instructors semester teacher teachers instructor assignment assignments composition teaching paper essay eng classes papers write	Scenes of Teaching (T49)	Response in real time: Bringing context to a semester's responses to student writing (56%) A critical discourse analysis of a university ESL classroom: Power and accommodation (54%) In five classrooms: A descriptive study of "before writing teaching practices" in encouraging college writers to write (51%)
3	5.2	discourse social public community identity power discursive discourses critical cultural process conflict dialogue political agency action values communication dialogic ideological	Rhetorics of Power, Conflict, and Politics (T21)	A pragmatics of power using Juergen Habermas' theory of communicative action (71%) Rhetorical in(ter)vention and the dialectic of conflict and conflict resolution: Sulh and Sadat's peacemaking rhetoric (53%) Transforming social conflict through an expanded theory of rhetoric (52%)

with the fundamental nature of a topic model as a detection mechanism for discourse streams, we see topics that hew toward a highly referential style (such as Reading Rhetoricians, Interpreting Philosophy, ranked tenth, with top words including *Burke, Aristotle, Plato, Kant, Gorgias, Nietzsche, Heidegger*, etc.) and others toward a more casual register (especially Personal Narrative and Oral History, leading off table 2.2 at rank 4, including *I'm, don't, it's, that's, you're, family*, and so on). Topics that emphasize direct observation (e.g., fifth-ranked Collaborative Learning, with social-science diction like *participants, data, interview, researcher, qualitative*, and *study*) are set against topics that emphasize

Table 2.2. Topics of rank 4–10, by aggregate percentage of tokens in the confirmed-RCWS corpus, continue to balance across dichotomies rather than reinforce dominance. N = 1,684 dissertations.

Topic rank	% of RCWS corpus	Most topic-specific keywords (by TF-ITF)	Assigned label (topic #)	Top titles (% of diss. text from this topic)
4	4.74	i'm don't it's that's school stories didn't write writing story lot people i've parents family life you're wanted experiences experience	Personal Narrative and Oral History (T26)	"A new lease on life": A narrative case study of an older adult, participant design writing group (50%) Trusting narrative beyond theory: One teacher's story (50%) Telling developments: Narrative interviews with writers as "acts of meaning" (46%)
5	4.69	participants research interview data interviews participant collaborative learning researcher qualitative study group collaboration community experiences researchers participation activity members writing	Collaborative Learning (T41)	That third hybrid thing: Locating a disciplinary view of collaboration and a conceptual model for exigency-based collaboration research (52%) Collaboration in a group of graduate writing teachers (48%) Listening to and learning from students: A case study of students' perceptions of collaboration in first-year composition (40%)
6	4.3	students faculty college writing education courses english colleges composition program teaching instructors programs student universities graduate curriculum academic higher developmental	Institutional Supports, Barriers, Constraints (T35)	University of Louisiana system freshman composition faculty: Instructor working conditions and student learning conditions (86%) Writing at the small liberal arts college: Implications for teaching and learning (59%) Exploring the Impact of WPAs' Leadership at Two-Year Colleges (57%)
7	4.02	visual memory images body image objects bodies art space embodied object affective experience meaning invention bodily design spatial brain materiality	Image, Body, Materiality (T2)	A memento of complexity: The rhetorics of memory, ambience, and emergence (57%) Bodies that move you: The rhetorical force of the dancing body (56%) Haptic visions: Rhetorics, subjectivities and visualization technologies in the case of the scanning tunneling microscope (52%)

continued on next page

Table 2.2.—*continued*

Topic rank	% of RCWS corpus	Most topic-specific keywords (by TF-ITF)	Label (topic #)	Top titles (% of diss. text from this topic)
8	3.77	literacy writing students literacies community classroom literate pedagogy reading critical practices service-learning learning education freire social texts experiences school print	Literacy Practices (T28)	Community action: A framework for egalitarian, reciprocal community engagement in the field of rhetoric and composition (44%) Redressing literacy narratives in composition (42%) Beyond hope: Rhetorics of mobility, possibility, and literacy (41%)
9	3.46	rhetoric rhetorical ethos audience argument arguments aristotle rhetor persuasion epideictic persuasive invention kairos rhetors classical pathos argumentation speech situation appeals	Rhetorical Frameworks (T33)	Practical reasoning as pedagogy: Chaim Perelman and the reasonable practice of argumentation in the composition classroom (43%) A brief history of topical invention in twentieth-century United States rhetorical studies (43%) The Human, the Machine, and the In-between: Identifying Rhetorical and Contextual Intelligence in Artificially Intelligent Programs and Device (42%)
10	3.05	burke aristotle truth plato philosophy burke's human philosophical rhetoric language kant gorgias nietzsche heidegger dialectic ethics thought dewey sophists art	Reading Rhetoricians, Interpreting Philosophy (T48)	Vico's counter-modern alternative: A new science of discourse (67%) The subject of ethos at the ends of rhetoric (53%) Writing beyond the art/chance binary: The ongoing debate about techne in rhetoric and composition (48%)

more abstract reasoning—such as ninth-ranked Rhetorical Frameworks, characterized by words like *argument(ation), audience, persuasion, ethos, kairos, epideictic*—alongside topics that explicitly connect material presence with theory, thus bridging a potential division between observation and reasoning. (See, for example, the seventh-ranked topic Image, Body, Materiality, with top words including *embodied, experience, object[s]* but also *meaning, memory, invention.*)

Given these top ten topics, which together account for just shy of half (46%) of the text in the analyzed corpus,[12] it would be difficult to say that doctoral programs in rhetoric and composition forbid students from developing theoretical arguments about the nature of writing; but it would be just as difficult to sustain a claim that the "teaching of writing per se" is only tangentially addressed. Both kinds of research are easy to find precedent for in recent graduate writing. Additional precedents visible here should also give committees pause before explaining that something "just isn't done"—or, to put that in a more positive light, the findings above should give committees license to support a wide range of dissertation writing styles and frameworks. For every graduate student worried that a dissertation is a difficult genre because it "has to be formal," we can point to the prominence of narrative, contractions, and personal pronouns (including first-person pronouns) to assuage that concern. Similarly, should grad students express anxiety around focusing too much on a single author or theorist, we've got examples of that, too. The Image, Body, Materiality topic, ranked seventh overall, demonstrates that expanded understandings of composing (e.g., the dancing body in motion) and of rhetorical action (e.g., microscopy) have a comfortable home in the field. If there's one thing we've learned about writing in all our time studying it, it's that writing is, as I suggested at the outset of this chapter, capacious: varied and adaptable. The same holds true even in the supposedly single genre of dissertation writing, even within a single consortium of doctoral programs.

ALL DISSERTATIONS ADDRESS MULTIPLE TOPICS

At the same time, it's worth remembering that none of these dissertations focus *exclusively* on the topics they exemplify, and as tables 2.1 and 2.2 also show, there is a good deal of variety with regard to how focused a given dissertation may be on a single topic. Though every dissertation shown above has the associated topic as its most common—which is to say, that topic accounts for more of the dissertation's words than any other single topic—the maximal percentage of this top topic in any given dissertation ranges from as high as 86% (Institutional Supports, Barriers, Constraints, in *University of Louisiana system freshman composition faculty: Instructor working conditions and student learning conditions*) to as low as 10% (Environment and Nature, a topic ranked thirty-ninth within the aggregate corpus, in *Toward sustainable literacies: An empirical study of journal writing in an ecocomposition course*). This variation is not surprising if we remember that topics are really sets of co-occurring words, with some sets related to methods of analysis and others to the objects being analyzed; even a dissertation laser-focused on one site of study will still move through several modes of discourse, and thus incorporate several

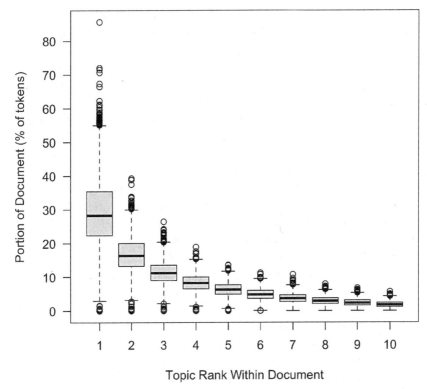

Figure 2.2. *Multiple topics are typically needed to account for even half of a dissertation's text. On the y-axis, proportions of text contributed by a given topic to an individual disser-tation, such that (e.g.) a value of 50% means the topic accounts for half of a dissertation's tokens. Each box-and-whisker shows the distribution of such contributions for the top-ranked, second-ranked, third-ranked (etc.) topic within each dissertation, ignoring which topics hold each rank. Box range shows the 25th to 75th percentile, with the median (50th percentile) contribution for that topic rank at the horizontal bar; dotted whiskers extend 1.5 times the interquartile distance.[13] Circles represent outliers. N = 1,684 dissertations from confirmed RCWS programs.*

topics (albeit at lower weight than that focal topic). At other times, we could expect the topical spread to be more evenly dispersed, as in the case I mentioned earlier, where various chapters consider a series of distinct methods or exhibits.

Even so, we can learn something about the expected topical focus or spread in a comp/rhet dissertation by describing, first, the *typical* distri-bution of topic weights, and second, alternate arrangements represented by relative outliers. The box plot in figure 2.2 shows the distribution of topic weights by their rank within individual dissertations—regardless of which specific topics hold those ranks—aggregated across the confirmed-RCWS corpus. As is standard for this kind of figure, the thick line in the center of each box represents the median value; the top and bottom of the box represent the upper and lower quartiles, respectively, so that 50% of the dissertations fall within each box; and the dotted "whisker" lines extend beyond that box for another 1.5 times the inter-quartile distance.[13] Data points lying beyond the whiskers (shown as circles) are considered outliers: unrepresentative of the distribution as a whole, but potentially interesting as edge cases. Many of the titles associated with the top topics in tables 2.1 and 2.2, for example, would appear in this figure as outliers above the leftmost box-and-whisker.

In the case of RCWS dissertations more generally, figure 2.2 shows that in fully half of the analyzed dissertations (represented by the box), the top-ranked topic accounts for only between 22% and 35% of the text, with a median of 28%, and the second-ranked topic represents between 13% and 20%, with a median of 16%. The third-ranked topic, for these middle two quartiles of dissertations, represents 9% to 14%, with 11% at the median. For topics beyond the top three, even the upper quartile lies at or below 10%, meaning that for 75% of dissertations in the dataset, each of the topics beyond their top three accounts for at most one-tenth of the included words (and often less).

The main takeaways from these numbers are twofold. First, a "typical" dissertation in comp/rhet is not focused solely or even primarily on a single topic, but instead requires a mixture of at least two topics to account for even half of its contents. The median dissertation (i.e., a dissertation with median values for all topic ranks) takes three topics to get just to that halfway point. One way to understand this is as an elaboration on the point made by Goldstone and Underwood (2014) that any text "participates in multiple thematic and rhetorical patterns." The distribution in figure 2.2 suggests that dissertations do not simply contain multiple topics; rather, their subject-matter focus is *constituted* by a multitopic cluster.

A second takeaway, though, is that topics beyond the top three in a given dissertation typically make up quite a small proportion of the dissertation's text: even the highest observed outlier topic for the fourth rank adds up to only about 20%. Typically, then, studying the top three topics—or top five, to be both generous and safe—will usually give a sufficient measure of what that dissertation is "about." The median dissertation's top five topics account for about 70% of the text; at the higher end of topical focus (75th percentile), these top five topics make up about 87% of the text; and even at the lower end (25th percentile), we'd be safely accounting for 56% of the text—still a clear majority of the dissertation—within the top five topics.

This pattern of top-topic proportions also makes clear that the dissertations listed in the top ten lists by topic (tables 2.1 and 2.2) are far more focused on individual topics than most dissertations in RCWS, with values for just the single top topic in the range of 40–80% of their respective documents. Therefore, while those dissertations are essential for clarifying what a given *topic* signals, and while the topics they represent further indicate sustained interests across doctoral writing as a whole, they are not, on their own, especially representative of RCWS dissertations as *documents*, written by individual graduate students. To better understand how dissertations integrate multiple topics—and to better understand what these topics look like in the context of real work, not just etherized upon a table, so to speak—let's look some more at the middle of the distribution.

Without wanting to put too much pressure on one dissertation, consider, as an illustrative case, Adela Licona's (2005) *Third-space sites, subjectivities and discourses: Reimagining the representational potentials of (b)orderlands' rhetorics* (Iowa State University), which falls very close to the median topic weights—that is, the midline proportions of topics at each rank, represented by the dark horizontal bars in figure 2.2. Licona's full abstract and top five topics read as follows:

> This dissertation identifies feminist third-space (both/and) consciousness in academic and non-academic contexts. Although dissimilar, both academic discourses and zines (self-published magazines) are comprised of complex rhetorical performances with implications for feminist practices of representation and the re-production of meaning. This dissertation analyzes academic third-space sites resulting from the crossing of disciplinary borders and activist zines as examples of nonacademic third space, with particular emphasis on representations of bodies and sexualities. Zines reveal (1) the transformative potentials beyond gender binaries; (2) the importance of revisioning histories; (3) the practices of what I term *reverso* (critical reversals of the normative gaze); (4) the deployment of *(e)motion* as embodied resistance; (5) the emergence of a coalitional consciousness and practices of articulation that have the potential to interrupt and reconfigure consumption patterns; and (6) the creation and mobilization of communities for social justice. (Licona 2005)

Here we can see three of the top-ten topics "in action," as it were, with Image, Body, Materiality (Topic 2) playing out in Licona's "particular emphasis on representations of bodies" and in her analysis of zines and

Table 2.3. Top 5 topics in a dissertation with median topic distribution. Topic weight and rank are given both for Adela Licona's (2005) *Third-space sites, subjectivities, and discourses* and for the RCWS corpus as a whole.

Assigned label (topic #)	Top words (by TF-ITF)	Topic weight & rank within doc (N = 1)	Topic weight & rank across corpus (N = 1684)
Reading (through) Feminisms (T38)	women feminist gender woman women's men female male power work feminism body family feminine girls social sex mother womens sexual	28.3% (rank 1)	2.5% (rank 16)
Image, Body, Materiality (T2)	visual memory body images image work space meaning experience art process material objects ways figure bodies sense text world time	16.6% (2)	4.0% (7)
Literacy Practices (T28)	literacy writing students practices work community social ways critical reading education texts classroom learning print pedagogy cultural literacies experiences school	9.5% (3)	3.8% (8)
Rhetorics of Power, Conflict, and Politics (T21)	social discourse public power community identity process cultural action critical individual analysis understanding values change people communication ways context language	8.0% (4)	5.2% (3)
LGBTQ and Gender Studies (T10)	gay identity sexual queer lesbian sex marriage sexuality jewish rights people lgbt gender activism violence jews men community coming lesbians	6.4% (5)	0.7% (40)

embodied resistance; Rhetorics of Power, Conflict, and Politics (T21), the third-ranked topic in the overall corpus, here accounts for a mere 8% of the dissertation, presumably in Licona's analysis of "the emergence of a coalitional consciousness" and "the creation and mobilization of communities for social justice." Both are strongly inflected by her feminist lens, an orientation to the work that is both explicitly named in the abstract and by this dissertation's top topic. I had already labeled this topic (T38) Reading (Through) Feminisms for the ways it seems both to structure rhetorical analyses and also to recursively assess or contribute to feminist theory itself—a double-orientation we see here in Licona's note that her sites of analysis are not only "comprised of complex rhetorical performances" worth studying as in themselves as "feminist practices of representation" but which also have "implications for . . . the re-production of meaning" and an expanded understanding of the contexts in which one can "identif[y] feminist third-space conscious-ness." This lens is further inflected by a particular concern for moving "beyond gender binaries," which shows up in the topic model through the presence of LGBTQ and Gender Studies (T10) in this dissertation's top five, despite its low frequency in the corpus as a whole (ranked for-tieth of forty-one content-bearing topics[14]).

The model, based as it is on the full text of the dissertation, also shows the strong presence of a topic that might not have been immediately obvious from the abstract alone: Literacy Practices (T28) emphasizes the ways that *literate* practices, in particular, are what's being considered in the analysis of "the crossing of disciplinary borders and activist zines," even though the terms *literacy* and *literate* do not themselves appear in Licona's one-paragraph abstract of her work.

In keeping with the pattern described more generally above, the top three topics in Licona's dissertation account for about 54% of the dissertation's content, and it is now more clear how the intersection of different topics might constitute a shared focus, especially where one primary topic is able to enfold or shape the inflection of those that fol-low. In this case, we might describe that combined focus as "embodied examples of feminist literacy practices," with the primary topic orienting the material and literacy analyses toward implications for feminism and feminist third-spaces more broadly. (I will further discuss the most com-mon topic combinations later in this chapter.)

BUT SOME TOPICS ARE MORE SINGULAR THAN OTHERS

An alternative pattern involves a single topic that by itself accounts for the majority of the dissertation. To find these, we can consider points at or above the upper whisker of figure 2.2, where the top-ranked topic alone accounts for 55% of the text. Here, for example, are the abstract and top five topics for Kate Brown's (2008) *Breaking into the tutor's toolbox: An investigation into strategies used in writing center tutorials* (University of Louisville):

> In this dissertation, I present the results of research conducted in the University Writing Center at the University of Louisville during the fall of 2006 and [which] serves as an example of an empirical study blend-ing qualitative and quantitative methods. It highlights and critiques the strategies tutors use to address students' concerns about their writing during writing tutorials by addressing two research questions: (1) What strategies do tutors employ during tutorials to address higher-order concerns? And, what strategies do tutors employ during tutorials to address later-order concerns? (2) How are these strategies perceived by

participants in tutorials? The data revealed that tutors tend to use three of the same strategies to address both higher-order and later-order concerns: Open-Ended Questioning, Reader Response, and Suggestion. Although tutors employed more strategies to address later-order concerns, which is congruent with advice from tutor-training manuals, they used these three strategies as default strategies throughout the observed tutorials. These strategies can be used effectively to address higher-order and later-order concerns; however, when used broadly, unique problems and potential pitfalls surfaced.

The data also revealed that strategies generally assumed by writing center scholars to lessen control over the student and his or her writing can be used just as easily as other strategies to dominate the tutorial. Other factors apart from the strategies themselves affect whether the tutor dominates the tutorial, including amount of time the tutor pauses to allow the student to answer questions or respond to suggestions, students' overall level of participation/interest in the tutorial, students' expectations for the tutorial, and tutors' listening to students' concerns (really *hearing* those concerns). Moreover, the use of praise and time spent on rapport building may have an effect on whether the tutor dominates the tutorial. These findings invite further investigation and research. (Brown 2008)

In Brown's abstract and topic distribution we can see how, even at 55% of the dissertation, a single topic can provide a sufficient focus and arena for an entire book-length project. Here, "writing center," "tutor," and "tutorial" are constant touchstones, with some form of those terms appearing twenty-two times in the twelve sentences of the abstract. Accompanying topics like Scenes of Teaching (T49), Writing Process (T18), and Collaborative Learning (T41) can, in this case, be nested within the research space carved out by the inquiry into writing centers, as they all provide ways of describing what happens in those writing center (WC) tutorial sessions. The final topic in Brown's top five, Disciplinary Formations (T32)—accounting for 9.1% of the dissertation text—stands in perhaps a different relation to that overarching thrust. Even so, it could reflect the degree to which the study's empirical approach builds on reference to "strategies generally assumed by writing center scholars," in that this topic often signals examination of the state of understanding within writing studies. If so, that literature review would, again, bear a distinctly writing-center slant even within the context of the disciplinarity-focused topic.

For dissertations with even higher proportions of their top topic—the outliers in figure 2.2, represented by circles above the upper whisker[15]—this enfolding pattern only intensifies. Because this suggests a degree of relative independence from other, more integrative topic combinations, it might be a useful metric for thinking about fields and

Table 2.4. Top 5 topics in a dissertation with relatively high top-topic focus. Topic weight and rank are given both for Kate Brown's (2008) *Breaking into the tutor's toolbox* and for the RCWS corpus as a whole.

Assigned label (topic #)	Top words (by TF-ITF)	Topic weight & rank within doc (N = 1)	Topic weight & rank across corpus (N = 1684)
Writing Centers (T27)	tutors writing tutor tutoring center centers tutorial student tutees session sessions consultants peer tutorials yeah conferences owl students um consultant	55% (rank 1)	1.3% (rank 28)
Scenes of teaching (T49)	students student class classroom writing instructors semester teacher teachers instructor assignment assignments composition teaching paper essay eng classes papers write	9.9% (2)	6.1% (2)
Disciplinary Formations (T32)	writing composition pedagogy students teachers teaching english writers classroom disciplinary pedagogical textbooks rhetoric academic writer pedagogies discipline theory write compositionists	9.1% (3)	6.6% (1)
Writing Process (T18)	writing writers essay feedback students write peer writer revision draft essays errors sentence drafts composing grammar paragraph sentences process comments	8.6% (4)	2.7% (14)
Collaborative Learning (T41)	participants research interview data interviews participant collaborative learning researcher qualitative study group collaboration community experiences researchers participation activity members writing	5.2% (5)	4.7% (5)

subfields in relation to RCWS. For example, professional writing and technical communication have sometimes been thought of as areas of focus within rhetoric and composition; at other times they've been considered "separate, rather than one subordinated to and within [composition]," according to Tim Peeples and Bill Hart-Davidson (2012, 54–56). Peeples and Hart-Davidson, pointing, among other things, to journals and book series (2012, 59–62), argue in favor of professional writing as a field in its own right. What does the evidence of dissertations point to? My dataset for this model consists of writing by PhD candidates within the Consortium of Doctoral Programs in Rhetoric and Composition, which does include programs and tracks in professional and technical writing, and can therefore point to differences in how students position themselves as they prepare to enter the field, or fields. While a topic model is not some perfect indicator of field independence or interdependence, and certainly should not be the only measure that matters in thinking about questions of disciplinary kinship and boundaries, it does provide one additional way of measuring how often certain topics stand apart or alone in organizing research. In other words, the more likely a topic is to produce highly single-topic-focused dissertations relative to the other topics in the dataset, the more likely it is that topic represents a discrete area of study.

As the boxplot of topic weights (figure 2.2) suggests, such outliers are far from the norm, but it turns out that the model does identify a handful of topics as more likely to dominate within dissertations than is otherwise observed. One of these is Writing Centers (T27), the top-ranked topic in Brown's dissertation, above. As shown in figure 2.3, the range of contributions when Writing Centers is in the top rank skews significantly higher than other topics ($p < .001$, Welch two-sample t-test).[16] In this figure, the "sample" in the boxplot at the left consists of all dissertations in the dataset where Writing Centers is the top-ranked topic; the "complement" is all other dissertations. The plot illustrates the degree to which the WC topic makes up more of the dissertations where it appears than other topics: what would be the 75th percentile of token-contribution for any other topic is only the median for Writing Centers, and conversely the median top-topic contribution for all other dissertations would be only a 25th-percentile WC dissertation. To put that somewhat differently, a highly focused dissertation like Brown's, discussed above, in which the top topic on its own accounts for more than 50% of the text, is not unusual for dissertations on Writing Centers, as it is for the rest of the dataset: it happens in about one out of every four WC dissertations.

Only one other topic in the model was as significantly offset above the norm: Technical Communication (T1; $p = 0.0005$), a research focus that, as discussed above, has already been suggested as essentially independent from RCWS more broadly. These higher top-topic values, indicating that one topic alone can account for the plurality or outright majority of the dissertation's text, support the idea that Tech Comm and Writing Center Studies are substantially distinct from the other topics in the model. However, that distinctness is not complete: it remains true even for dissertations in these focal areas that the median percentage of the text accounted for by their top topics is still below 50%.

To be clear, I show this range of possibilities not to imply that the level of focus found in dissertations is all over the place; rather, my intended takeaway from the distribution of topic proportions is that the topical

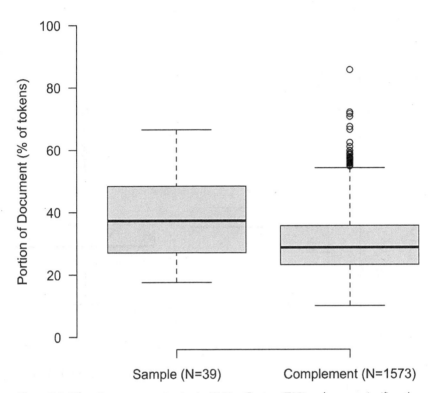

Figure 2.3. *When it appears as a top topic, Writing Centers (T27) makes up a significantly greater proportion of the dissertation than is typical of other topics. Left side, the distribution of within-document topic weights for topic 27 (Writing Centers) in dissertations where it is the most prominent topic; at right, within-document topic weights for top-ranked topics of all other dissertations. The distributions are different at a high level of significance (p = 0.0002, Welch two-sample t-test).*

focus is usually formed jointly among several topics. It's very rare that a third-ranked topic makes up more than 20% of a dissertation, but very common that the third-ranked topic makes up more than 10%. In other words, to assess what a given rhetoric-and-composition dissertation is about, we would want to look at least at the first two or three topics in combination.

ANOTHER VIEW OF "ABOUTNESS": TOP TOPIC COMBINATIONS

Thus far in the quest to understand what graduate students in RCWS are writing about, we've seen the individual topics that occur most

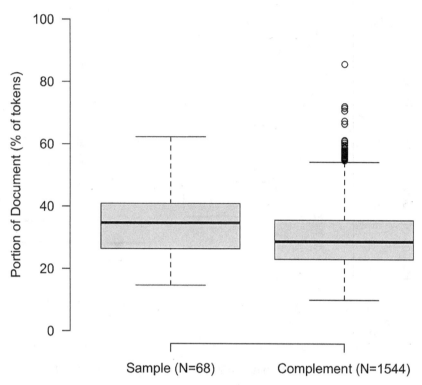

Figure 2.4. When it appears as a top topic, Technical Communication (T1) makes up a significantly greater proportion of the dissertation than is typical of other topics. Left side, the distribution of within-document topic weights for topic 1 (Technical Communication) in dissertations where it is the most prominent topic; at right, within-document topic weights for top-ranked topics of all other dissertations. The distributions are different at a high level of significance (p = 0.0005, Welch two-sample t-test).

frequently across the entire composite corpus, that is, the combined text of all the dissertations taken together (tables 2.1 and 2.2); and we've seen the degree to which the top-ranked topics in any given individual dissertation combine together to constitute that one dissertation's focus, regardless of which specific topics those are (figure 2.2). I then showed a few specific examples both of dissertations and of their top-ranked topics, as a way of clarifying how the model works: what a topic looks like, and how topics can combine to describe a document. I now want to extend the latter discussion by looking at the topics that appear in those top-ranked slots most often.

Disregarding for now *where* in the top three they occur, the most common combination of three topics at the top of a dissertation in the RCWS dataset is the blend of Image, Body, Materiality (T2), Rhetorical Frameworks (T33), and Reading Rhetoricians, Interpreting Philosophy (T48). This combination—which suggests a focus on how the three terms labeling topic 2 act rhetorically, as seen through the lens of particular theorists' work—occurs fifteen times in the dataset. As a most-frequent value, 15 out of 1,684 is not especially compelling: it includes less than 1% of the documents in the corpus. A handful of other combinations account for twelve to fourteen dissertations each, and then the frequency drops even lower from there. What this tells us is that, while the third-ranked topic does often provide an important inflection to a dissertation's subject-area focus, the selection of three-topic combinations, even allowing for order-changes to maximize overlap, is sufficiently varied as to preclude the detection of strong patterns.[17]

Instead, therefore, I want to focus for now on combinations of only two highly ranked topics per dissertation as an indicator of what subject areas most commonly command the attention of graduate-student writers. To ensure that the topics really were part of the dissertation's focus, I required that one of the two topics be the top-ranked in its dissertation, and looked for other topics that were frequently paired with it in the same dissertation—as either the second- *or* third-most-common topic, to increase the detection rate of these pairings. The top-line results of that analysis are shown in table 2.5.

Here, a version of the top three-topic combination seen above returns, but as only the eighth-most common pairing: Image, Body, Materiality (T2) and Reading Rhetoricians, Interpreting Philosophy (T48). Surprisingly, but in keeping with that reduction in rank, highly theory-focused topics like these are less represented here than in the aggregate top 10 presented earlier in the chapter (tables 2.1 and 2.2). Instead, the topics that recur are more like Scenes of Teaching (T49) and Disciplinary Formations (T32), which appear as part of the focal mix six and four times of the top ten, respectively—including twice in combination with each other. (The combined frequency when one is in the top slot and the other is in slot two or three is seventy-two dissertations, or 4.3% of the corpus: higher than any other two-topic combination.)

This does not necessarily mean that theoretical topics only rarely form the focus of dissertations, but rather that, if they do, they are less consistent in what secondary topics they pair with. Scenes of Teaching (T49) has a clear affinity with a pedagogically applicable

Table 2.5. Top 10 two-topic foci for individual dissertations. Most frequent combinations of two topics within dissertations when one topic is top-ranked within the dissertation and the other is in the top 3 for the same document. This lens emphasizes teaching and disciplinarity over theory and rhetoric. Total N = 1,684 dissertations confirmed to be from RCWS programs.

Top-ranked topic	Common pairing (rank 2 or 3 within diss)	Frequency of pairing (% of disses)	Rank by frequency of pairing
Scenes of Teaching (T49)	Collaborative Learning (T41)	41 (2.43%)	1
Disciplinary Formations (T32)	Scenes of Teaching (T49)	39 (2.32)	2
Disciplinary Formations (T32)	Rhetorics of Power, Conflict, and Politics (T21)	34 (2.02)	3
Institutional Supports, Barriers, Constraints (T35)	Disciplinary Formations (T32)	33 (1.96)	4 (tie)
Technical Communication (T1)	Collaborative Learning (T41)	33 (1.96)	4 (tie)
Scenes of Teaching (T49)	Disciplinary Formations (T32)	33 (1.96)	4 (tie)
Scenes of Teaching (T49)	Personal Narrative and Oral History (T26)	31 (1.84)	7
Scenes of Teaching (T49)	Writing Process (T18)	27 (1.6)	8 (tie)
Image, Body, Materiality (T2)	Reading Rhetoricians, Interpreting Philosophy (T48)	27 (1.6)	8 (tie)
Institutional Supports, Barriers, Constraints (T35)	Scenes of Teaching (T49)	25 (1.48)	10

topic like Collaborative Learning (T41), or with Writing Process (T18) as something likely to be discussed or studied in a classroom setting. Disciplinary Formations (T32), which considers the development of composition-rhetoric within the academy, makes a natural pairing with historical sites of that development, which includes Scenes of Teaching (T49) as well as Institutional Supports, Barriers, Constraints (T35). By contrast, a topic like Rhetorical Frameworks (T33)—ranked ninth in the aggregate corpus but absent here, and including common analytical terms such as *audience* and *argument*—can pair with just about anything.

In a way, then, the topic pairings in table 2.5 could help explain some of the perception, voiced by Kopelson and Dobrin, that teaching-related subjects dominate dissertation-writers: maybe it's just easier to envision how a classroom-based study would develop—for example, through personal narratives (T26) of collaborative learning (T41) or writing process (T18)—because it's easier to find a pattern in examples of dissertations that develop along these teaching-related lines than it is to find a pattern among dissertations on rhetoric or literacy. That doesn't mean, though, that theoretically focused dissertations don't exist. Maybe we just need computers to help us discern the patterns that are less obvious to human readers.

And so, having begun this section with three-topic focal combinations, and then moved to two-topic combinations, I want to close it with the single topics that most commonly occupy the top slot within their dissertations. While it's true that, as I established above, these topics do not in themselves usually make up more than half of their dissertation's text, they should nevertheless begin to tell us whether the practical focus of the two-topic combinations seen above is really the most common pattern, or whether theoretical topics, too, regularly form the primary seeds around which dissertations develop.

As it turns out, the top-ten list for topics at the highest rank (table 2.6) is overall quite similar to the top-ten list for the composite corpus, though there are a few key differences.

Image, Body, Materiality (T2) remains prominent, in fact moving up in rank: it is the fourth most-common top-ranked topic in the dataset, with seventy dissertations: over four times as many as we found when looking only for three-topic combinations. Its partner theory-invested topic, Reading Rhetoricians, Interpreting Philosophy (T48), remains in the top ten as well, adding another fifty-three dissertations, so that the percentage of dissertations focusing on one of these topics is closer to 8%: not a huge number in absolute terms, but still fairly robust, considering forty-one content-bearing topics were possible. Another topic that ranks high both by overall representation in the aggregate corpus and in the top slot is Literacy Practices (T28), which similarly seems not to have as many consistent partners as teaching and disciplinary formations. Given the ways literacy is distributed across academic, workplace, community, and home spaces, this is perhaps not surprising, but the correlation of the data with our prior expectations should give us more confidence in surprises that the data does reveal.

Three of the top ten topics by frequency as the largest topic within dissertations (table 2.6) are different from the top ten topics by proportion of the aggregate corpus (tables 2.1 and 2.2). Among those newly surfacing is Technical Communication (T1), one of the two topics discussed above as accounting for a significantly higher-than-typical proportion of the text in dissertations where it appears as the top-ranked topic. We can now see that this was the case for about one in twenty-five dissertations in the dataset, often enough to make Technical Communication the fifth-most-common topic to take that top slot within a dissertation; it was ranked twelfth as a portion of the overall corpus.[18] The two remaining new topics in this top ten list are Digital Media Affordances (T45), which moved

Table 2.6. Top 10 top-ranked topics within individual dissertations. This vantage is more balanced across theory and practice than topic pairs—and, relative to aggregate rankings, reveals hidden foci that were not visible in top topics aggregated across dissertations. N = 1,684 dissertations confirmed to be from RCWS programs.

Assigned label (topic #)	Top words (TF-ITF)	Count as top topic (% of disses)	Rank by count as top topic	Rank by portion of aggregate corpus
Disciplinary Formations (T32)	writing composition pedagogy students teachers teaching english writers classroom disciplinary pedagogical textbooks rhetoric academic writer pedagogies discipline theory write compositionists	132 (7.84%)	1	1
Scenes of teaching (T49)	students student class classroom writing instructors semester teacher teachers instructor assignment assignments composition teaching paper essay eng classes papers write	131 (7.78)	2	2
Institutional Supports, Barriers, Constraints (T35)	students faculty college writing education courses english colleges composition program teaching instructors programs student universities graduate curriculum academic higher developmental	90 (5.34)	3	6
Image, Body, Materiality (T2)	visual memory images body image objects bodies art space embodied object affective experience meaning invention bodily design spatial brain materiality	70 (4.16)	4	7
Technical Communication (T1)	technical communication design engineering workplace professional business team employees management information usability documents user engineers organizational document users company organizations	68 (4.04)	5	12
Personal Narrative and Oral History (T26)	i'm don't it's that's school stories didn't write writing story lot people i've parents family life you're wanted experiences experience	64 (3.8)	6	4
Literacy Practices (T28)	literacy writing students literacies community classroom literate pedagogy reading critical practices service-learning learning education freire social texts experiences school print	62 (3.68)	7	8
Digital Media Affordances (T45)	digital technology computers computer technologies hypertext online software electronic multimodal technological media composition writing composing selfe internet web design interface	61 (3.62)	8	15

continued on next page

Table 2.6—*continued*

Assigned Label (topic #)	Top words (TF-ITF)	Count as top topic (% of disses)	Rank by count as top topic	Rank by portion of aggregate corpus
Race and Ethnicity (T5)	african black race racial white racism american identity immigrants ethnic americans language cultural immigrant racist mexican whiteness asian color immigration	54 (3.21)	9	19
Reading Rhetoricians, Interpreting Philosophy (T48)	burke aristotle truth plato philosophy burke's human philosophical rhetoric language kant gorgias nietzsche heidegger dialectic ethics thought dewey sophists art	53 (3.15)	10	10

from fifteenth place as a portion of all dissertations to the eighth-most-common when considering only dissertations' most-prominent topics; and Race and Ethnicity (T5), with an even bigger jump from nineteenth place in the previous ranking to ninth by this measure, representing the top topic in about one in thirty-two dissertations.

What does it mean that these three topics, despite being among those most-often selected for a primary focus by graduate students, are less visible in a distant reading of the full corpus? For one thing, it points to a high degree of variability in how topics attain their high ranks in the aggregate list: while some dissertations take up technical communication, digital media, and racial or ethnic identity and spend a good deal of time and text on them, many others must all but avoid those issues, pulling the overall average attention-level down. Meanwhile, the top topics that they replace—Rhetorics of Power, Conflict, and Politics (T21), which had been the third-ranked topic by portion of the aggregate corpus; Collaborative Learning (T41), ranked fifth by the same measure; and Rhetorical Frameworks (T33), previously ranked ninth—must attain their high rank not through small numbers of highly focused dissertations but rather through lower-level attention spread more broadly. I will address the question of topic distribution across documents in the next section.

For another thing, though, even to say that there are topics persistently chosen but not widespread is to say that those topics are, in a sense, on the margins; they are, in the words of bell hooks ([1984] 2014), "part of the whole but outside the main body" (xvii). As in hooks's argument in the context of race and class as lacking in earlier feminism, this has a doubled and contradictory import: even as the marginalization remains a problem, the margin *remains*, even when unseen from the center, and only by seeing the center and margin together do we get a complete sense of the whole. This is why we need *multiple* digital lenses: the first pass would have left unseen the actual prominence of these topics.

Carmen Kynard (2013) makes a related point in *Vernacular Insurrections*, where she traces the joint histories of composition/rhetoric and Black freedom movements. Despite the white-centered narratives that have often dominated the origin stories of the field, from the Anglo-American Dartmouth Seminar to Mina Shaughnessy's introduction of basic writing at the City University of New York (CUNY), Kynard documents the extensive influence of Black student activists, artists, and writers on the educational environments in which comp/rhet was founded—including, crucially, at CUNY. As both her research and experience demonstrate, and as my own foregoing analysis of top dissertation topics affirms, race-conscious subjects that have been hidden by first-pass representations "are always right there in the mix, no matter how much you have been written out, spanning much wider than the token representation that you have been allowed" (Kynard 2013, 12). Kynard's use of the second person makes explicit the stakes of extending representation beyond tokenization: it's not just the *topics* of race and ethnicity but scholars, writers, and rhetors themselves (especially Black and Latinx scholars, writers, and rhetors) who get written out when the field acts as if those topics are not a major concern.

It's only a minor consolation that Race and Ethnicity (topic 5) is in the top ten list for primary topics taken up by RCWS dissertation writers: the model also shows that this topic is concentrated rather than distributed across most dissertations, which suggests that critiques of the field's race-blindness have not caused wide-spread corrections in light of those critiques, or led race and ethnicity to become part of the everyday language of all dissertation writers. At the same time, though, the thread has not been dropped: the evidence of table 2.6 demonstrates that the work not only continues but lies solidly within the scope of the discipline's accustomed pursuits. As I argued above, seeing these top topics listed should give graduate students and their advisory committees some reassurance that the intellectual work they signal is, indeed, valued within comp/rhet. In Kynard's (2013) words, "The light at the end of the tunnel is this: we have precedents, examples, and inspiration if we clear out what has gotten in the way" (248). There may always be more left *unseen*. But we can choose to take that seeming invisibility not as disincentive, but as invitation to look again, to look more closely.

A THIRD VIEW: TOPIC REACH ACROSS DISSERTATIONS

As I noted above, the shifts in topic rank between the aggregate-corpus approach and the top-topic approach point to an important distinction in how topics acquire their ranks in the overall corpus, with some becoming prominent through a large number of small references and others through a small number of highly focused studies. (In neither of those cases does it seem to be the result of a major constraint on topic selection.) This distinction is also visible in the example dissertations discussed earlier, in that topics from the aggregate top ten list appear in both Licona's (2005) and Brown's (2008) dissertations, but not as major players: each of the overall top three, for example, account for less than 10% of either text.

In this section, I probe the data for evidence of how widely distributed topics are *across* dissertations, regardless of where those topics rank *within* dissertations. If we think of the number of different dissertations showing a discernable presence of a given topic as representing that topic's "reach," we can rerank topics by that criterion rather than by their make-up of either the aggregated text or individual documents. The greater a topic's reach, the closer we might be to identifying an "imperative" of the kind that Kopelson (2008) believed pedagogy held over graduate students; or, viewed more positively, topics that are consistently present, even at small levels, would seem to form a shared touchstone across programs, a throughline for the discipline.

For the sake of argument, suppose "a discernable presence" means that the topic accounts for 5% of the dissertation's text: a rounded value taken from the lower hinge (4.87%) of the fifth-ranked topic in figure 2.2. (In other words, if you see a topic with at least this level of contribution to a dissertation, roughly three quarters of the time it will be one of the top five topics for that dissertation.) Table 2.7 shows the topics that "reach" more than 20% of the documents in the corpus by this criterion.

Notably, the top topics in this ranking are the same as by the overall contribution to the corpus discussed above, which treated all the text as a single aggregate "bag of words." Earlier, that is, we could not tell the difference between a few dissertations highly focused on the top topics and a large number of dissertations only briefly mentioning them; we were only measuring overall total mentions. Here, we are testing for the presence of the topic one dissertation at a time.

That the ranks of top topics are unchanged between these two views should strengthen our sense that these are important discursive throughlines for the field's self-understanding. The trend continues right up to the top: the top five are the same top five; the top three are the same top

Table 2.7. Top topics by "5% reach," defined as the percentage of dissertations (N = 1,684) for which the topic accounts for at least 5% of the text.

Assigned label (topic #)	5% reach	Rank by 5% reach	Rank by aggregated corpus	Top words (TF-ITF)
Disciplinary Formations (T32)	39.01%	1	1	writing composition pedagogy students teachers teaching english writers classroom disciplinary pedagogical textbooks rhetoric academic writer pedagogies discipline theory write compositionists
Rhetorics of Power, Conflict, and Politics (T21)	36.76	2	3	discourse social public community identity power discursive discourses critical cultural process conflict dialogue political agency action values communication dialogic ideological
Scenes of Teaching (T49)	33.79	3	2	students student class classroom writing instructors semester teacher teachers instructor assignment assignments composition teaching paper essay eng classes papers write
Collaborative Learning (T41)	32.84	4	5	participants research interview data interviews participant collaborative learning researcher qualitative study group collaboration community experiences researchers participation activity members writing
Personal Narrative and Oral History (T26)	29.81	5	4	i'm don't it's that's school stories didn't write writing story lot people i've parents family life you're wanted experiences experience
Literacy Practices (T28)	23.28	6	8	literacy writing students literacies community classroom literate pedagogy reading critical practices service-learning learning education freire social texts experiences school print
Rhetorical Frameworks (T33)	23.22	7	9	rhetoric rhetorical ethos audience argument arguments aristotle rhetor persuasion epideictic persuasive invention kairos rhetors classical pathos argumentation speech situation appeals
Image, Body, Mind (T2)	22.03	8	7	visual memory images body image objects bodies art space embodied object affective experience meaning invention bodily design spatial brain materiality
Institutional Supports, Barriers, Constraints (T35)	21.5	9	6	students faculty college writing education courses english colleges composition program teaching instructors programs student universities graduate curriculum academic higher developmental

Note: The reach column can sum to more than 100%. Consider a hypothetical topic that accounted for 5% of every dissertation. This topic alone would have a 5%-reach value of 100%, even though its aggregate contribution was still only 5% of the corpus.

three. Topic 32, which I've labeled Disciplinary Formations, is both the first-ranked by portion of the aggregate corpus and also the topic with the greatest reach across documents.

This is not guaranteed to be the case: at higher required levels of each document, the reach for these topics falls off at different rates, such that (for example) at a criterion level of 13%,[19] Rhetorical Frameworks (T33) drops down from seventh to thirteenth place, while Institutional Supports, Barriers, Constraints (T35) jumps up from ninth to fifth, and Scenes of Teaching (T49) rises from rank three to take the top slot—a configuration closer to the ranks by top-topic within dissertations (table 2.5 and 2.6). And these changes do point to some potentially important distinctions. For instance, given that Institutional Supports, Barriers, Constraints is the most administrative/WPA-focused of the top-ten topics, it seems noteworthy that its weight overall seems to come more from dissertations where it has a relatively higher focus than from merely having broad low-level reach, like some of the other topics shown in table 2.6. Administration, that is, looks more like a subfield than like an essential component of RCWS identity.

Nevertheless, the stability of the full set of top topics at the 5% criterion level may well signal a kind of hierarchy of obligatory nods in RCWS dissertations, whereby many graduate student authors feel the need to gesture toward these topics, even when they're not the true focus. In this interpretation, which aligns with Kopelson's (2008) idea of a "pedagogical imperative," PhD students with little or no research interest in, say, scenes of teaching, still feel compelled by tradition or the academic job market to describe assignments or classroom applications of the phenomena they spend the bulk of their time and energy on. But even if that's the case, the data make clear that pedagogy would not be the only such mandatory topic of discussion: a similar share of dissertations make at least glancing reference to critical theory and rhetorics of power, whether or not cultural conflict and political agency form the main thrust of the research project. Likewise for rhetorical terminology like *ethos* and *kairos*; for terms that recognize situated behaviors like *literacies, embodied,* and *practices*; and above all for the disciplinary framing terms of *composition* and *rhetoric* themselves.

These latter sets of terms also point toward a more positive interpretation of the same underlying evidence than the feared "imperative": the pervasiveness of these topics could represent a disciplinary lingua franca, a means of translating one's work to be more legible across subfields and subject areas. From this perspective, the gesture toward shared language can be a generous one, motivated less by unwelcome peer pressure and more by the pleasure of welcoming peers into new conversations, through vocabulary they're likely to find familiar.

Regardless of how dissertation writers may have felt in the past (and we know from Kopelson's [2008] study that at least some students felt less compelled *by* than compelled *into* some topics), we can emphasize this more positive motivation moving forward. In other words, having identified shared language through topic modeling, graduate students (and their advisors) can choose to use the network sense made possible by the model as an invitation to write inclusively, offering such shared language as a way into the areas of their preferred greatest focus.[20]

FROM TOPICS TO TOPIC CLUSTERS

In the previous section, I described the individual topics that, in their specific combinations of terms, are discernably present in a large number of dissertations. Sharp-eyed observers may have noticed that even the furthest-reaching of these topics, at a relatively easy-to-reach criterion (5% of a dissertation's text), reaches fewer than two-fifths (39%) of the documents. This, it's true, complicates our ability to draw clear conclusions about the field as a whole from the ranks of individual topics, unless we were to concede that there simply is no shared discourse that runs through even half of the graduate writing in rhetoric and composition in this time period. However, before we fully declare the death of that "paradigm hope" (North 1997), I'd like to offer a corrective measure: considering topics not just individually but in clusters. As we shall see, many of the conclusions drawn above about the mix of top subject areas are borne out in an analysis of consolidated topic groups.

The LDA topic model I'm using in this chapter, as implemented in the MALLET software, requires users to choose the number of topics ahead of time: I chose fifty topics based on an informed sense of their interpretability (see appendix A; see also Pääkkönen 2021), after experimenting with a range of possible values. But there is nothing inevitable about the topic sizes that result, even as their relative weights are still meaningful. In particular, choosing a greater number of topics would result in more narrow slices of the total corpus, while choosing a smaller number of topics would lead some of these topics to combine.

Consider, for example, the three topics in table 2.8. Topics 44 (which I've labeled Online Circulation and Media) and 45 (Digital Media Affordances) are clearly connected by their attention to digital technologies and what happens in those spaces, even as they have some different valences: they share top words like *online, internet,* and *digital,*

Table 2.8. Illustration of topic similarity/dissimilarity. Ranks shown in the last two columns are out of 41 content-bearing topics. Percentages attached to top titles are portions of those individual documents accounted for by the given topic.

Topic number	Assigned label (topic #)	Top words (TF-ITF) and top titles	Portion of aggregate corpus (rank)	5% reach across documents (rank)
T44	Online Circulation and Social Media	online blog blogs web internet posts facebook virtual users site media sites websites blogging digital posted website post user twitter	2.0% (20)	9.7% (21)
		Building an interdisciplinary framework for experience design: The use of social software in the aftermath of the London Bombings (56%)		
		Rhetoric, social media, and privacy (47%)		
		What we talk about when we talk about talking: Ethos at work in an online community (46%)		
T45	Digital Media Affordances	digital technology computers computer technologies hypertext online software electronic multimodal technological media composition writing composing selfe internet web design interface	2.7% (15)	14.4% (14)
		Mapping a geographical history of digital technology in rhetoric and composition (72%)		
		Toward a new literacy: Technology, policy, and control (46%) An art of emergent visual rhetoric (42%)		
T13	Politics, Empire, Radicalism	political politics democracy war radical violence freedom democratic critique power liberal capitalism public ibid social american revolution ideology critical ideological	2.5% (17)	14.4% (15)
		Without content: Rhetoric, American anarchism, and the end(s) of radical politics (47%)		
		Entering the fray: The slogan's place in Bolshevik organizational communication (47%)		
		Agent and Event: Rhetorical Dissent in the Context of Globalization (39%)		

and in some instances the top words in T44 are specific instances or applications of more abstract terms in T45 (*facebook* for *software*, for instance, or *blogging* for *composing*). It is easy to imagine how these could combine into a single "digital media" subject area. Topic 13 (Politics, Empire, Radicalism), on the other hand, feels less directly connected: while it's certainly possible (and even important) to talk about politics

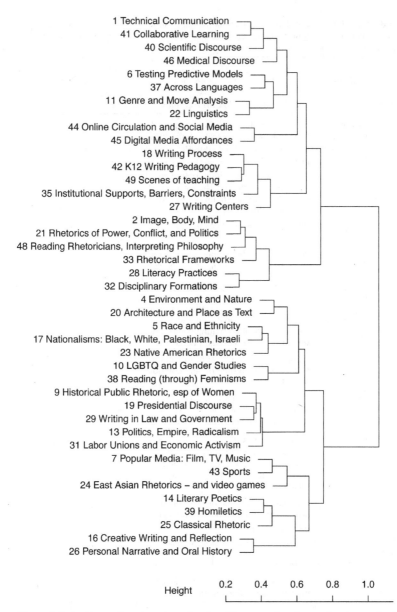

Figure 2.5. *Agglomerative clustering of topics. 41 content-bearing topics shown; for full list of topics, see appendix C. Distance matrix calculated using Jensen-Shannon Distance among topic-word assignment probabilities; clustering calculated using Ward's method.*

and power in digital spaces, it's also very possible to exclude the digital entirely from a discussion centered on this topic; it would not so easily fuse with the other two.

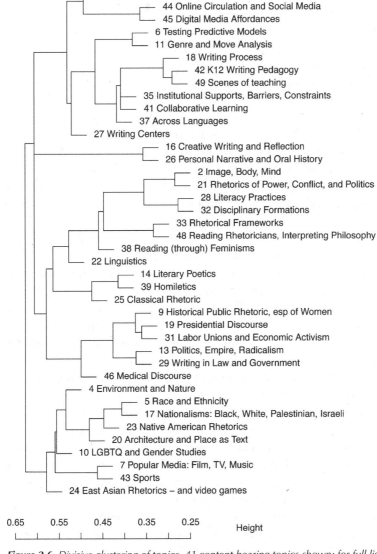

Dendrogram of diana(x = twm, diss = TRUE)

- 1 Technical Communication
- 40 Scientific Discourse
- 44 Online Circulation and Social Media
- 45 Digital Media Affordances
- 6 Testing Predictive Models
- 11 Genre and Move Analysis
- 18 Writing Process
- 42 K12 Writing Pedagogy
- 49 Scenes of teaching
- 35 Institutional Supports, Barriers, Constraints
- 41 Collaborative Learning
- 37 Across Languages
- 27 Writing Centers
- 16 Creative Writing and Reflection
- 26 Personal Narrative and Oral History
- 2 Image, Body, Mind
- 21 Rhetorics of Power, Conflict, and Politics
- 28 Literacy Practices
- 32 Disciplinary Formations
- 33 Rhetorical Frameworks
- 48 Reading Rhetoricians, Interpreting Philosophy
- 38 Reading (through) Feminisms
- 22 Linguistics
- 14 Literary Poetics
- 39 Homiletics
- 25 Classical Rhetoric
- 9 Historical Public Rhetoric, esp of Women
- 19 Presidential Discourse
- 31 Labor Unions and Economic Activism
- 13 Politics, Empire, Radicalism
- 29 Writing in Law and Government
- 46 Medical Discourse
- 4 Environment and Nature
- 5 Race and Ethnicity
- 17 Nationalisms: Black, White, Palestinian, Israeli
- 23 Native American Rhetorics
- 20 Architecture and Place as Text
- 10 LGBTQ and Gender Studies
- 7 Popular Media: Film, TV, Music
- 43 Sports
- 24 East Asian Rhetorics – and video games

0.65 0.55 0.45 0.35 0.25

Height

Figure 2.6. *Divisive clustering of topics. 41 content-bearing topics shown; for full list of topics, see appendix C. Distance matrix calculated using Jensen-Shannon Distance among topic-word assignment probabilities; clustering calculated using Diana.*

To generalize this insight across the topic model, I constructed figures 2.5 and 2.6, both of which show a hierarchical clustering of the forty-one content-bearing topics in the model.[21] Because each topic can be thought of as a vector of probabilities distributed across all the words in the corpus, we can find the distance from one such vector to another using a kind of high-dimensional Pythagorean theorem.[22] Figure 2.5 starts at the left with each separate topic-word vector, and at each branch point the algorithm joins the two vectors with the lowest distance between them, until all are joined: a process known as *agglomerative* clustering.[23] Figure 2.6 also moves from left to right, but through *divisive* clustering, an opposite process. In divisive clustering, each new intermediate cluster is constructed around the topic-word vector with the greatest distance from its current cluster mates (Maechler et al. 2019; Maechler n.d.). This process helps to empha-size distinguishing features at each step from the most zoomed-out (one megacluster) to the most zoomed-in (each topic on its own).

I'll present both figures in their entirety first, and then walk through the most interesting clusters in each—and how they change from one clustering strategy to the other. Please bear with me through this next complicated bit.

These diagrams are *hierarchical* in the sense that they don't uniquely assign a topic to a specific cluster but rather specify the order in which to form alternative clusters of various sizes, depending on where you "cut" the diagram, which is known as a *dendrogram* for its similarity to a branch-ing tree. (It helps if you squint, or haven't looked too closely at real-world trees.) For example, a vertical line drawn through figure 2.5 where the "height" reads 0.9 would cut the "tree" into just two groups; a little far-ther to the left, at a height of 0.75, would create four groups; and so on. In agglomerative clustering, groups of topics that cluster at relatively low heights (that is: toward the left in figure 2.5) are more similar to each other than topics that become cluster mates only high in the tree. Thus, for example, about a quarter of the way down from the top of figure 2.5, we can see that Online Circulation and Social Media (T44) and Digital Media Affordances (Topic 45) join with each other before they join with anything else, confirming our sense from table 2.8 that these two topics could also be seen as two aspects of one subject area.

Politics, Empire, Radicalism (T13), our third example from table 2.8, appears down at the opposite end of the diagram in figure 2.5: it would not join up with the other two until all topic clusters were combined into one. Instead it forms a local cluster with four other topics that, together, we might think of as considering Public Rhetorics and Political Writing: topics whose top distinguishing words, dissertation titles, and abstracts led me to label them as Labor Unions and Economic Activism (T31), Writing in Law and Government (T29), Presidential Discourse (T19), and Historical Public Rhetoric, Especially of Women (T9). (For

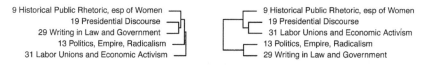

9 Historical Public Rhetoric, esp of Women
19 Presidential Discourse
29 Writing in Law and Government
13 Politics, Empire, Radicalism
31 Labor Unions and Economic Activism

9 Historical Public Rhetoric, esp of Women
19 Presidential Discourse
31 Labor Unions and Economic Activism
13 Politics, Empire, Radicalism
29 Writing in Law and Government

Figure 2.7. Minor differences of local clustering within an otherwise stable group. Agglomerative clustering shown at left (detail from figure 2.5) and divisive clustering at right (detail from figure 2.6). The same five topics appear in both hierarchical trees, with no additions or subtractions, but form pairs in a different order.

an overview of this local cluster, see figure 2.7; for more detail on these topics, see appendix C.)

Agglomerative clustering tells us that these topics are more similar to each other than to any other topic or cluster of topics. This impression is affirmed by the divisive clustering in figure 2.6, where the same group of five topics breaks off from the rest of the pack as a unit.

True, the division of topics within the cluster happens in a slightly different order (see figure 2.7), suggesting that, for example, Historical Public Rhetoric (T9) joined with Presidential Discourse (T19) and Writing in Law and Government (T29) more because it is like the former than because it is like the latter; or that Writing in Law and Government (T29) in turn is more like Politics, Empire, Radicalism (T13). But these subtleties mostly just confirm that these five topics are worth considering as a set, rather than focusing on the minor gradations of difference within their overall similarity.

Looking across the two large clustering diagrams, other stable clusters become visible, as shown in figure 2.8 and with more detail in table 2.9. Only one major branch of the agglomerative clustering shifts its groupings significantly in the divisive hierarchy; I will discuss those topics after outlining the major stable clusters in the table.

In addition to the cluster on public rhetorics discussed above (now outlined in salmon pink and labeled E), five groups of topics stand out as being both sufficiently different from the others to cluster divisively and sufficiently similar to each other to cluster agglomeratively. These include a cluster centered on teaching and working within the constraints of academic institutions (labeled B in figure 2.8 and outlined in green);[24] one small but distinct[25] cluster linking creative writing to personal narrative and oral history (labeled H, and outlined in indigo); one collecting topics on specific places and groups of people along lines of race, nationality, gender, and sexuality (labeled D, and outlined in yellow). Of the two smallest[26] clusters in table 2.9, one seems to link topics that focus on (composing for) oral delivery, while the other joins a pair of topics addressing various kinds of entertainment.

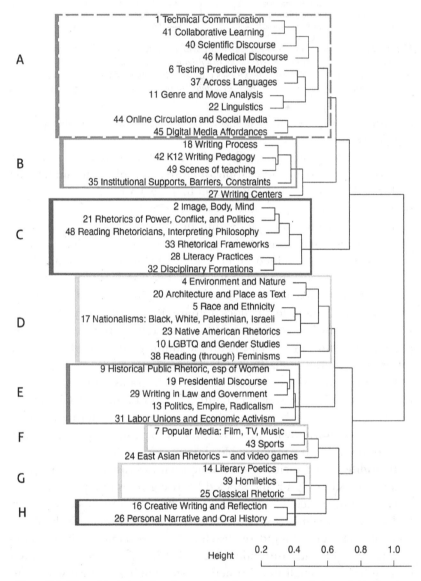

Agglomerative clustering (Ward's method)

A
- 1 Technical Communication
- 41 Collaborative Learning
- 40 Scientific Discourse
- 46 Medical Discourse
- 6 Testing Predictive Models
- 37 Across Languages
- 11 Genre and Move Analysis
- 22 Linguistics
- 44 Online Circulation and Social Media
- 45 Digital Media Affordances

B
- 18 Writing Process
- 42 K12 Writing Pedagogy
- 49 Scenes of teaching
- 35 Institutional Supports, Barriers, Constraints
- 27 Writing Centers

C
- 2 Image, Body, Mind
- 21 Rhetorics of Power, Conflict, and Politics
- 48 Reading Rhetoricians, Interpreting Philosophy
- 33 Rhetorical Frameworks
- 28 Literacy Practices
- 32 Disciplinary Formations

D
- 4 Environment and Nature
- 20 Architecture and Place as Text
- 5 Race and Ethnicity
- 17 Nationalisms: Black, White, Palestinian, Israeli
- 23 Native American Rhetorics
- 10 LGBTQ and Gender Studies
- 38 Reading (through) Feminisms

E
- 9 Historical Public Rhetoric, esp of Women
- 19 Presidential Discourse
- 29 Writing in Law and Government
- 13 Politics, Empire, Radicalism
- 31 Labor Unions and Economic Activism

F
- 7 Popular Media: Film, TV, Music
- 43 Sports
- 24 East Asian Rhetorics – and video games

G
- 14 Literary Poetics
- 39 Homiletics
- 25 Classical Rhetoric

H
- 16 Creative Writing and Reflection
- 26 Personal Narrative and Oral History

Height   0.2   0.4   0.6   0.8   1.0

Figure 2.8. Hierarchical clustering diagrams showing topic groups that are stable (i.e., have the same members) under both agglomerative clustering (left, as in figure 2.5) and divisive clustering (right, as in figure 2.6). Outer edges of boxes are positioned to preserve cluster rank by portion of aggregate text, meaning that the highest-ranked cluster is furthest to the left in agglomerative and right in divisive clustering. Inner edges are positioned to show the lowest branch-point in the hierarchical tree at which the cluster forms. For more detail about cluster membership, see table 2.9. Clusters with dotted lines are not quite stable across clustering methods, and are discussed further in the chapter.

Divisive clustering (diana)

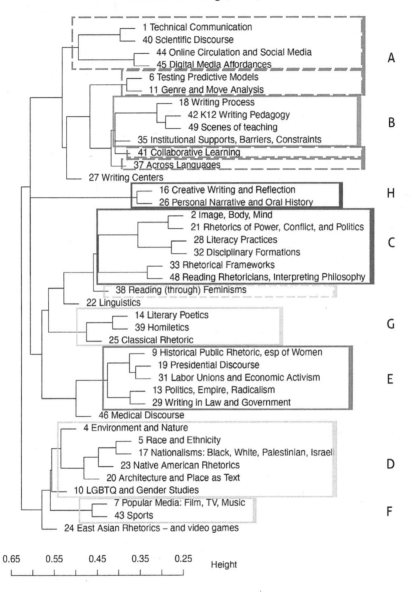

1 Technical Communication
40 Scientific Discourse
44 Online Circulation and Social Media
45 Digital Media Affordances

A

6 Testing Predictive Models
11 Genre and Move Analysis

18 Writing Process
42 K12 Writing Pedagogy
49 Scenes of teaching
35 Institutional Supports, Barriers, Constraints
41 Collaborative Learning
37 Across Languages

B

27 Writing Centers

16 Creative Writing and Reflection
26 Personal Narrative and Oral History

H

2 Image, Body, Mind
21 Rhetorics of Power, Conflict, and Politics
28 Literacy Practices
32 Disciplinary Formations
33 Rhetorical Frameworks
48 Reading Rhetoricians, Interpreting Philosophy

C

38 Reading (through) Feminisms
22 Linguistics

14 Literary Poetics
39 Homiletics
25 Classical Rhetoric

G

9 Historical Public Rhetoric, esp of Women
19 Presidential Discourse
31 Labor Unions and Economic Activism
13 Politics, Empire, Radicalism
29 Writing in Law and Government

E

46 Medical Discourse

4 Environment and Nature
5 Race and Ethnicity
17 Nationalisms: Black, White, Palestinian, Israeli
23 Native American Rhetorics
20 Architecture and Place as Text
10 LGBTQ and Gender Studies

D

7 Popular Media: Film, TV, Music
43 Sports

F

24 East Asian Rhetorics – and video games

0.65   0.55   0.45   0.35   0.25   Height

Table 2.9. Topic clusters that are stable under both agglomerative and divisive clustering. Cell values in column "X% reach" give the percentage of dissertations (N = 1,684) for which the topics in the given cluster cumulatively account for at least X% of the words in that document. The cutoff points of 5, 13, and 22% were derived from the lower hinge of top-topic distributions (see figure 2.2).

Cluster label (label in figure 2.8)	Topics in cluster	% of aggregated corpus	50% reach	22% reach	13% reach	5% reach
Theoretical Orientations (Group C)	Image, Body, Materiality (T2) Rhetorics of Power, Conflict, and Politics (T21) Reading Rhetoricians, Interpreting Philosophy (T48) Rhetorical Frameworks (T33) Literacy Practices (T28) Disciplinary Formations (T32)	26.1%	11.94%	51.13%	72.92%	90.44%
Teaching and Administration (Group B)	Writing Process (T18) Institutional Supports, Barriers, Constraints (T35) K12 Writing Pedagogy (T42) Scenes of Teaching (T49)	15.1	5.52	27.2	41.03	57.78
Public Rhetorics and Political Writing (Group E)	Historical Public Rhetoric, esp of Women (T9) Politics, Empire, Radicalism (T13) Presidential Discourse (T19) Writing in Law and Government (T29) Labor Unions and Economic Activism (T31)	9.2	1.96	13.9	23.28	45.49
Narrative and Reflection (Group H)	Creative Writing and Reflection (T16) Personal Narrative and Oral History (T26)	6.5	0.53	6.53	14.73	40.44
Peoples and Places (Group D)	Environment and Nature (T4) Architecture and Place as Text (T20) Race and Ethnicity (T5) Nationalisms: Black, White, Palestinian, Israeli (T17) Native American Rhetorics (T23) LGBTQ and Gender Studies (T10)	6.7	0.89	11.7	17.99	30.17
Poetics and Oratory (Group G)	Literary Poetics (T14) Classical Rhetoric (T25) Homiletics (T39)	4.3	0.65	4.81	10.45	22.21
Popular Entertainment (Group F)	Popular Media: Film, TV, Music (T7) Sports (T43)	1.89	0.00	1.9	4.22	9.26

Note: The reach columns can sum to more than 100%. Consider a hypothetical topic that accounted for 5% of every dissertation. This topic alone would have a 5% reach of 100%, even though its aggregate contribution was still only 5% of the corpus.

I've saved the largest cluster in the table for last. Outlined in magenta and labeled C in figure 2.8, it is interesting for several reasons. It includes six of the top ten topics by contribution to the aggregate corpus, adding up to more than a quarter (26.1%) of the total text in the dataset. It reaches a whopping 90% of dissertations if we stick to the 5% criterion level; the next-largest stable cluster, reaching 57.8%, doesn't even come close. This top cluster is pervasive enough to reach more than half (51%) of dissertations even at a 22% criterion level, meaning that the majority of RCWS dissertations devote more than one-fifth of their text (roughly the equivalent of a full chapter) to these topics. Understanding this cluster, then, would seem to be an important part of understanding the expertise performed in composition/rhetoric dissertations.

Yet here the common thread among the labels is not as immediately clear as in other clusters: Literacy Practices (T28) seems attuned to observations and interviews in a way that Rhetorical Frameworks (T33) or Reading Rhetoricians, Interpreting Philosophy (T48), operating dialectically through text and idea, are not. And how do these integrate with the largely historical emphasis of Disciplinary Formations (T32)? Looking at the dissertations with the greatest percentage of their text accounted for by this cluster of topics (table 2.10), though, it becomes clear that this is in many ways "the theory cluster": these dissertations feature various orientations toward language as epistemic, as seen in dissertations like *Of a certain persuasion: Rhetoric, complexity, and the emergence of subjectivity* or *The substance of style: Invention, arrangement, and paralogic rhetoric in the composition classroom.* They engage in arguments about what counts as rhetorical, or should fall under consideration of rhetorical criticism, as in *A sound form of knowledge: Composition and the rhetorical problem of music* and *Arts of concealment rhetoric and ethics in the age of wireless computing.* Several explicitly state their aim to articulate a coherent ethics, or theory, or rhetorical framework in their own right (such as *Catalyzing persuasion: Toward a theory of kairos and repetition*), as opposed to forwarding an existing framework as part of their method (though that is present here, as well, as in *Vico's counter-modern alternative: A new science of discourse*).

Seen from this perspective, the Literacy Practices topic (T28) fits here by virtue of defining and redefining the nature of literacy, and Disciplinary Formations (T32) signals not (or not only) passages tracking the history of the discipline but (especially) those making claims about disciplinarity as such: text that proposes an overall shape or form through which to understand that history.

Clustering topics, then, contributes to our understanding of the model: it adds nuance to the sense of constituent topics within each

Table 2.10. Titles of dissertations in which topics in the top-ranked cluster from table 2.9 cumulatively account for more than 80% of the text.

Dissertation title	Portion of text attributed to this cluster
The subject of ethos at the ends of rhetoric	85.18%
An institutional critique of writing process	85.08
Re-articulating postprocess: Affect, neuroscience, and institutional discourse	84.72
Of a certain persuasion: Rhetoric, complexity, and the emergence of subjectivity	84.06
Arts of concealment rhetoric and ethics in the age of wireless computing	84.00
"Resources of ambiguity": An exploration of pathos	83.80
Vico's counter-modern alternative: A new science of discourse	82.93
Moving thumos: Emotion, image, and the enthymeme	82.89
Towards consequence and collaboration in composition studies: Theorizing collaboration after the social turn	82.53
The substance of style: Invention, arrangement, and paralogic rhetoric in the composition classroom	82.43
Rhetoric and revelation: In search of a foundation for a postmodern ethics	82.01
A sound form of knowledge: Composition and the rhetorical problem of music	81.99
Rhetorical inventions/inventional rhetorics: Opening possibilities	81.93
Organizing rhetoric: situation, ethos, identification, and the institution of social form	81.53
Writing beyond the art/chance binary: The ongoing debate about techne in rhetoric and composition	81.04
Rhetorical memory, synaptic mapping, and ethical grounding	80.48
Catalyzing persuasion: Toward a theory of kairos and repetition	80.30

cluster. Whereas earlier I discussed the topics in light of only twenty words associated with each topic—a common-enough procedure in many topic-modeling studies—the clustering algorithm takes into account a far greater number of the topic's constituent term frequencies, revealing deeper similarities (and some hidden differences) than

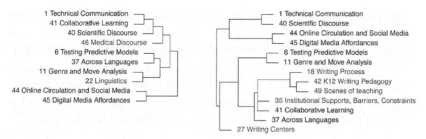

Figure 2.9. *Unstable topic clustering between two clustering methods. Comparing in either direction between agglomerative clustering (left, detail from figure 2.5) and divisive clustering (right, detail from figure 2.6), several topics are added or subtracted (shown here in gray text).*

were visible on the surface. This demonstrates a key affordance of using computers to study writing: they don't simply tell us what we already know, as some have alleged, but prompt us to reconsider how we organize what we know.

The topics just described leave out a fairly significant chunk of figure 2.8: ten topics that don't appear in any of the clusters discussed above. Here's why: they seem to form a cluster under the agglomerative process, but not under divisive clustering. Let's look at them now. In figure 2.8, I outlined in blue (and labeled A) a large branch of the agglomerative clustering diagram, reproduced as figure 2.9.

This agglomerative cluster accounts for 20.9% of the aggregated corpus: more, that is, than the teaching cluster (outlined in green and labeled B in figure 2.8). Yet the "cluster" splinters under divisive clustering: only four of the original ten topics fall into one contiguous branch (Technical Communication [T1], Scientific Discourse [T40], Online Circulation and Social Media [T44], and Digital Media Affordances [T45])—and the latter two of those had not been especially close to the others under agglomerative clustering, joining only in the final step. Two topics appearing in the agglomerative cluster (Medical Discourse [T46] and Linguistics [T22]) are split so far away from this remnant that to display them in figure 2.9 would be to essentially reproduce the hierarchical tree for the entire model.

Leaving those two topics aside for the moment, though, two other patterns are still discernable. The first is that the four consistent topics, for all that their proximity is shuffled by the clustering methods, do seem to share a semantic connection in technology and technical writing. The second is that the four remaining topics of the ten in the agglomerative cluster all move, in the divisive hierarchy, to join what I've labeled the teaching cluster: Testing Predictive Models (T6), Across Languages (T37), Genre and Move Analysis (T11), and Collaborative Learning (T41). On the surface, there is nothing inherently classroom-y about these topics: Collaborative Learning, for example, includes dissertations on practices of business teams and scientific labs, with the latter perhaps explaining its close affinity for both Technical Communication (T1) and Scientific Discourse (T41) in the agglomerative model. But given the ways they move between the two trees, it is tempting to see these topics as perhaps especially capable of linking, or hinging between, classroom applications and applications beyond the university. (In the same vein, the one remaining topic not mentioned above that changes position significantly between the hierarchical trees—Reading [Through] Feminisms [T38]—could be seen as hinging between the Theoretical Orientations cluster, in the divisive clustering, and the People and Places cluster, in the agglomerative.)

We might, then, think of both the splintering technical cluster in figure 2.9 and the more stable teaching cluster as belonging to a larger grouping we could call Applied Composition. Such a cluster (which could now expand to also include Topic 27, Writing Centers, otherwise off on its own in the divisive hierarchy) is described in table 2.10. Note that two topics in the agglomerative clustering (T22: Linguistics, and T46: Medical Discourse) are not included even in this more expansive divisive clustering, and are thus left out here.

As we might expect from combining such a large number of topics, this grouping now surpasses our previous largest cluster (labeled Theoretical Orientations) in raw size, accounting for almost 35% of the text in the aggregated corpus, compared to theory's 26% (see table 2.9). It significantly closes the gap in the number of dissertations incorporating this cluster at least in passing: 87% of dissertations spend at least 5% of their words on these applied topics, approaching the 90% incorporating at least some theoretical orientation by the same criterion. Interestingly, while only about 12% of dissertations in the dataset devoted more than half of their text to topics in the Theoretical Orientations cluster (i.e., 12% of individual documents in the corpus hit the 50% reach level), the number of dissertation writers focusing on some combination of applied composition topics is higher: about 29% devote more than half their text to topics in this super-cluster. That's between a quarter and a third of RCWS dissertations primarily focused on Applied Composition in this time period, compared to about one eighth comparably focused on theory.

This may at first seem an unfair comparison, especially as a way of thinking through the real balances underlying theory/practice splits

Table 2.11. Clusters related to technical writing, genre analysis, and teaching form a stable super-group. Cell values in column "X% reach" give the percentage of dissertations (N = 1,684) for which the topics in the given cluster cumulatively account for at least X% of the words in that document. The cutoff points of 5, 13, and 22%were derived from the lower hinge of top-topic distributions (see figure 2.2).

Cluster label (label in figure 2.8)	Topics in cluster	% of aggregated corpus	50% reach	22% reach	13% reach	5% reach
Applied Composition (Groups A and B)	Technical Communication (T1) Scientific Discourse (T40) Online Circulation and Social Media (T44) Digital Media Affordances (T45) Testing Predictive Models (T6) Genre and Move Analysis (T11) Writing Process (T18) K12 Writing Pedagogy (T42) Scenes of teaching (T49) Institutional Supports, Barriers, Constraints (T35) Collaborative Learning (T41) Across Languages (T37) Writing Centers (T27)	34.86%	29.45%	58.08%	72.8%	87.17%

Note: The reach columns can sum to more than 100%. Consider a hypothetical topic that accounted for 5% of every dissertation. This topic alone would have a 5% reach of 100%, even though its aggregate contribution was still only 5% of the corpus.

bemoaned by Kopelson (2008), Dobrin (2011), and others. After all, I have not combined the theory cluster with anything, as I just combined the teaching cluster. But the truth is, the model does not seem to facilitate such a combination. Perhaps signaling again the important role that theory plays as a touchstone for all groups, in looking across the hierarchical trees in figure 2.8, the cluster I've labeled Theoretical Orientations (marked in magenta, and labeled C) does not consistently combine with any one other group. Its nearest neighbors under divisive clustering are Poetics and Oratory (group G, in light blue) and Public Rhetorics and Political Writing (group E, in salmon pink)—and even to do that, we need to incorporate three topics that belong to none of those three clusters in the agglomerative hierarchy. And under agglomerative clustering, theory's nearest neighbor is, ironically or not, the blue/green supercluster of Applied Composition (groups A and B); the divisive-clustering neighbors I just mentioned are on the far side of the highest-level division in the agglomerative tree, meaning they wouldn't combine with our theory cluster until *all* clusters were combined.

I suggested above that topics without stable clusters, like Collaborative Learning (T41), Genre and Move Analysis (T11), and Reading (Through) Feminisms (T38), might act as hinges between the neighbors they move among when we shift our attention between agglomerative and divisive forms of cluster building. If so, then the same might be said about Theoretical Orientations as a group: this cluster on meaning-making hinges between study of writing and teaching of writing, between acquisition of writing knowledge and applications of writing knowledge.[27] And even if direct advancement of such theory is only engaged in by a minority of the field's doctoral students, its near-universal presence across dissertations signals how essential it is for students across subfields to be at least somewhat familiar with the theoretical advancements the field has, collectively, made.[28]

WHERE WE STAND SHOULD NOT LIMIT WHERE WE LAND

This chapter set out to characterize the range of subjects taken up in RCWS research: to help members of the field find places to stand, so to speak, in relation to the broad flux of topics in rhetoric, composition, and writing studies. Especially for those who are new to the field, like graduate students, as well as those advising them, the topics and clusters described above should help with the process of orientation. To the extent that they are stable, *topic clusters help us name our places* in the complex space of the discipline—and do so with confidence that we understand the adjacent contexts those names imply, the additional topics we might be expected to be familiar with. Topic modeling could provide a way of grounding subject-area clusters at CCCC, for example, usefully distinguishing the different threads and throughlines as they change over time, and helping new scholars to "find their people," as the expression has it.

I also aimed to investigate the degree of balance between theory and practice: research orientations sometimes seen as directly opposed, or at least mutually limiting. The analyses above make clear that *the theory/ practice balance is actually fairly even across RCWS writ large*. Roughly the same proportion of dissertations (about nine in ten) pay at least some attention to theoretical orientations as to applied composition (5% reach level); and each cluster gets at least a chapter's worth (22% reach) in about half of the dissertations.

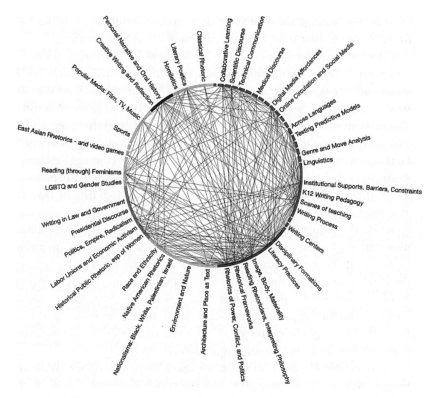

Figure 2.10. *Topics co-occurring within dissertations regularly connect across topic clusters. Topics are arranged according to hierarchical agglomerative clustering (agnes, using Ward's method), as in figure 2.5; slight variations in placement are the result of local left/ right swaps in the layout algorithm. Lines running across the center connect pairs of topics that each account for at least 13% of the same dissertation, in at least 3 dissertations. Clusters are marked using the same color scheme as in figure 2.8.*

Why all the angst, then, about whether composition should return to "pedagogical roots" or whether rhetoric is limited by a "pedagogical imperative"? Well, different ways of asking what the field is writing about yield different answers. The same data showing the balance described above also shows that teaching-related topics specifically (just the green-marked cluster) reach only about 58% of dissertations, and make up more than half of only around 6%, so advocates for more attention to teaching can find evidence to support that view. Conversely, advocates for theory can point to the only 12% of dissertations that are *not* reached by applied topics to say that "pure" theory is rare in the field. By revealing the different frames that lead to these seemingly contradictory conclusions, my approach should help advocates on both sides of this debate to acknowledge the source of their opponents' concerns—and, in so doing, assuage some of their own anxiety about what's being lost. In many cases, what they seek to promote is already happening.

Ultimately, purity is probably not the best lens through which to understand what's happening in composition/rhetoric. *As useful as the clusters above can be for locating one's primary home in the field, we shouldn't let that stop us from working outside our homes.* To have a place to stand is also to have solid ground from which to push off, and the data suggest that many dissertation writers do indeed work *across* content clusters. Figure 2.10 takes the hierarchical tree of figure 2.5 (the agglomerative clustering) and spins it around a circle, the better to draw lines across the middle that connect pairs of topics appearing together at discernable levels in the same dissertations.

While this figure may look complex, the main story it tells is simple: dissertations regularly combine topics from across clusters, including topics from the farthest branches of the hierarchical tree. To increase the confidence of this finding, I've set up the figure to display only pairs in which both topics represent at least 13% of the shared dissertation, and then further stipulated that each such pairing must occur at least three times. Even under this relatively stringent criterion, every cluster is joined, and in most cases multiple times.

Far from their being isolated or opposed, then, dense threads of connection link applications and theory, the concrete and the abstract, the analog and the digital, composition and rhetoric.

3

HOW DO YOU KNOW?
Unevenly Distributed Dappling in Dissertation Methods

> *All things counter, original, spare, strange;*
> *Whatever is fickle, freckled (who knows how?)*
> —G. M. Hopkins, "Pied Beauty"

In chapter 2, I argue that the language of theory, especially framings and definitions of rhetoric and literacy, form a common backbone, or at least a common touchstone, for the great majority of dissertations in composition/rhetoric (more than 90%). And yet, the same evidence shows that a *focus* on theoretical language is far less common: in only about 12% of dissertations do such topics make up the majority of the writing. This suggests that most dissertation writers are not actively developing new framings and definitions as one of their primary modes of inquiry. In this chapter, I ask what modes of inquiry *are* common at the entry points to the field. What methods are graduate students marshalling in the pursuit of their PhDs? Which is to say, what kinds of evidence do they gather, and by what means do they evaluate that evidence? It matters not only *that* such methods vary (which is, perhaps, obvious) but also *how* they vary, and in what proportions: it affects the degree to which modes not taken up are nevertheless mutually understood, and therefore valued, and whether or not graduate programs see a need to teach a given method.

This quest to identify research modes in RCWS, and the question of whether practitioners of different modes can understand each other, can arguably be traced to North's (1987) *Making of Knowledge in Composition* (henceforward, MKC). That book's motivating claim, derived from the work of Paul Diesing (1971), was that knowledge-making communities form and survive based more on shared methods than on shared subject matter (North 1987, 2, 364–65), making the stakes no less than existential for the field. North's (1987) concern, stated most clearly in his concluding chapter, was that "Composition faces a peculiar methodological paradox: its communities cannot get along well enough to live with one another, and yet they seem unlikely to survive, as any sort of an integral

https://doi.org/10.7330/9781646423224.c003

whole called Composition, without one another" (369). This question of internal research "communities" has often been framed via a distinction between humanistic, text-based approaches (a group North calls "Scholars," summarizing their central question as "What does it mean?" [1987, 3]) and social-scientific, empiricist methods ("Researchers," summarized as "What happened [or happens]?" [1987, 3]). A third category, the "Practitioners," characterized by the question "What do we do?" [1987, 3], were seen as borrowing from all sides, sometimes in inconsistent ways (see, e.g., Fulkerson 1990).[1] While North (1987) claimed that these camps were by and large opposed or in competition, a view reinforced by arguments around the supposed "theory/practice split" discussed in chapter 2, other scholars have argued that RCWS necessarily draws on *both* social-scientific and humanistic approaches. Cindy Johanek (2000), in particular, points to the power of empirical "what happens" kinds of research to provide important context for interpretive "what does it mean" kinds of research. A number of essays and articles have been written in support of such "methodological pluralism" (see, e.g., Liggett, Jordan, and Price 2011; Fleckenstein et al. 2008), but only a handful of studies (especially Driscoll and Perdue 2012; Hansen 2011; Juzwik et al. 2006) have sought to track the balance of different methods actually in practice. Almost all of these studies limit the context to journal articles.

In this chapter, I contribute a new source of evidence by analyzing dissertation abstracts to address two questions:

• What is the methodological landscape of doctoral research in composition and rhetoric? That is, what methods do graduate students turn to in constructing their identities as composition/rhetoric researchers, and in what proportions?

• How do doctoral programs cover this territory? That is, do schools tend to produce graduates specializing in the same one or two methods or methodological groups, or to span the range of possibilities?

ACCOUNTING FOR METHODOLOGICAL PLURALISM, OR METHODS FOR STUDYING METHODS

A sense of that methodological range can be seen in Kristine Hansen's (2011) analysis of textbooks commonly used in introductory graduate research methods courses, which she presented as part of a collective reevaluation of MKC's legacy (Massey and Gebhardt 2011). Across five books chosen for providing "an overview of a range of methods with enough detail about each that students could use the descriptions to plan and conduct their own research" (245),[2] Hansen identified no fewer than twelve methods:

- Practitioner/Teacher research;
- Historical;
- Philosophical/Theoretical;
- Critical;
- Experimental;
- Clinical/Case Study;
- Formalist/Cognitive Studies;
- Ethnographic;
- Survey;
- Interview/Focus Group;
- Discourse or Text Analysis; and
- Meta-Analysis.

What's more, several chapters in *The Dissertation and the Discipline: Reinventing Composition Studies* (Welch et al. 2002) highlight another kind of practitioner study not included in the taxonomy above, namely the use of creative writing, including poetry and fiction, as an act of academic investigation (see especially Moore and Woods 2002; Cook and Fike 2002).

Discussions of possibility do not in themselves tell us what methods students take up for extended projects such as dissertations. As Hansen (2011) writes, echoing Brown et al.'s (2008) notes on the *Rhetoric Review* surveys of graduate programs, "*In the absence of more reliable data, we don't know the present state of the field.* Even if all graduate programs required a course entitled Research Methods, we wouldn't know what was taught in those courses or whether they are required or elective without asking more detailed questions" (Hansen 2011, 248, emphasis added). Hansen is talking here about the shortcomings of existing survey instruments, but response rates are also a source of concern, as is the question of where to send the surveys. Moreover, as Rebecca Rickly (2012) points out, even if we knew perfectly what was supposed to be in each of those courses, the experience of students taking it can vary widely depending on which faculty member teaches it (235). For these reasons, the dissertations themselves are a particularly promising source of data on methodological uptake.

The analyses that follow are based on the same set of 1,684 dissertations as in the previous chapter, which were confirmed to have been completed between 2001 and 2015 at PhD programs in rhetmap.org and/or the

Consortium of Doctoral Programs in Rhetoric and Composition. Methods were coded[3] primarily through a close reading of dissertation abstracts, assisted by skimming the tables of contents and chapters when readers initially disagreed. We used a coding schema derived from Hansen (2011) (see table 3.1), with a few important modifications added during the initial round of reading. First, I renamed some of her tags to maximize clarity: for example, her "Critical" became "Critical/Hermeneutical" to avoid confusion with cultural-critical studies; "Formalist/Cognitive Studies" became "Model-Building" both to avoid confusion with formalist pedagogies and to distinguish the cognitive subject matter from the approach used to research it; and "Meta-Analysis" became "Meta-Analytical/Discipliniographic" to link these studies to the work of Maureen Daly Goggin (2000) and Derek Mueller (Mueller 2009; 2012a; 2017), who extends Goggin's term for scholarly activity that "writes the field" to encompass the study of such activity (Mueller 2009, xviii). Second, I added a new category of "Rhetorical-Analytical" to distinguish between two kinds of work with texts I had observed in the data. Third, I added a category for creative writing, "Poetic/Fictive/Craft-Based," which bears the oft-raised questions of voice, alternate academic discourses, and the knowledge-making of practitioners.[4]

The method tags in table 3.1 are further grouped according to larger methodologies that signal not only the particular ways of gathering evidence but also the underlying theoretical beliefs about how evidence behaves and thus how arguments proceed and knowledge advances. The first group, the *Dialectical*, generally corresponds to North's (1987) "Scholar" approaches; these draw on research from primarily textual sources that are subject to competing interpretations and emphasize authors' individual reasoning as the basis for persuasion. A second group treats evidence as *Aggregable*, with the expectation that the amount of data—and here *data* is more likely than not to be the term used—is proportional to the persuasive power of the claims made about what that data shows. As an empirical methodology, emphasizing "what happens," the Aggregable group falls within North's (1987) set of "Researcher" approaches but does not exhaust that set, because there is also a *Phenomenological* methodology: here, researchers assume that each site of observation is in many ways unique, defying the ability to aggregate across contexts. The emphasis here is not, then, on finding sameness or widespread pattern but on highlighting variation and revealing differences. What is persuasive by these methods is the richness, or thickness (a la Geertz), of the description, especially given that any given locus of research is presumed to be essentially inexhaustible.

Table 3.1. Method tags. The following 14 tags, adapted from Hansen (2011, 246), were used to describe the methods and methodologies used in the full dataset of 3,647 dissertations: both the confirmed RCWS subset of 1,684 dissertations described in this chapter and the remaining dissertations to be discussed in chapter 4. Note that while I have attempted to make tags mutually distinguishable, any given dissertation may engage in multiple methodologies and so receive more than one tag. They are presented here in groups loosely derived from Michael Carter's (2007) "meta-genres" in order to highlight similarities and contrasts.

I. Research from Sources/Dialectical Methodology

Philosophical/Theoretical (PHIL): Inductive or deductive argument based primarily on reason, rather than empirical evidence. Proceeds dialectically from prior arguments. May include claims about what *should* happen, such as proposed curricula that have not yet been tried. Re-definitions of terms and their significance will generally be classified as Philosophical/Theoretical.

Historical/Archival (HIST): Generally speaking, asks "what happened, and why?" and seeks answers via artifacts (including texts). When paired with other terms, may also indicate explicit "situating" of particular phenomena within historical and contemporaneous cultural contexts. Biographies of historical figures are included here, rather than under Clinical/Case Study (CLIN), because textual or second-hand evidence tends to dominate in such studies.

Critical/Hermeneutical (CRIT): Qualitative interpretation of texts' content, meaning, and significance, as in literary criticism: asks, "what can we see in the text if we view it through the lens of _____?" or "what does _____ argue?" Texts are treated as crafted cultural artifacts, so claims about them are subject to disagreements among interpreters. In its "critical" aspect, often involved in curation of value, arguing that some set of texts is worthy of scholarly attention. Similar to Rhetorical Analytical (RHET) in its subjective analysis of textual features; distinct from Rhetorical Analytical in its emphasis on content—the unique *what* of the text—as opposed to structure (the repeatable *how*).

Rhetorical-Analytical (RHET): Attempts to determine extractable writerly "moves" or authorial intent (e.g., with regard to effects on readers) through close or contextual reading of texts. Similar to Critical/Hermeneutical (CRIT) in its subjective analysis of textual features; distinct from Critical/Hermeneutical in its focus on "meta" elements such as motivation, structure, and effect, rather than identifying elements or value in textual content. Genre analysis will generally be tagged Rhetorical Analytical.

Model-Building (MODL): What North (1987) called "Formalist" and Hansen (2011) called "Formalist/Cognitive Studies": abstract modeling that looks to capture algorithmically or symbolically the relations among parts of a system, with an understanding of the system's dynamics as a primary goal. For example, actor-network theory would be one rubric (or lens) for formalist analysis; Flower & Hayes' (1979) cognitive model would represent another, drawing on computer science for its rubric. Grounded Theory approaches will generally be tagged Model-Building, as will dissertations that explicitly propose new methodologies. This new name was chosen to distinguish this approach from formalist pedagogies and assessments; see Fulkerson (1990, 412–13).

II. Empirical Inquiry

(a) Aggregable methodology

Discourse/Text Analytical (DISC): Systematic, often quantitative coding and analysis of formal features in a "text," broadly construed. Distinct from Critical/Hermeneutical (CRIT) in that whole texts are treated as data archives, so claims are aggregable and findings potentially replicable.

Experimental/Quasi-Experimental (EXPT): Hypothesis-driven empirical studies conducted under controlled conditions (or as close as the researchers can get). Whether quantitative or qualitative, the expectation is that the results would be replicable and aggregable.

continued on next page

Table 3.1.—*continued*

Interview/Focus Group (INTV): Studying some external phenomenon through the reactions and "knowledge about" of many individuals or groups. Distinguished from Clinical/Case Study (CLIN) in that interviews are instrumental ("third person"): the people interviewed are not what is being studied. Likely to have questions set in advance, rather than emerging from open-ended conversation, and as such includes questionnaires distributed directly to participants (as opposed to being widely broadcast, as in Survey).

Meta-Analytical/Discipliniographic (META): An analysis that generates and/or analyzes meta-data about disciplinary formation, especially within comp/rhet. In practice, this often takes the form of synchronic analyses of other comp/rhet research materials (e.g., articles, books, conference talks), as a way of capturing the overall state of disciplinary knowledge or identity. May include explicit aggregation of prior research findings as per Hillocks (1986), or merely aggregation of research or teaching epiphenomena such as authorship (cf. Goggin 2000), conference attendance, curricular requirements, etc. Compare to historiography as opposed to history.

Survey (SURV): Research via (widely distributed) quantitative or qualitative questionnaires that do not involve direct interaction between the researcher and those filling out the survey (thus distinct from Interview/Focus Group). Includes quantitative analysis of survey results, as well as data-mining that does not fall under Discourse/Text Analytical (DISC) or Meta-Analytical/Discipliniographic (META).

(b) Phenomenological methodology

Clinical/Case Study (CLIN): Rich portraits of individuals to learn about those individuals' behavior or motivations. Distinguished from Ethnographic (ETHN) by emphasis on individuals, as opposed to systems, even though both take context into account. May involve interviews as well as observations but distinguished from Interview in that the interviews will favor "first person" reflection over "third person" knowledge.

Ethnographic (ETHN): Direct (embedded) observations of a community's systems of interaction. Distinguished from Clinical/Case Study (CLIN) by emphasis on community and system vs. individual portraits, and as such includes studies of online/classroom/workplace communities, even when these are referred to as "case studies." Note that this does not rule out examination of textual evidence, especially transcripts or field notes, but does suggest that such texts will be treated as secondary evidence for context and recall about the studied system, rather than as the primary locus of investigation.

III. Performance/enactment-based methodology

Poetic/Fictive/Craft-Based (POET): Original poetry, fiction, or creative nonfiction writing (including memoir and autoethnography) composed by the author, perhaps as a way of exploring the process of such composition; see Johnson (2010) on "craft knowledge," Liggett et al. (2011) on "narrative inquiry."

Practitioner/Teacher Research (PRAC): Narrative or anecdotal descriptions of "what worked" in a classroom, writing center, writing program, etc, or in the author's personal experiences of writing or performance. Distinguished from Ethnographic (ETHN) classroom studies in its orientation toward future action and enactment vs. understanding of a (possibly unique) system.

Finally, I include a group of methods in which research is enacted through *Performance*, including the crafting of experiences or artifacts (see Carter 2007, 400ff), and in which reflection is key to advancing knowledge, making concrete and/or explicit what had been implicit or inchoate in the performance itself.

Every analytical schema must make some tradeoffs between specificity and simplicity—adding enough categories to reveal distinctions without becoming so complex as to obscure high-level patterns. In combining Critical/Hermeneutical approaches under one tag, I chose this time to sacrifice the distinctions among various critical lenses that in another context might be readable as methods of their own, such as feminist, queer, or socioeconomic approaches to working with sources. For another pass at the same materials, a different breakdown would give a different but also valuable view.

The methodological groupings loosely align with Michael Carter's (2007) "meta-genres," a term he coined in the context of writing across the curriculum (WAC) to describe rhetorical strategies that both signal and transcend disciplinary alignments and thus constitute "meta-disciplines" (403). By emphasizing "similar ways of doing that point to similar ways of writing and knowing" (393), these meta-genres highlight distinct techniques for gathering evidence and extending knowledge, making them a useful framework for identifying the methodological modes at play in each dissertation.

Missing from my schema is Carter's final meta-genre, of responses that call for problem-solving (2007, 395); though a handful of dissertations, especially related to technical communication and usability testing, might have fit this description, as a rubric for seeing what was happening it was largely unneeded, and the coding schema was already large enough to make tests of statistical significance challenging. Given the very small number of problem-solving methods observed, I decided to include them in the catch-all category coded as using "Other" methods, tagged OTHR.

In assigning these tags to abstracts, we paid particular attention to the dissertations' "exhibits"—Joseph Bizup's (2008) term for "materials a writer offers for explication, analysis, or interpretation" (75). Not only was it instructive to determine what was offered up for examination (full documents, individual sentences or phrases, student behaviors, archival photographs, etc.) but methodological affiliations were also revealed by attending to the questions asked *of* those exhibits, as well as how the exhibits were obtained. One consequence of this focus on exhibits as opposed to other sources is that the presence of other texts in a literature review would not be sufficient to merit a Critical/Hermeneutical tag, because those texts act instead either as background ("materials whose claims a writer accepts as fact" [Bizup 2008, 75]) or as arguments "whose claims a writer affirms, disputes, refines, or extends in some way" (Bizup 2008, 75). Given that virtually all dissertations engage both background and argument sources, these would not have been sufficient to distinguish among the methods employed. Similarly, mere mention of pedagogical applications, without the presence of hands-on evidence from teaching situations, would not be tagged as a practitioner study, but rather as contributing a Philosophical/Theoretical claim with teaching as the content.[5] Where Method sources "from which a writer derives a governing concept or a manner of working" (Bizup 2008, 76) were explicitly mentioned, they did guide the tagging, but, as Bizup notes, such sources often go uncited, slipping instead into prose style or oblique reference.

Finally, rather than treat "multimodal" as a separate category, as Hansen (2011) did, I allowed each dissertation to have multiple method tags. Todd Taylor (2003), in his study of dissertations, claimed that "because these abstracts rarely declare a methodology per se, putting them into appropriate categories is difficult. If there *is* a pattern among the methodologies in these dissertations, it is that they defy placement in clear methodological categories" (143). To support his claim, he demonstrates that one abstract could arguably fit into seven of the eight methodologies in North's (1987) *MKC*. Rather than give up on categorization, though, I believe we should follow through on the implications of that multiplicity. Cultural anthropologist Michael Wesch (2007) has suggested that mutually exclusive categories are a holdover from file folders and shelves used for sorting and storing physical objects (books, pages, card-based catalog entries), and that in digital environments, information can and should be "stored" in multiple "places" at once (Wesch 2007, n.p.). In this way, we can avoid the problem of artificially or arbitrarily deciding which method in a hybrid project is "primary," and instead code for all methods observed. This also allows us to further examine the correlations among specific methods within individual dissertations.

WHEN WE ALLOW THEM TO, MOST
DISSERTATIONS USE MULTIPLE METHODS

To illustrate how this nonexclusive tagging works, consider the abstract of Douglas Walls's (2011) dissertation, "The 'human' network: Digital, professional, and cultural access enacted" (Michigan State University):

> The idea of technological access has been a core concern in the field of rhetoric and composition (computers and composition). Traditionally, access has been understood as a literacy issue located in classrooms and framed in political terms such as race, class, gender, technological materiality and activity in networked writing environments. That is to say, access has been a trait to learn or to be possessed. Yet, with the emergence of

pervasive socially networked writing environments like Facebook and Twitter, issues of social, cultural, and technological access express themselves much earlier in students' lives and linger throughout professional careers. Such writing technologies collapse moments of access in activities that are enacted across traditional private/public divides. These social writing technologies make access harder to theorize and locate than it was even five years ago by moving across academic disciplinary divides like cultural rhetoric, professional writing, and computers and composition. In this work, I update the definition of access as enacted to ask two important questions: what does access mean today and can we locate access as it happens?

To address these questions, this dissertation builds a methodology at the level of theory and empirical research that enables researchers, theorists, and rhetors to find specific moments of access that span both the cultural and the technological simultaneously. I theorize and trace access not as a trait to be assigned to individuals or in reference to specific technologies but instead as moments of accessing enacted by people, tools, and cultures in professional and personal lifespheres. I build my definition and methodology of access-as-enacted by drawing on a variety of research methods (creative non-fiction, theory building critical analysis, network analysis, and participant interview). These methods trace the professional and personal/cultural lifesphere issues that are coordinated around and through writing technologies not by defining access but rather by locating when and where access occurs.

This dissertation demonstrates that attention to social media, careers, and lived cultural experiences when placed alongside traditional concerns of access give us new insights into the interconnectedness of new media writing. Women and nonwhite ethnicities with lower social power have spent more time struggling with the practices of access, which now include social writing technologies. As such, their actions in social writing environments highlight the cultural and career relationships of social writing technologies. Their actions and lived experiences index a more accurate understanding of both cultural and technological rhetorical issues than others who might not have to work as hard to deploy such rhetorically loaded technologies. This dissertation helps us to understand new concerns in the field of Rhetoric and Composition about the relationship between careers, culture, and technologically supported social media writing.

Walls helpfully signals his research methods in the abstract's second paragraph: "creative non-fiction" signaled the presence of what the schema labels a "Poetic/Fictive" method. "Participant interview" was tagged as "Clinical/Case Study," a decision reinforced by the table of contents' inclusion of specific interviewees' names as headers of large chunks of the document: these are interviews toward profiles of individuals rather than pieces of an aggregate puzzle. "Theory building critical analysis" was a bit trickier but was ultimately tagged as "Philosophical/

Table 3.2. Most dissertations use multiple methods. Frequency with which a given number of method tags was assigned to a dissertation in the dataset. The median method count is 2. Percentages are given in parentheses.

Method count	1	2	3	4	5
Dissertation count (out of 1,684)	457 (27%)	663 (39.4%)	429 (25.5%)	120 (7.1%)	15 (0.9%)

Theoretical" to reflect Walls's emphasis on redefining the key terms of the dissertation (especially *access*), again reinforced by the table of contents, which shows prominent sections engaged in direct dialectical argument with prior theorists. Network analysis was rare enough in the dataset that we decided against including it outright in the coding schema, but it was marked as "Other," and could thus be retrieved later if additional data suggests the need to update the schema.

We should not be surprised to see multiple methods in use: after all, as Lynn Z. Bloom (2011) points out, "Composition studies researchers generally do not choose North's labels (say formalists or clinicians) and most would not restrict themselves to such a categorization system" (38–39). Taylor (2003), similarly, celebrates that "the dissertations in [his] study display a wide array of methodologies for gathering evidence, both within and amongst themselves" (144). And indeed, multiple methods were more the rule than the exception for dissertations in this study as well. As shown in table 3.2, the great majority of dissertations—over 70%—engage in two or more methodologies.

Where I disagree with Bloom and Taylor, however, is in concluding that the categories themselves are not useful once we acknowledge this variety. What's important, instead, is to recognize that a researcher—indeed, even a single research project—can wear more than one label at a time. Treating the system as a set of nonexclusive tags, rather than folders into which researchers and their work must be uniquely sorted, we can more aptly represent the work being done and still gain useful perspectives and contrasts.

Updating Taylor's (2003) comment, then, I would say that most (but not all) of these abstracts defy *unique* placement in such categories. This contrasts with Hansen's (2011) findings that only 10 of 184 articles (~5%) she examined in *CCC* and *RTE* were "multimodal." To some extent, it makes sense that articles edited for publication would be more focused, whereas dissertations spanning multiple chapters can be more expansive. I also wonder, though, whether some approaches were uncounted because they played a secondary, but perhaps still significant, role. This

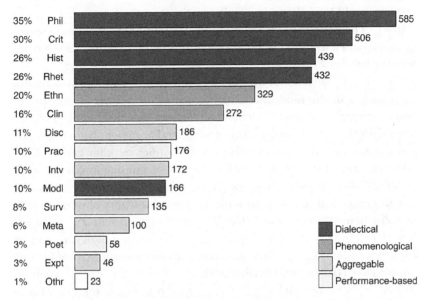

Frequency of Assigned Method Tags

35%	Phil		585
30%	Crit		506
26%	Hist		439
26%	Rhet		432
20%	Ethn		329
16%	Clin		272
11%	Disc		186
10%	Prac		176
10%	Intv		172
10%	Modl		166
8%	Surv		135
6%	Meta		100
3%	Poet		58
3%	Expt		46
1%	Othr		23

Dialectical
Phenomenological
Aggregable
Performance-based

Tags are non–exclusive, so sum will be greater than the 1684 included dissertations.

Figure 3.1. Frequency of Method Tags assigned to dissertations completed at RCWS-affiliated programs 2001–2015 (N = 1,684). Tags are nonexclusive, so the sum of all methods will be higher than 1,684; similarly, the sum of percentages will exceed 100.

raises the question: what gets undercounted if only the dominant methods are recorded?

EVEN SO, NOT ALL METHODS ARE EQUALLY ADOPTED

For all that we do see multiple methodologies in use, some are pretty clearly more in use than others. Figure 3.1 summarizes the prevalence of individual method tags across the 1,684 dissertations in the RCWS dataset.

Four of the Dialectical methods—Philosophical/Theoretical, Critical/Hermeneutical, Historical/Archival, and Rhetorical-Analytical—loom especially large, taking all of the top four slots. At least one of these tags appears in some 1,168 dissertations,[6] or 69% of confirmed RCWS dissertations in the dataset; adding the remaining Dialectical method, Model-Building, brings that figure up to 74% (1,242 dissertations). No other methodological cluster is nearly as extensive. The Empirical/Phenomenological group (Clinical/Case Study and Ethnographic), which takes up the next tier by frequency, appears as part

of the methodological mix in 515 dissertations (31%), and Empirical/
Aggregable methods (Discourse Analytics, Interview, Survey, Metadisciplinary, and Quasi/Experimental) reach a very similar 511 dissertations
(30%).[7] The Enactment-based methods (Practitioner/Teacher Research
and Poetic/Fictive, that is, creative writing) taken together have a reach
of only 226 (13%).

In terms of balance between humanistic and social-scientific
approaches in the field, this evidence seems to indicate a clear preference among graduate students for humanistic dissertation projects,
especially those that involve close reading and argument from texts. This
proportion generally aligns with previous studies in other genres. Dana
Driscoll and Sherry Wynn Perdue (2012), examining twenty years of
Writing Center Journal (1980–2009), found that 66% of the articles did not
involve empirical research, with the largest subcategory of nonempirical
articles being "theoretical," that is, "those that present an argument,
frame or new way of seeing" (32.2%); articles scoring high on an index
of replicability, aggregability, and data support were much fewer: only
around 6% (Driscoll and Perdue 2012, 25). Juzwik et al. (2006), similarly,
found that 68% of articles (3,222 of 4,739) did not meet their criteria for
empirical research when trawling several databases[8] for articles on writing, composition, or written language (Juzwik et al. 2006, 460).

On the one hand, it is not too surprising to see a preference for
dialectical/humanistic methods, nor that the qualitative-leaning phenomenological group within empirical methods would appear more
often than the quantitative-leaning aggregable group: after all, many
PhD programs in rhetoric and composition are still housed in English
departments, with many graduate faculty trained in literary analysis
supervising rising "generations" within the field. Even so, it is good to
see the same pattern emerge across several datasets because it gives data-
backed support to the intuition and does so at scale.

GRADUATE PROGRAMS VARY CONSIDERABLY
IN METHODOLOGICAL FOCUS

On the other hand, the very mention of scale should remind us that
more local patterns may buck the general disciplinary trend. Consider
the case of New Mexico State University, whose doctoral program
in Rhetoric and Professional Communication was founded in 1991
("Ph.D. Rhetoric & Professional Communication"). Among the thirty-
five confirmed dissertations from this department in 2001–2015, about
twice as many were tagged as Clinical/Case Study than were tagged

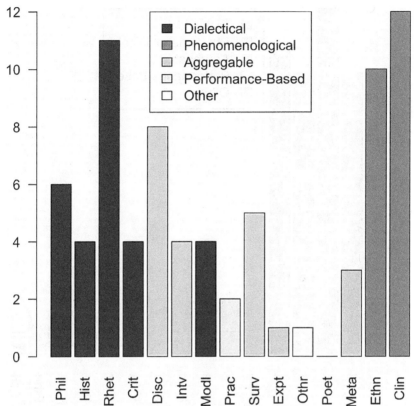

Figure 3.2. *Method tag count for a program with higher-than-average empirical focus, New Mexico State University, 2001–2015. N of 35 includes only confirmed RCWS dissertations. Total of individual tag counts exceeds N because dissertations may be tagged several times.*

as Philosophical/Theoretical; the number of dissertations tagged Historical/Archival was about half of those tagged Discourse Analytical (see figure 3.2.).

Though just about all of the methodologies are accounted for—the only one missing is Poetic/Fictive—the ratios are significantly different from those in RCWS dissertations overall, with both aggregable and especially phenomenological empirical methods considerably more common relative to dialectical methods at NMSU than in the field at large. Being able to visualize these differences could help schools like NMSU recruit new students and faculty: from this vantage point, the opportunity to think systematically about individual writers and communities, whether through distant (DISC) or close readings (ETHN, CLIN), could become part of the identity of the program.

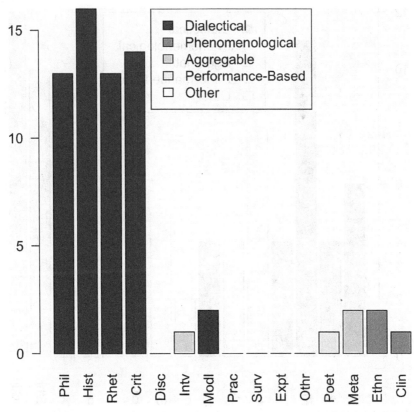

Figure 3.3. *Method tag count for a program with higher-than-average dialectical focus, Pennsylvania State University, 2001–2015. N of 32 includes only confirmed RCWS dissertations. Total of individual tag counts exceeds N because dissertations may be tagged several times.*

Other programs will have different tendencies that these analyses can help to make visible. Figure 3.3 shows an even more methodologically concentrated program, Penn State's doctorate in English with a specialization in rhetoric and composition.

With a similar number of confirmed RCWS dissertations in the same time period (thirty-two compared to NMSU's thirty-five), Penn State's output is almost entirely within the Dialectical method group, and in particular the top four methods in the overall dataset: Philosophical/Theoretical, Historical/Archival, Critical/Hermeneutical, and Rhetorical-Analytical. Methods outside that group appear in only one or two dissertations each, and four methods in the schema don't appear at all. That's not to say there's no diversity within this set of approaches; archival work on the history of a college's writing course (which would be tagged HIST) has

Figure 3.4. *Example of bargraph values converted to heatmap values.*

different entailments, to take just one example, than theoretical work on notions of writerly self (PHIL). But at Penn State in this time period there does seem to have been a consistent focus on reading and the persuasiveness of the individual student-scholar's account of the texts read—as opposed to gathering survey data (SURV), say, or trying something out in a classroom and reporting on student reception and outcomes (PRAC). Again, as I'd suggested with NMSU, a school like Penn State can choose to make these methodological commitments explicit, so that incoming students can feel confident that even when their particular dissertation topics will vary, they will be able to draw on the insights of a cohort of peers and faculty with hands-on experience doing a similar *kind* of research.

As with any such a programmatic decision, there are tradeoffs. A student may not know early on what methods will work best for their research questions, or those questions may shift; in programs with a clear methodological specialization, going outside that specialization may be difficult or may require coursework and advisors from outside the program. On the other hand, maintaining a wide methodological range is itself challenging, between the difficulty of securing many faculty lines to cover that range of expertise and the potential for imbalances in student demand for those faculty members to chair dissertation committees.

To see how more schools have weighed these competing considerations, figure 3.5 combines the method distributions of individual programs into a single visual field. To help all schools fit in one figure, rather than use bar heights to represent values, I used a *heatmap*—a graph type in which values are converted into a color, with white in this case representing zero, progressively darker shades representing increasing values, and black representing 100%. Figure 3.4, for example, shows how the two schools above are rerendered for consolidation into heatmap form: The more concentrated focus of dialectical methods at Penn State appears as a darker patch of gray on the lower left side of the figure; the wider distribution at NMSU shows in the top line as lighter gray spreading across the top line, with only one spot of white. These contrasts become easier to see as we aggregate and cluster schools across the dataset.

In figure 3.5, to make programs of different sizes more readily comparable, dissertation counts for each method are normed by dividing over the total number of dissertations from that program, meaning that shading now represents a percentage of the program's output. In addition, schools with fewer than five dissertations across the fifteen-year span in the dataset are excluded from this figure, to avoid over-emphasizing the methods used in a small number of dissertations simply by virtue of having fewer opportunities for variation within its program.

The first thing to notice is that none of the lines in figure 3.5 displays a uniform shade of gray all the way across, and most aren't even close to uniform: in other words, few schools present a close balance among the methods and methodologies described in this chapter.[9] This in itself gives us an initial answer to the question of how graduate programs, writ large, address the challenge of such a methodologically diverse field: by focusing on a subset of possibilities. Only 3 schools of the 66 included here have all 15 methods in the schema represented in their dissertation output: Indiana University of Pennsylvania (119 dissertations), the University of Arizona (96 dissertations), and Purdue University (96 dissertations).

It's worth noting that these are the three largest programs in the time period, with a considerably high average of more than six students graduating per year, giving these programs that much more opportunity for methodological variation. (The next-highest number of dissertations is sixty-one at the University of Louisville, an average of four students per year; most schools have fewer than forty students over the fifteen years in the dataset.) As shown in figure 3.6, there is indeed a positive relationship between the number of dissertations completed in a given program, on the x-axis, and the number of methods observed in those dissertations, on the y-axis.

That said, it's not as though small programs *can't* have a wide range of methods represented: the University of South Carolina at Columbia, with only twenty-two dissertations in the dataset, still spans fourteen method tags, as do the University of Texas at El Paso and Wayne State University, with twenty-five dissertations each. Florida State University hits twelve methods with only fifteen dissertations in the dataset.

Conversely, even at the largest programs, some methods are more common for students to pursue than others: at IUP, for example, which appears just left of the vertical line at the center of figure 3.5 and in the top right corner of figure 3.6, Phenomenological methods (and especially Clinical/Case Study) are better represented than those in any other methodological group. At the University of Arizona—located about a quarter of the way across figure 3.5, halfway between the left two vertical lines—the focus is skewed heavily toward Dialectical approaches, much as we saw earlier in the case of Penn State.

And indeed, Penn State appears in figure 3.5 just a few rows to the right of the University of Arizona. This similar placement is the result of a divisive clustering algorithm: that is, the columns have been arranged to group programs with related methodological focus, with the dendrogram at the bottom indicating where groups of graduate programs were iteratively divided to maximize the differences between the subgroups that remained, until each group contained only one program. I added the vertical lines mentioned above to mark some major division points in this hierarchical tree—which is to say, the major methodological patterns into which schools fall.

In the group containing both Penn State and the University of Arizona, for example, the big four Dialectical methods (PHIL, HIST, RHET, CRIT) tend to dominate, showing up in figure 3.5 as a dark block at the bottom left of the figure. The frequency of other methods is variable within this cluster, with some schools also producing dissertations with solid levels of Ethnographic and Clinical/Case Study work, and a couple of individual programs having quite strong representation of Model-Building (East Carolina University) and Practitioner/Teacher Research (University of Texas at San Antonio). However, the two schools just mentioned have very few dissertations in the dataset, possibly making small numbers weigh more heavily; and these variations do not override the general trend within this group that methods outside the top four are significantly less common. This cluster of dialectical methodological focus is fairly extensive, with the pattern encompassing some 24 graduate programs of the 66 in the figure, for a total of 548 dissertations.

Larger still is the cluster at the right of figure 3.5, which includes 742 dissertations from 25 schools. Dialectical methods are also well-represented at this group of schools, but here other methods balance them out more often. In fact, the distribution of methods in this cluster seems largely to mirror the distribution in the overall dataset, as shown in figure 3.2: After the top method group of PHIL + HIST + RHET + CRIT, Phenomenological methods (ETHN, CLIN) come close behind. Next is a set of largely aggregable methods: Discourse Analytical, Interview/Focus Group, and Survey, but also Practitioner/Teacher Research—an enactment-based method—and Model-Building (which I've labeled dialectical; more on that in a moment). Finally, at the low end of the distribution, come Experimental/Quasi-Experimental and Poetic/Fictive methods, plus a smattering of other, even less-common methods. Related, perhaps, to the way this cluster matches the average distribution of methods, schools within the cluster seem to include more methods than schools in other clusters: sixteen of twenty-five programs

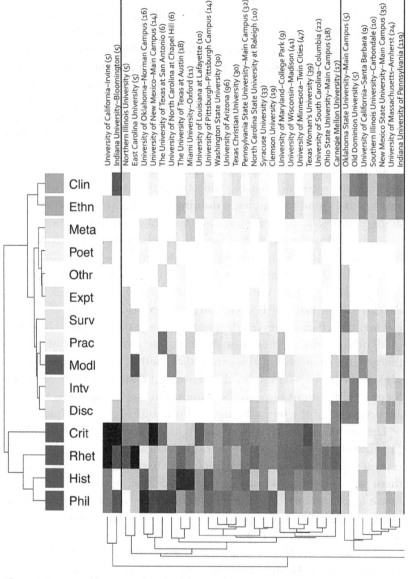

Figure 3.5. *Normed heatmap of methodological distribution across RCWS programs, 2001–2015. The shading of each cell gives the frequency with which a dissertation in the dataset from the school in row Y is tagged with the method in column X, with white = 0 and black = 100%. N = 1,647 confirmed RCWS dissertations at 66 schools with 5 or more such dissertations in the time period. The number of included dissertations at each school is given in parentheses. Dendrograms at top and left indicate divisive hierarchical clustering (diana); major divisions in the school (row) dendrogram are marked by black horizontal lines extending across the figure.*

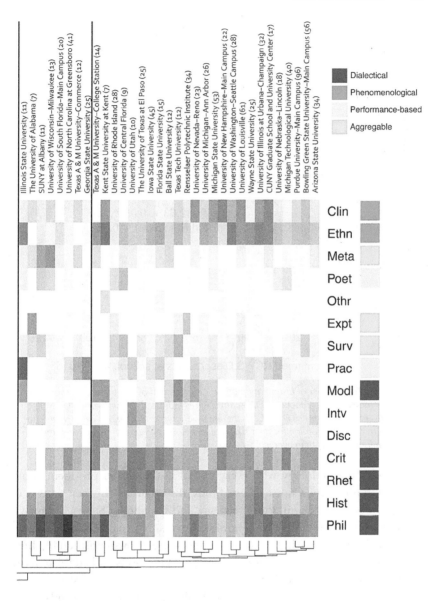

had four-fifths or more of the methods tagged at least once, the most schools of any cluster in figure 3.5 to meet that criterion.

Just left of the center in the figure is a cluster that, while including only seven programs, nevertheless includes 207 dissertations, mostly because it includes the very large program at IUP. This is also the cluster of schools containing NMSU. As suggested above, the pattern of method distribution here tilts more heavily toward the phenomenological than

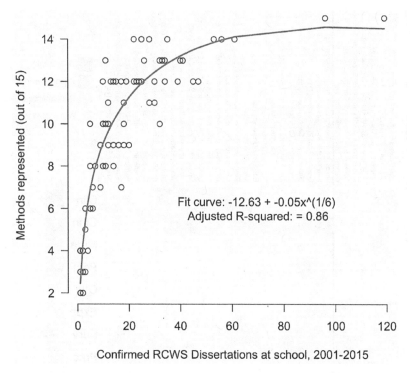

Figure 3.6. *The number of distinct method tags represented by the dissertations of a given program increases as a function of program size (as indicated by confirmed RCWS dissertations in the dataset). Points above the fit curve represent programs with wider-than-average method distribution for their size; points below represent programs with more methodological focus than average.*

any other methodology, with every school in the cluster producing both Ethnographic and Clinical/Case Study dissertations. In fact, at two of the schools (Old Dominion University and Oklahoma State University), the dialectical methods that dominate elsewhere are all but nonexistent within the dataset. This cluster of schools also shows considerably high representation for the mostly empirical set of methods ranked third in the large cluster discussed above: DISC + INTV + SURV + PRAC + MODL. Every school in this cluster had both Model-Building and Survey methods represented, which further distinguishes this cluster from the others.

Just right of that cluster is a set of eight schools, representing 140 dissertations, in which the dialectical methods look a lot less like a cohesive bloc: here, the Philosophical/Theoretical tag is the most common, and the strength of the Rhetorical/Analytical tag is much less visible; interestingly, the Meta-Analytical/Discipliniographic tag seems to have taken its place—or, perhaps, META plus Practitioner/Teacher Study, which at

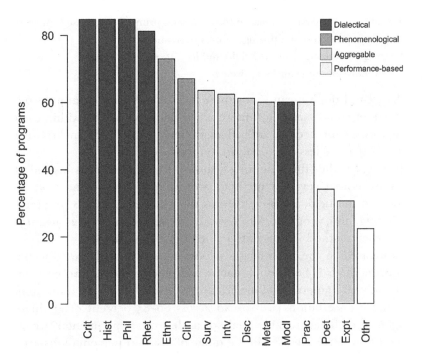

Figure 3.7. *Presence of methods across schools is broader than overall dissertation counts would suggest. Percentage of programs with at least one confirmed RCWS dissertation using each indicated method, 2001–2015. N = 85 possible programs. The maximum observed value is 84.7% (72 programs).*

some programs comes in the top slot. Given the latter, I suspect these PHIL tags include theorizing about teaching, a subset perhaps worth further study and disambiguation.

The last cluster in figure 3.5 is a very small group at the far left (only two schools, with only ten dissertations between them), seemingly distinguished from the rest of the dataset because it covers a smaller range of methods than the others: at each school, only six of fifteen method tags were needed to categorize the research output. This could well be an artifact of the small sample size, but even so it's likely no coincidence that the methods we do see represented are the top methods in the full dataset: Dialectical, then Phenomenological. (Let it not be said that these trends are absolute, though: the overall quite rare Poetic/Fictive is one of those six methods at the University of Califorina, Irvine.)

These clusters demonstrate a range of "flavors" for methodological focus within graduate programs, when taking fifteen years of dissertations into account. Summarizing the groups from left to right in figure 3.5, we might say the choices so far visible are these:

- all-in on dialectical research from sources, primarily text-based sources;
- empirically focused through observation and survey;
- philosophizing about the field and its history;
- a more all-of-the-above approach.

To be clear, I don't mean to say these are the *only* choices an individual program could make, and there are certainly variations within each group, especially because individual students can and do incorporate methods that are less common within those programs.

In fact, another thing figure 3.5 shows, if we look at rows instead of columns, is that very few methods are entirely *un*represented across schools in the field. Figure 3.7 shows the number of RCWS programs (including, now, programs with fewer than five dissertations 2001–2015) where each method was tagged in at least one dissertation.

Compared to the percentages of *dissertations*, overall, this distribution of methods is both much flatter and much closer to 100 percent: while only 26–35 percent of dissertations use one of the top four methods, those dissertations are spread across 80–85 percent of graduate programs. While aggregable methods aside from Experimental (which remains low here) are used in the range of just 6–11 percent of dissertations, these methods are in use at over 60 percent of programs.

So I'm not posing any kind of purity test in describing the patterns of methodological focus that seem to have prevailed at programs in this time period. Even so, it does seem that the four major "flavors" above can generally describe the roads most taken by graduate programs in RCWS.

(If anything, knowing that the already low frequency of aggregable dissertations is so spread out only heightens the degree to which graduate students writing these dissertations are more isolated than students writing with the more-common dialectical or phenomenological methods. With 186 Discourse-Analytical dissertations produced at 52 programs, that leaves an average of only 3–4 DISC-tagged dissertations per school over the 15-year period in the dataset; the comparable value for CRIT is more than twice that.)

It would be interesting to see whether any consistent patterns of staffing or curriculum seem to undergird these different models, such as faculty-student ratio; the availability and duration of funding for graduate students; whether methods courses are required, how often they are offered, and what methods are included; or how the characteristics of graduate programs that faculty themselves attended might influence the methods of students they advise. We might hypothesize, for example, that RCWS programs hiring faculty with backgrounds in Linguistics

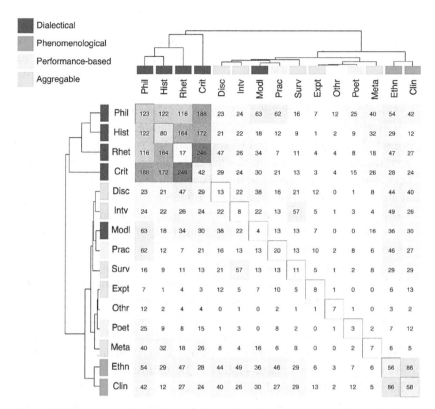

Figure 3.8. *Raw counts of method correlations within dissertations suggest that methods mostly cohere within methodological groups. In this figure, a box in row Y, column X shows the number of dissertations tagged Y that are also tagged X; note the symmetry across the diagonal. Numbers on the diagonal, where each method crosses itself, show counts of single-method dissertations rather than total counts. Note that the sum of values in each row may exceed total counts for that row's method, because some dissertations have more than two tags. Dendrograms outside the grid show complete-linkage hierarchical clustering based on Euclidean distance. N = 1,684 confirmed RCWS dissertations, 2001–2015.*

might support more Discourse-Analytical dissertations, or that time-intensive Ethnographic studies would be more common at institutions with strong funding packages obviating the need for additional work outside of school. However, determining the answers to these questions would require data that was beyond the scope of the present study.

"SCHOLAR" AND "RESEARCHER" METHODS REMAIN LARGELY SEPARATE, BUT NOT ENTIRELY

While the heatmap in figure 3.5 shows which methods tend to co-occur at programs, it cannot, in itself, confirm that these patterns hold in individual dissertations. For example, are the dialectical methods so high-ranked because they provide interpretive or contextualizing frameworks alongside more empirical or enactment-based methods? Or are these modes of engagement largely happening in parallel, nearby but not touching?

Consider figures 3.8 and 3.9, which show the co-occurrences of methods within individual dissertations. In each figure, the same method tags are set along both the x- and y-axes; where the rows and columns intersect, the box is shaded as in the heatmap above, to make higher numbers (darker colors) easier to find. To avoid maxing out this color scale along the diagonal, where a method intersects itself, I have replaced the total counts for each method (which are given above in figure 3.1) with the counts for dissertations where that method occurs alone, that is, where it intersects *only* itself.

The most prominent feature in figure 3.8 is the dark square at the top left: the intersections of the four Dialectical methods that topped the ranks of methods in general, demonstrating how they tend to co-occur primarily with each other. The single most common combination observed was Critical/Hermeneutical with Rhetorical-Analytical—246 of 1684 dissertations share these two methods, or about 15 percent of the dissertations in the dataset—followed by Critical/Hermeneutical with Philosophical/Theoretical (188, or about 11 percent), then Rhetorical-Analytical with Historical/Archival (164, or ~10 percent of dissertations). As might be expected for the method with the highest overall frequency, the Philosophical/Theoretical tag was the one most likely to occur on its own (123 times, about 7 percent of the dissertations), but it is also the method tag that co-occurs with the most *other* tags, as seen in the shading that extends across the first row (and, equivalently, down the first column) of figure 3.8. This observation is in keeping with the finding from chapter 2 that topics related to theory run through the entire dataset, even though theory wasn't often the *primary* subject of the writer's inquiry. Combining that insight with the current figures, we can infer that, even when theoretical arguments made up less than half of the dissertation's text, such claims were still treated prominently in the abstract (on which these method tags were primarily based)—another way of signaling the value of theory to graduating PhD students and their committees.

Strikingly, however, the relationship is not symmetrical, as the next figure demonstrates. Whereas figure 3.8 shows the observed *number* of dissertations with each pair of tags, figure 3.9 scales these values within each row, dividing them by the total frequency of that row's method (as given above, in figure 3.1). The axes remain the same, but now

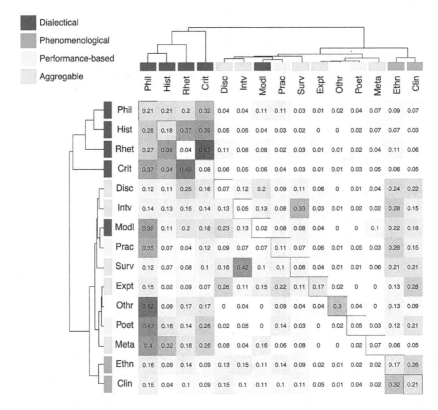

Figure 3.9. *Scaling method correlations within dissertations highlights linkages across methodological groups—but less so for the top four dialectical methods. A box in row Y and column X shows the observed probability (where 1 = 100%) that a dissertation tagged with method Y will also be tagged with method X. Note that the resulting heatmap is not symmetrical; in addition, the sum of values in each row may exceed 1 because some dissertations have more than two tags. As in the previous figure, diagonals indicate the rate of single-method dissertations, rather than totals (which would otherwise all be 1). N = 1,684 confirmed RCWS dissertations, 2001–2015.*

each cell shows the *proportion* of dissertations tagged with the method at the left that were also tagged with the method at the top: it shows, for example, that 35% of Practitioner/Teacher-Research dissertations were also tagged Philosophical/Theoretical, while only 6% were tagged (Quasi-)Experimental. Note that the figure is no longer symmetrical around the diagonal. That is, these relationships are no longer reciprocal: only 11% of Philosophical/Theoretical dissertations were also tagged as Practitioner studies, and for a (Quasi-)Experimental dissertation to be tagged Practitioner is almost four times as likely (22%) as the reverse.

Seen from this new angle, the commonality of pairing with the Philosophical/Theoretical tag is revealed to be more one-sided than

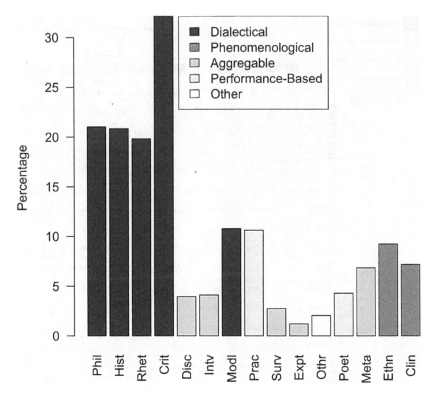

Figure 3.10. Rates of method co-occurrence for dissertations tagged "Philosophical/ Theoretical." N = 585 confirmed-RCWS dissertations, 2001–2015. These values correspond to the top row of figure 3.9. Values for PHIL indicate dissertations tagged only with that method.

figure 3.8 alone might have suggested: the shaded band is still present down the leftmost column, but no longer across the top row. This indicates that while dissertations employing a wide range of methods are relatively likely[10] to also employ Philosophical/Theoretical methods, the presence of Philosophical-Theoretical methods is more selectively predictive: these dissertations engage in Dialectical methods far more often than otherwise (20–32% of the time vs. 1–11% of the time), and specifically the other members of the top four methods overall: Critical/ Hermeneutical, Rhetorical-Analytical, and Historical/Archival.

Indeed, that whole dialectical corner at the top left of figure 3.9 is followed by a long stretch of white to the right across all four rows, indicating that a randomly selected dissertation tagged with one of these four methods is much less likely to also be tagged with any of the methods in the schema than the other three. This reinforces my impression from the method/school heatmap in figure 3.5 that many programs are "all-in" on this kind of research from sources: it's not just the programmatic view that suggests these methods form an integrated and often separate cluster, but also the view based on individual documents.

A similar pattern, albeit not quite as strong, occurs with the next-most common group of methods, Ethnographic and Clinical/Case Study. A solid block of gray along the right side of figure 3.9 demonstrates that—apart from the first four methods discussed above—many other methods co-occur with these phenomenological approaches at relatively high rates. When a dissertation uses Interviews, for example, 28% of the time it's in the context of Ethnography; over a quarter of Practitioner/ Teacher Research studies use Ethnographic methods, as well, and 22% of dissertations engaging in Discourse Analysis are trying to build portraits of individuals' behavior or motivations (CLIN). But the mostly white bottom rows show that this relationship isn't symmetrical: both phenomenological methods are most likely to co-occur with each other.

In a way, this asymmetry makes some sense: as Cindy Johanek (2000) points out, it's far easier to go from numbers to the story behind and around them (what she calls "the rich, multiple, and diverse layers of texts that exist in traditional research that relies on numerical data") than it is to pivot from phenomenological narrative to telling a quantitative story based on numbers that weren't collected initially (Johanek 2000, 120). Still, as I suggested above, the difference isn't as stark as with the top-four dialectical methods, and so we see relatively high rates of Philosophical/ Theoretical work in both Ethnographic and Clinical/Case Study dissertations, and one peak each at 15%: the correlations with Interview/Focus Group in the case of ETHN, and Discourse Analytical in the case of CLIN.

The co-occurrence of aggregable and phenomenological methods within dissertations could be somewhat surprising, because the epistemologies of the two methodological groups would seem to be opposed. As Max van Manen (1989) put it in *Researching Lived Experience*:

> In the sense that traditional, hypothesizing, or experimental research is largely interested in knowledge that is generalizable, true for one and all [. . . so that] actions and interventions, like exercises, are seen as repeatable; while subjects and samples, like soldiers, are replaceable. In contrast, phenomenology is, in a broad sense, a philosophy or *theory of the unique*; it is interested in what is essentially not replaceable. (Van Manen 1989, 6–7, emphasis in original)

For Van Manen, what aggregable research treats as a feature, the phenomenological treats as a bug, and vice versa: the unique is by definition what resists or defies pattern, and it's pattern that aggregation seeks to discern. To see graduate students working *across* these two modes, though, is a good reminder that ultimately it's impossible to know what is unique without knowing the pattern from which it deviates. As Johanek (2000) notes, pushing back on a resistance to quantification she sees in Peter Elbow's (1990) *What Is English?*,

> When joined with the "complexity" of moral evidence, scientific evidence adds information and helps make sense of the complexity of moral evidence . . . the "single number" never *replaces* the "valuable perceptions and data"; instead, the number *summarizes* the perceptions and data, which remain very much intact and are even enhanced by the new language given as a summary. (Johanek 2000, 51; italics in original. Words in quotation marks from Elbow 1990, 251)

In other words, in some ways it makes even more sense to combine the two groups of empirical methods than to keep them apart: by turns centering and decentering the individual perspective or the narrative of experience, the combination gives us more to see and more lenses through which to describe what we see; it helps paint a more nuanced picture. The relatively high rates at which dissertations using Discourse-Analytical (DISC), Interview/Focus Group (INTV), Survey (SURV), and even Experimental (EXPT) methods also engage in Ethnographic (ETHN) or Clinical / Case-Study (CASE) research suggests that at least some graduate students see the appeal of arguments like Johanek's; likewise for the use of DISC methods in ETHN dissertations and INTV methods in CLIN.

At the same time, the relatively low numbers of dissertations using aggregable methods in general also suggest that quantification is still far from standard practice. Whether this is an active decision on the part of dissertation-writers or a function of what graduate curricula emphasize (or de-emphasize), and how that relates to the training of doctoral faculty, remains to be seen. I do hope the analyses in this book help readers reflect on both how they've considered aggregable and empirical research in the past, and on what quantification makes possible—and thus whether they would want to further develop their capacities for it in the future. I can say that recent advances in technology have steadily lowered the barriers to entry for data analysis and visualization; for more examples of why and how writing studies might want to engage in these processes, see the collection I edited with Amanda Licastro, *Composition and Big Data* (Licastro and Miller 2021). As the foregoing discussion in this chapter demonstrates, quantitative and qualitative methods are far from mutually exclusive.

Further demonstrating how those lines are already blurred, two methods stand out in figure 3.9 as different from the others within their methodological group: Meta-Analytical/Discipliniographic (META) and Model-Building (MODL). Unlike other aggregable methods, which I

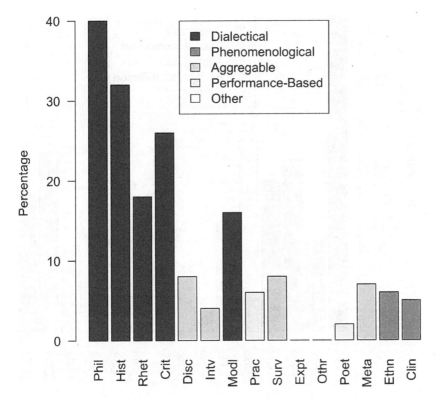

Figure 3.11. *Rates of method co-occurrence for dissertations tagged "Meta-Analytical/ Discipliniographic." N = 100 confirmed-RCWS dissertations, 2001–2015. These values correspond to the* META *row of figure 3.9. Values for* META *indicate dissertations tagged only with that method.*

described above, the META tag is far more likely to co-occur with *dialectical* methods than with either phenomenological or other aggregable ones (see figure 3.11).

A dissertation tagged META is tagged Philosophical/Theoretical 40% of the time, one of the highest rates of co-occurrence between two methods observed in the whole dataset. The remaining four dialectical methods appear in META-tagged dissertations at a rate of at least 15% each (and Historical/Archival is more than twice that), while nondialectical methods appear 8% of the time or less. I believe this reflects the *discipliniographic* nature of the evidence drawn on by this method: whereas meta-analysis in many fields involves synthesizing and summarizing other RAD studies, for Rhetoric and Composition, with its relatively limited supply of aggregable data, the most commonly available data to synthesize is text: journal articles, conference presentations,

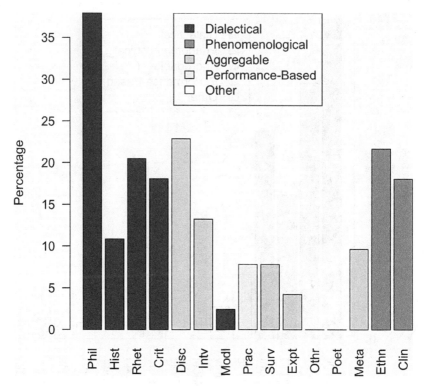

Figure 3.12. *Rates of method co-occurrence for dissertations tagged "Model-Building."* N = 166 confirmed-RCWS dissertations, 2001–2015. These values correspond to the MODL row of figure 3.9. Values for MODL indicate dissertations tagged only with that method.

syllabi. These kinds of data lend themselves to histories of the field and to philosophical discussions about its purpose and its future, or to scale-shifting between distant and close readings of the items under analysis.

The Model-Building method, which involves a systematizing imaginary, is far less common in this dataset than the other four dialectical methods; in both overall frequency (as seen in figure 3.1) and distribution across schools (as seen in figure 3.7), it is more in line with aggregable methods. It is reasonable to wonder whether model-building is less popular because the phenomena it works to explain are more likely to be data derived from empirical studies than the text-based sources most commonly at the heart of the other four dialectical methods—the paired opposite, that is, of Meta-Analysis/Discipliniography. In other words, is the frequency of the MODL tag "pulled down" by the general unpopularity of RAD studies in this time period?

The data can help us test this hypothesis. As it turns out, while Model-Building does tend to appear in different contexts than other dialectical methods, it's not as straightforward as saying that it pairs with data-focused replicable/aggregable methods.

Figure 3.12, which expands one line of the heatmap in figure 3.9, shows that the method most likely to appear in the same dissertation as Model-Building is actually Philosophical/Theoretical (63 of 166 dissertations tagged as Model-Building, or 38%). The next-most common pairing is, though, an empirical method, namely Discourse-Analytical (23%): studies treating text as a mine-able corpus of recurring features. But the third falls in yet another methodological group: a little more than one in five Model-Building dissertations also engage in Ethnography (22%). Nearly as many employ Rhetorical-Analytical methods (20%). In a way, then, Model-Building is an equal-opportunity method for dissertation writers in composition/rhetoric, despite appearing in only about 10% of dissertations overall in this time period.

PACKING FOR A JOURNEY THROUGH
A DISCIPLINARY LANDSCAPE

I had categorized Model-Building as a dialectical method, not an empirical one, because the models people build are ultimately both developed and accepted based not on direct observations and descriptions ("what happens/happened?") but on explanations ("what does it mean?" in the sense of "*why* did that happen?"). But the difference points to the limits of such groupings, and the importance of interrogating assumptions.

When Liggett, Jordan, and Price (2011) surveyed the landscape of research in writing center studies, they initially developed a cleanly separable taxonomy, splitting research into three main clusters (55):

1. *Practitioner Inquiry* (further subdivided into narrative and pragmatic inquiry, or what I have here labeled, respectively, Poetic/Fictive and Practitioner/Teacher Research);

2. *Conceptual Inquiry* (historical, critical, theoretical; note that this seems to map onto North's Scholarly set of approaches); and

3. *Empirical Inquiry* (with two subclusters, descriptive and experimental/quasiexperimental, the first of which breaks down further into survey, text analysis, and a pair of "contextual methods," i.e., case study and ethnographic inquiry, or the pair I have referred to above as having phenomenological methodology).

However, after realizing the extent to which methodologies were more pluralistic in practice, they re-imagined that top-down hierarchy as a more geographical map, with the three branches as points on a triangle: some methods, they realized, are closer to conceptual inquiry than to empirical, or vice versa, without being entirely captured by either; some approaches are pulled in by practitioner inquiry, and some pull away from it. This allowed them to label the landscape in between as "Methodological Pluralism" (81, their figure 2).

Like Liggett, Jordan, and Price (2011), I find the body of evidence suggests that the clean categories identified by North (1987) are not, in practice, as separate as he thought or feared. To the extent that there are methodological subcommunities within rhetoric, composition, and writing studies, there appear to be many people who commute among them.

Having said that, though, is not license to give up on characterizing the field: the methodological landscape is not flat, nor evenly distributed in population density. The maps I've drawn in this chapter seem to point to two major conclusions, each with an accompanying caution—not quite a *hic sunt dracones*, but a risk of misinterpretation I want to forestall—as well as a question each doctoral program must ask about where it wants to be, and go.

A first conclusion: the dialectical methods of conceptual inquiry constitute a city center, as it were, that attracts far more inbound commuters than it sends back into the metaphorical suburbs.[11] Graduate programs that focus on dialectical methods can be seen, in that sense, as metropolitan, no matter where they might be situated in the real world.

The richness and range of approaches to history, hermeneutics, rhetoric, and theory provide these programs with an internal diversity that is surely attractive and sustaining. At the same time, like real-world big cities, we must be mindful of the potential for an ironic metropolitan parochialism that sees this range as entirely sufficient. I think of the famous *New Yorker* cover showing the "View of the World from 9th Avenue": two city blocks fill half the page, and everything from the city-bordering Hudson River to the far-off Pacific Ocean is collapsed into a quarter-page, half that size; the rest is empty sky (Steinberg and Wikipedia contributors 2021). A first caution, then: if we allowed our methodological perspectives to echo the attitude that illustration both lampoons and indulges—if we were to say, there's dialectical work here and phenomenological work dimly visible out there, and isn't that all there is?—then the dappling of our discipline would have lost quite a few shades of meaning.

A second conclusion. All programs have methods beyond those they spend most of their energies on, as this chapter has shown; how they want to consider or describe the methods not included (or not included equally) is a question for local consideration and reflection. Dissertation writers thinking about how they will gather evidence, toward what kinds of questions, should know better using the charts and graphs above what kinds of questions and evidence (which is to say, what methodologies) are most likely to be familiar to their most likely readers across the field as a whole—for example, hiring committees, journal readers, and to some extent dissertation committees—from those readers' own graduate work or work with graduate students.

A second caution, though: such an outward-facing familiarity with common methods should not stop student researchers from practicing less-common ones. On the contrary, one might say that the rarity-but-persistent-presence of a method is an invitation to shore up what we can learn about writing, rhetoric, and composition by means of that method. Data visualization can help identify these less turned-to approaches just as readily as it does the most customary ones. For instance, the lower-frequency values in the bar chart of figure 3.1 (such as Poetic/Fictive, Experimental, or Meta-Analytical) or in the heatmaps of figures 3.8 and 3.9 (e.g., the pairing of Historical/Archival with Practitioner/Teacher Research) should help to identify these less obvious throughlines and tracks, and how they have historically combined—or left gaps for future writers to explore.

But this also raises the question of who will mentor writers in navigating such tracks and gaps, and so for doctoral curriculum designers and hiring committees, the charts and graphs in this chapter offer an opportunity to reflect on their current capacity to do so, and to decide how they want to move forward: whether they will specialize in a particular group of methods; try to expand what they can offer in terms of direct methodological mentoring (perhaps through the hiring of new faculty); or perhaps just to gesture toward the existence of other methods in a course on disciplinary history and practices, as a way of at least increasing students' familiarity and literacy in absorbing such research, if not producing it themselves.

Our understanding of "the field" is, by and large, local. At our home campuses, we see a range of methods and know the field to be diverse, and so we meet colleagues from elsewhere and agree that yes, this is a "dappled discipline" (Lauer 1984). But as this chapter has shown, the variation itself varies from place to place. Understanding the range of methodological options currently in use can help us appreciate both the common ground we share and the paths that are (in Hopkins's words) "counter, original, spare, strange."

4

BUT DOESN'T EVERYONE KNOW ABOUT WRITING?
Distinguishing RCWS from Allied Fields

There will be time, there will be time
To prepare a face to meet the faces that you meet;
—T. S. Eliot, "The Love Song of J. Alfred Prufrock"

The success of Writing Across the Curriculum and Writing in the Disciplines (WAC/WID) initiatives over the last few decades is a reminder of something that might have seemed obvious without departments of composition and writing studies: writing knowledge and expertise is not the domain only of writing specialists. In every field of academia (and beyond), part of professional development and training is the development of genre awareness, writerly skills, and habits of mind suited to those domains. Interdisciplinary or metadisciplinary scholarship of teaching and learning (SoTL) can turn, in part, on how students acquire this awareness, or these skills and habits. And to the extent that all cultural productions are composed—are "texts" of one kind or another—historical and cultural studies through a wide variety of lenses can be seen as a way of studying composition, rhetoric, or writing.

It should come as no surprise, then, that some graduate students working outside the familiar Consortium of Doctoral Programs in Rhetoric and Composition would also tag their dissertations "language, rhetoric and composition" when submitting to the ProQuest database. In the timespan examined in the earlier chapters (2001–2015), in addition to the 1,684 dissertations confirmed to be from known RCWS programs, the dataset I received from ProQuest also contains 733 dissertations that were clearly from *other* programs—plus another 1,230 for which I was unable to determine the program of origin.[1] After removing dissertations with top topics that were non–content bearing (see appendix C), I was left with 695 dissertations. In the analyses that follow, I will focus on these 695 confirmed-non-RCWS dissertations as a way of seeing from a new angle what it means to study writing, rhetoric,

https://doi.org/10.7330/9781646423224.c004

and/or composition under the disciplinary affiliation of rhetoric and composition/writing studies.

The dissertations in this new subcorpus were from a wide range of departments. Of those whose programs could be determined, the plurality were from communication studies or a variant thereof[2] (132 dissertations); many came from departments related to languages and literatures (55) or education (35), including educational psychology. Other programs included political science, linguistics, philosophy, classical studies, journalism, and psychology; a number of department names also had terms referring to culture or society in combination with those mentioned above. For 447 of the dissertations even in the confirmed subcorpus, the departments were not indicated, but I nevertheless categorized them as non-RCWS because they were either completed at schools outside the lists in rhetmap.org and the Consortium of Doctoral Programs in Rhetoric and Composition, or because they were not included in departmental alumni lists I was able to obtain from known RCWS programs.

The presence of rhetoric and composition research outside of rhetoric and composition is, on the one hand, exciting. It means that there is wider interest in formal study of writing and learning to write than we sometimes give credit for—when, for example, the authors of *Naming What We Know* feel it necessary to declare that "Writing is an activity and a subject of study" is a threshold concept: a form of "troublesome knowledge" that not all would accept (Adler-Kassner and Wardle 2015, 15, 2). On the other hand, as that book makes clear, there are many ways of framing that subject of study, and not all of them will be shared widely across all the contexts of studying it. As members of a community of practice, graduate students in RCWS are enculturated into these concepts, or something like them, and the concepts in turn evolve through the practice and experience of those same student and faculty researchers, scholars, teachers, and writers. Different communities of practice, working from different shared experiences and citation networks, will enculturate their members to some different threshold concepts. But that doesn't mean we can't understand and communicate and even collaborate across such differences. And in fact, as Adler-Kassner and Wardle (2020) argue in their follow-up collection, *Re-Considering What We Know*, articulating these differences or gaps can be important for bridging across them (2020, 16–19).

Before we start to talk about what these other fields are focusing on, it's important to first acknowledge the variety of what I'm examining here. As I mentioned above, there are a lot of departments represented

in the dataset, along with a lot of dissertations that I couldn't find departments for; because of that breadth, the sample size of any one discipline
is actually quite small. Whereas just about everything in RCWS should
be captured by a search for rhetoric, composition, and writing,[3] we can't
expect that these areas would form anything close to the majority of
dissertation topics in political science, or psychology, or even linguistics.
Communication, the largest sample of confirmed-department studies
I have, is represented here by only 132 dissertations, or something less
than 10% the size of the confirmed-RCWS sample.

So rather than saying something clear about trends in these *other*
disciplines, the comparisons I'm elaborating in this chapter are better
suited for telling us what's *distinctive* about RCWS: what makes rhet-
comp dissertators recognizable as a coherent group compared to the
mixed multitude of other graduate-level researchers on similar subjects.

ROADS NOT TAKEN: DIFFERENTIALLY POPULAR TOPICS AND METHODS IN RHETORIC, COMPOSITION, AND WRITING OUTSIDE RHETORIC, COMPOSITION, AND WRITING STUDIES

Despite the variety of disciplinary influences merging in this dataset,
some clear patterns do emerge: topics and methods that RCWS dissertations engage with only rarely, but that are taken up often in other
departmental contexts. Table 4.1 shows the top ten topics by aggregate
percentage of tokens in the non-RCWS corpus, along with the corresponding ranks and percentages in the RCWS corpus.

Let's focus, first, on what's the same. Fully half of these topics appear
also in the corresponding top ten list for RCWS: "Rhetorics of Power,
Conflict, and Politics" (Topic 21), "Personal Narrative and Oral History"
(T2), "Reading Rhetoricians, Interpreting Philosophy" (T48), "Scenes
of Teaching" (T49), and "Collaborative Learning" (T41). That list also
includes four of the top five topics in the RCWS corpus, measured either
by aggregate tokens or by 5% reach across dissertations (which is the
same top five; see chapter 2). Another way of saying that: many of the
most common topics for graduate research that composition/rhetoric is
sponsoring are *not* actually that unique to composition/rhetoric.

This suggests grounds for collaboration and cross-citation with other
fields, some of which already happens but more of which might mutually benefit all concerned. That said, this finding does not preclude
other differences in the *way* we go about researching these topics; we'll
need to look at methods, for starters, and there may be additional genre
markers that closer readings could reveal. In addition, it could be that

Table 4.1. Topics of rank 1–10, by aggregate percentage of tokens in the confirmed non-RCWS corpus (across 695 dissertations). Topics in italics are in the top 10 for the confirmed RCWS corpus as well; topics in bold are ranked much lower in that corpus.

Non-RCWS rank	% of non-RCWS corpus	Assigned label (topic #)	% of RCWS corpus	RCWS rank
1	6.2	**Presidential Discourse** (T19)	1.26	29
2	5.73	*Rhetorics of Power, Conflict, and Politics* (T21)	5.2	3
3	4.5	*Personal Narrative and Oral History* (T26)	4.74	4
4	4.36	*Reading Rhetoricians, Interpreting Philosophy* (T48)	3.05	10
5	4.36	**Politics, Empire, Radicalism** (T13)	2.48	17
6	4.26	**Writing Process** (T18)	2.67	14
7	3.91	**Testing Predictive Models** (T6)	0.95	34
8	3.55	**K12 Writing Pedagogy** (T42)	2.01	21
9	3.33	*Scenes of teaching* (T49)	6.1	2
10	3.22	*Collaborative Learning* (T41)	4.69	5

these potential collaborators might not share all of the common threshold concepts as identified, for example, in *Naming What We Know*. (Doug Hesse and Peggy O'Neill [2020] offer a case in point through a study of learning outcomes and guiding principles in journalism and creative writing.) But even those points of contention are opportunities for dialogue, negotiation, and growth.

The exceptions can tell us more about what does set composition-rhetoricians apart. The most common non-RCWS topic is "Presidential Discourse" (T19), which includes keywords such as *bush president presidential war clinton reagan campaign policy presidents military public iraq political news obama u.s nuclear media speech election*. While this topic does appear in RCWS dissertations, at an aggregate rate of 1.26% of that corpus, this rate puts it in the bottom half of topics represented in the model for those dissertations. There is a disjunction, then, between RCWS writers' interest in "Rhetorics of Power, Conflict, and

Politics" (T21), third-ranked overall, and presidential discourse specifically. Seeing that students in other programs do not, on average, make
the same choice—they are collectively able to attend to both, and to
"Politics, Empire, Radicalism" (T13) as well—raises a question about why
RCWS might trend otherwise.

Consider the different emphases in these three political topics, as
shown in table 4.2.

The topics are listed here in their order of prominence within the
confirmed-RCWS corpus; this arrangement also has the effect of ordering them in decreasing order of theoretical orientation. Whereas top
titles in RCWS for topic 21 talk about broad "pragmatics of power" and
"an expanded theory of rhetoric," seeking to move from the specific
to the general, for topic 19 (Presidential Discourse) the RCWS titles
project a more descriptive orientation, moving from the general to the
specific: the "role of ethos and parrhesia" in *one* presidential candidate's
discourse, the cases of two vice-presidential nominees, dialogism in one
campaign. Topic 13 (Politics, Empire, Radicalism) occupies a middle
space, with named contexts that are both more explicit than in T21 and
broader than in T19, such as "American anarchism" and "Bolshevik
organizational communication." The non-RCWS titles, on the other
hand, are more descriptive across the board. Even in the more theory-
oriented "Rhetorics of Power, Conflict, and Politics" (T21) we see more
discrete exhibits under analysis: multiculturalism applied to analysis of
negotiations around European Union membership, cosmopolitanism as
a lens on Carter, Havel, and Said, and so on. While neither trend is uni-
versal (e.g., the non-RCWS corpus includes a dissertation moving outward "toward a rhetorical theory for democratic politics"), the overall
pattern suggests that the more a political topic manifests through concrete reading of a specific exhibit, the less representative that topic is of
rhetoric and composition's approach to politics and power. Conversely,
the more a political topic builds toward a general theory of power, the
more rhet/comp takes up that topic.

This difference is in keeping with a generally low-empirical tendency
within the RCWS corpus in this time period (2001–2015), as shown
both in chapter 3's study of dissertation methods and in the turn away
from statistical modeling and verification shown in table 4.1. Testing
Predictive Models (topic 6) is the seventh-most-common topic for non-
RCWS dissertations, accounting for something like one of every twenty-
five tokens in the aggregate corpus. In the RCWS corpus, by contrast,
that topic made up less than one in a hundred tokens, ranking thirty-
fourth. The most topic-specific[4] key terms for topic 6, *study group table*

Table 4.2. Comparing 3 politically oriented topics differently ranked by aggregate percentage of tokens in the confirmed RCWS and non-RCWS corpora.

Assigned label (topic #)	Most topic-specific keywords (TF-ITF)	Top RCWS titles (% of diss. text from this topic)	Top non-RCWS titles (% of diss. text from this topic)
Rhetorics of Power, Conflict, and Politics (T21)	discourse public social community identity power discursive discourses political critical cultural conflict dialogue process agency action individuals ideological values communication	A pragmatics of power using Juergen Habermas' theory of communicative action (71%) Rhetorical in(ter)vention and the dialectic of conflict and conflict resolution: Sulh and Sadat's peacemaking rhetoric (53%) Transforming social conflict through an expanded theory of rhetoric (52%)	The return of the Serbian other: Interpretative repertoires of nationalism and identity politics in online news discourses on Serbia's integration in the European Union (63%) The rhetorical uses of multiculturalism: An ideographic analysis of the European Union and Macedonian discourses in the dialogue for EU accession (46%) Communicating cosmopolitanism: An analysis of the rhetoric of Jimmy Carter, Vaclav Havel, and Edward Said (34%)
Politics, Empire, Radicalism (T13)	political politics democracy war violence democratic radical capitalism freedom power liberal critique public ideology ibid american revolution ideological utopian conservative	Without content: Rhetoric, American anarchism, and the end(s) of radical politics (47%) Entering the fray: The slogan's place in Bolshevik organizational communication (47%) Agent and Event: Rhetorical Dissent in the Context of Globalization (39%)	Constituting conservatism: The Goldwater/Paul analog (39%) The rhetorical pursuit of political advantage: Toward a rhetorical theory for democratic politics (38%) A rhetoric of moral imagination: The persuasions of Russell Kirk (38%)
Presidential Discourse (T19)	bush presidential president war clinton reagan presidents iraq campaign obama policy political public military news u.s presidency election nuclear speeches	The role of ethos and parrhesia in the presidential reelection discourse of George Herbert Walker Bush (60%) Women's political rhetoric: The cases of United States vice-presidential nominees Geraldine Ferraro and Sarah Palin (57%) Blogs and dialogism in the 2008 United States presidential campaign (48%)	Framing national security threats: An analysis of the arguments in the missile defense controversy (80%) Part of something larger than ourselves: George H.W. Bush and the rhetoric of the first United States war in the Persian Gulf (80%) The reverend, the terrorist, and a web of rumors: The image repair discourse of Barack Obama (69%)

scores results research significant participants test score data groups total number differences model variables level effect scale, are not exactly foreign to the history of composition/rhetoric research; however, what they most call to mind is an earlier era in that history, when research into writing process was conducted primarily through experimental and quasi-experimental studies. Indeed, while the RCWS corpus does address Writing Process (T18) moderately often (2.67% of the aggregate corpus, rank 14), the non-RCWS corpus does so more regularly: 4.26% of the aggregate corpus, for rank 6 overall.

This difference in attention to empiricism—and especially quantitative or aggregable empiricism—is visible as well in the methods and methodologies given priority across dissertations in RCWS programs compared to those outside of them. Figure 4.1 shows the relative ranks of assigned method tags in the two groups; lines connect corresponding tags to make the shifts easier to see.

Six of the method tags show statistically significant differences between the two corpora, with the most dramatic being the rate of the Experimental/Quasi-Experimental tag, which appears more than three times as often in dissertations completed at non-RCWS programs than in those at RCWS programs. Philosophical/Theoretical, on the other hand, appears significantly more often in the RCWS corpus (about 1.5 times as often), earning the top rank for that group of dissertations but dropping to the bottom of the cluster of dialectical methods in the non-RCWS corpus. Rhetorical-Analytical methods, oriented toward identifying repeatable writerly "moves," were less representative of RCWS than of non-RCWS dissertations. (Note that this corroborates from a different angle the finding that rhetorically oriented subjects were not distinctive to rhetoric and composition in the topic model.)

I want to be clear: I am *not* saying that empirical, statistical, or even experimental studies cannot be seen as "truly" part of RCWS. On the contrary, part of what I aimed to demonstrate in the previous chapter is that such studies are regularly used as passports to the PhD, across a wide array of RCWS graduate programs. Moreover, I would expect to see the prevalence of modeling and statistical work persist and even grow in the period since the 2001–2015 dataset under consideration here, as better computer hardware and software has become more readily available. In *Composition and Big Data,* for example (Licastro and Miller 2021), scholars use large-scale computational methods to analyze sentence-level stylistic complexity; the frequency with which writers synthesize multiple sources within paragraphs; the shifting subject lines in disciplinary listservs; the topical focus of peer review comments; and

Confirmed RCWS dissertations
(N=1684)

Confirmed non–RCWS dissertations
(N=695)

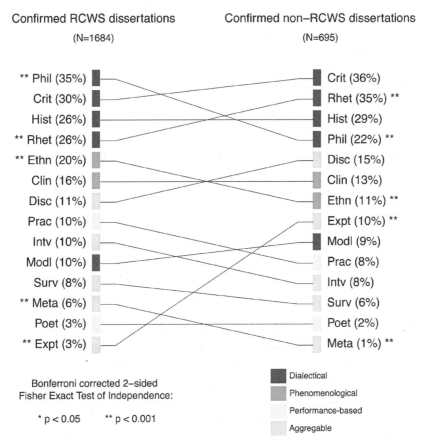

Figure 4.1. *Method tag frequency comparison between confirmed RCWS corpus (N = 1,684) and confirmed non-RCWS (N = 695) dissertation corpora. In both columns, method tags are arranged in descending order of frequency, with percentages of each corpus given in parentheses. Significance was computed using each method's odds ratio of tagged vs. not-tagged across the two corpora (Fisher's exact test), with possible correlations among methods accounted for (Bonferroni correction). Method tag abbreviations and descriptions are as in table 3.1.*

more. And many of these authors began that work while completing PhD programs.

What I am saying, though, is that empirical/statistical studies were very much in the minority of dissertations in RCWS in the early twenty-first century, both overall and at most graduate programs in the field. Considering the work outside those departments from the same time period establishes that this tendency is not merely part of a broader shift in academic culture, nor is there something inherent in the subject matter to require the imbalance observed in RCWS dissertation work. The pattern may, then, reflect a disciplinary culture that valorizes theory over empiricism; how much we wish to sustain such a culture, or where we should strike the balance, is a question that graduate faculty and students should consider.

METHODOLOGICAL COMMITMENTS AND CORRELATIONS

When we looked at the methods that tend to co-occur in RCWS dissertations, in chapter 3, Dialectical methods mostly appeared with each other (marked in the graph by a dark block in the upper left of figure 3.9) and Phenomenological methods did the same (forming another block in the lower right), with only a few methods occurring across the board regardless of what else was going on methodologically (as signaled by vertical lines of shading in the graph). Philosophical/Theoretical (PHIL) was the strongest of these across-the-board methods, followed by Clinical/Case Study (CLIN), that is, close descriptions of individual writers. In figure 4.2, which uses the same row and column order for dissertation methods outside of RCWS, the Dialectical and Phenomenological clusters in the upper left and lower right continue, as we might expect. But a number of other patterns diverge from the RCWS method correlations, pointing to different disciplinary expectations of what constitutes a "normal" combination of methods for a dissertation.

There is a notable gap about midway down the left side of the graph: Experimental (EXPT) and Survey (SURV) studies are much less likely in this dataset to also engage in Philosophical/Theoretical methods than they were in the RCWS dataset, and, as the darker squares along the middle of the diagonal indicate, much more likely to appear as methods unto themselves (31% for EXPT and 26% for SURV, as opposed to 17% and 8%, respectively, in RCWS). Practitioner/Teacher Research (PRAC), in RCWS, was most associated with Philosophical/Theoretical and Ethnographic (ETHN) methods; in the confirmed non-RCWS dissertations, these PRAC studies are more likely to be paired with Experimental (40%) or Clinical/Case Study methods (23% of the time).

To better illustrate these changes, consider figure 4.3, which represents the mathematical difference between the observed rates of method co-occurrence in the two datasets. In other words, the values here indicate percentage point changes in likelihood that a dissertation using the method in a given row will use the method in the corresponding column.

As in the other figures of this type, the rates here are determined by dividing by dissertation counts in each row; this bears repeating because

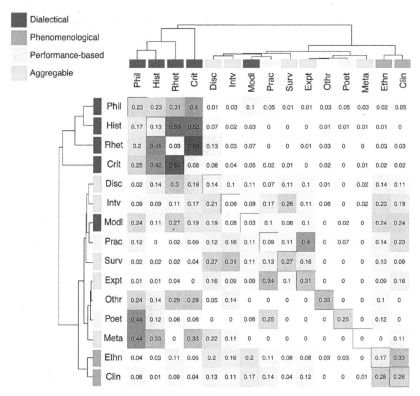

Legend: Dialectical, Phenomenological, Performance-based, Aggregable

	Phil	Hist	Rhet	Crit	Disc	Intv	Modl	Prac	Surv	Expt	Othr	Poet	Meta	Ethn	Clin
Phil	0.23	0.23	0.31	0.4	0.01	0.03	0.1	0.05	0.01	0.01	0.03	0.05	0.03	0.02	0.05
Hist	0.17	0.13	0.53	0.52	0.07	0.02	0.03	0	0	0	0.01	0.01	0.01	0.01	0
Rhet	0.2	0.45	0.03	0.62	0.13	0.03	0.07	0	0	0.01	0.03	0	0	0.03	0.03
Crit	0.25	0.42	0.59	0.08	0.08	0.04	0.05	0.02	0.01	0	0.02	0	0.01	0.02	0.02
Disc	0.02	0.14	0.3	0.19	0.14	0.1	0.11	0.07	0.11	0.1	0.01	0	0.02	0.14	0.11
Intv	0.09	0.09	0.11	0.17	0.21	0.06	0.09	0.17	0.26	0.11	0.06	0	0.02	0.23	0.19
Modl	0.24	0.11	0.27	0.19	0.19	0.08	0.03	0.1	0.08	0.1	0	0.02	0	0.24	0.24
Prac	0.12	0	0.02	0.09	0.12	0.16	0.11	0.09	0.11	0.4	0	0.07	0	0.14	0.23
Surv	0.02	0.02	0.02	0.04	0.27	0.31	0.11	0.13	0.27	0.16	0	0	0	0.13	0.09
Expt	0.01	0.01	0.04	0	0.16	0.09	0.09	0.34	0.1	0.31	0	0	0	0.09	0.16
Othr	0.24	0.14	0.29	0.29	0.05	0.14	0	0	0	0	0.33	0	0	0.1	0
Poet	0.44	0.12	0.06	0.06	0	0	0.06	0.25	0	0	0	0.25	0	0.12	0
Meta	0.44	0.33	0	0.33	0.22	0.11	0	0	0	0	0	0	0	0	0.11
Ethn	0.04	0.03	0.11	0.05	0.2	0.16	0.2	0.11	0.08	0.08	0.03	0.03	0	0.17	0.33
Clin	0.08	0.01	0.09	0.04	0.13	0.11	0.17	0.14	0.04	0.12	0	0	0.01	0.28	0.26

Figure 4.2. Method correlations within dissertations (normed by row), N = 695 confirmed non-RCWS dissertations, 2001–2015. A box in row Y and column X shows the observed probability (where 1 = 100%) that a dissertation tagged with method Y will also be tagged with method X. Note that the resulting heatmap[5] is not symmetrical; in addition, the sum of values in each row may exceed 1 because some dissertations have more than two tags. As in figure 3.9, the corresponding figure for RCWS dissertations, the diagonals indicate the rate of single-method dissertations, rather than totals (which would otherwise all be 1).

it means that some of the more dramatic swings here are merely artifacts caused by low sample sizes. We can safely discount the twenty-point differences in the Poetic/Fictive (POET) row, for example, because there are only fourteen dissertations using that method in the non-RCWS dataset. That said, the *direction* of change is still likely to be meaningful: single-method narrative or poetic dissertations are indeed less common in RCWS, whereas Clinical/Case Studies involving creative writers (the intersection of POET and CLIN) are more common in RCWS, if still not common overall. Similar concerns apply to the highest values in the rows for META (Meta-Analytical/Discipliniographic) and OTHR (with the latter signaling methods even less common in RCWS, not explicitly named in the schema).

Change in Methodological Pairing Likelihood

(Percentage point difference, RCWS minus non-RCWS)

More common in non-RCWS corpus   -30   +30   More common in RCWS corpus

	Phil	Hist	Rhet	Crit	Disc	Intv	Modl	Prac	Surv	Expt	Othr	Poet	Meta	Ethn	Clin
Phil	-2	-2	-11	-8	3	1	1	6	2	0	-1	-1	4	7	2
Hist	11	5	-16	-13	-2	3	1	3	2	0	-1	1	6	6	3
Rhet	7	-7	1	-5	-2	4	1	2	3	0	-1	2	4	8	3
Crit	12	-8	-10	0	-2	1	1	2	2	1	-1	3	4	4	3
Disc	10	-3	-5	-3	-7	2	9	2	0	-4	-1	1	2	10	11
Intv	5	4	4	-3	-8	-1	4	-9	7	-8	-5	2	0	5	-4
Modl	14	0	-7	-1	4	5	-1	-2	0	-6	0	-2	10	-2	-6
Prac	23	7	2	3	-3	-9	-4	2	-4	-34	1	-2	3	12	-8
Surv	10	5	6	6	-11	11	-1	-3	-19	-12	1	1	6	8	12
Expt	14	1	5	7	10	2	6	-12	1	-14	2	0	0	4	12
Othr	28	-5	-12	-12	-5	-10	0	9	4	4	-3	4	0	3	9
Poet	-1	4	8	20	2	5	-6	-11	3	0	2	-20	3	0	21
Meta	-4	-1	18	-7	-14	-7	16	6	8	0	0	2	7	6	-6
Ethn	12	6	3	4	-7	-1	-9	3	1	-6	-2	-1	2	0	-7
Clin	7	3	1	5	2	-1	-6	-4	7	-7	1	4	1	4	-5

Figure 4.3. Change in methodological pairing likelihood, RCWS vs. non-RCWS, 2001–2015. Values in row Y, column X represent percentage point changes between the observed probability that a dissertation in the confirmed-RCWS dataset (N = 1,684) tagged with method Y will also be tagged with method X and the corresponding probability for a dissertation in the confirmed-non-RCWS dataset (N = 695). Positive values, in red, mean that the pairing is more likely in the RCWS data; negative values, in blue, mean that the pairing is less likely in RCWS than outside of it. Darker shades represent greater absolute value of the difference. Values along the diagonal refer to dissertations tagged with only one method.

In rows with more robust representation, the strengths of the swings are more meaningful. Halfway down the figure, for example, figure 4.3 draws more attention to the striking difference in how Practitioner/Teacher Research (PRAC) is handled inside and outside RCWS, mentioned briefly above. Dissertations in other disciplines are 34 percentage points more likely to link such classroom studies to Experimental/Quasi-experimental (EXPT) methods; dissertations in rhetoric and composition, by contrast, are far more likely to link them to Philosophical/Theoretical (PHIL) arguments, by a margin of 23 percentage points. They are also more likely to use Ethnographic (ETHN) methods—that is, to study the full activity system—while non-RCWS dissertations are more likely to produce Clinical/Case Study (CLIN) portraits of individuals alongside their Practitioner research (albeit by a smaller margin of 8 percentage points).

Survey research (SURV) is another row in which figure 4.3 shows large differences in associated methods. While both RCWS and non-RCWS dissertations commonly pair surveys with interviews (INTV), that pairing is more likely in RCWS: 42% of the SURV-tagged dissertations versus 31%. In the non-RCWS dataset, by contrast, there was a higher rate of discourse analysis (DISC) in the same dissertation (27% versus 16%) and a much higher likelihood of surveys (SURV) being used as the sole research method: also 27%, compared to just 8% in the RCWS dataset, for a 19-point spread.

Some of the largest differences between the two datasets in terms of method pairings come from Experimental/Quasi-experimental (EXPT) and Philosophical/Theoretical (PHIL) methods, as might be expected from the large slopes of their relative overall frequencies shown in figure 4.1. The mostly blue column for EXPT near the center of figure 4.3 suggests that hypothesis-driven, data-supported studies are a more common part of the methodological mix for non-RCWS programs' graduates than for rhet/comp PhDs. Again, this is not a huge surprise, given the earlier discussion of aggregable empirical studies' low frequency in RCWS contexts; even so, seeing the same signal repeated across many rows reinforces the impression that the EXPT tag's relatively high rank in the non-RCWS corpus indicates its status as a "normal" practice to incorporate, rather than stemming from solo experimental studies alone.

Conversely, the solid line of red along the left side of the figure (i.e., the PHIL column) indicates that the tendency of RCWS dissertations to signal Philosophical/Theoretical methodology in abstracts across a wide range of topics—as discussed in chapter 3—does not seem to be shared widely outside of RCWS. Interestingly, this applies even within the dialectical cluster at the top left of the figure, which includes the four methods that ranked highest in both corpora: Historical/Archival (HIST), Rhetorical-Analytical (RHET), and Critical/Hermeneutical (CRIT), along with Philosophical/Theoretical itself. While these methods cluster with each other in both RCWS and non-RCWS dissertations, the blue in that corner signals that the proportions are not the same: in disciplines outside of writing studies, CRIT and especially RHET are the more go-to dialectical methods, appearing in more than half of HIST-tagged dissertations and appearing together around 60% of the time either one appears.

It's tempting to say this pattern points to something about the nature of "rhetoric" in rhetoric & composition, for example, that it's more separable from hermeneutics than in other fields. But that's more of a leap that we can make based on the present data: even with the 10-percentage-point gap between corpora, Rhetorical-Analytical and Critical/Hermeneutical methods are still commonly found together in the RCWS corpus—57% of RHET-tagged dissertations are also tagged CRIT—and in fact this pairing has the single highest co-occurrence rate in figure 3.9. Rather than say rhetorical analysis and textual criticism are separable, then, it might be more useful to see them as often linked, and to see their linkage as a highly recognizable starting point for interdisciplinary conversations—even in cases where the next step in that conversation might be to separate them, for example, to rhetorically analyze something beyond a text or without interpretation of particular content.

IN-FIELD INDICATORS: META-TOPICS ARE MORE COMMON IN RCWS-AFFILIATED PROGRAMS THAN OUTSIDE OF THEM

If the previous sections point to investigative roads not taken, what are the paths *more* traveled-by in RCWS than among those studying writing and rhetoric elsewhere? In other words, what topics and methods are revealed through contrast as most distinctive to rhetoric and composition/writing studies as a discipline? Table 4.3 repeats the comparison of table 4.1 from the other direction, recapitulating the top ten RCWS topics by aggregate token (from chapter 2) and adding the corresponding percentages and ranks in the non-RCWS corpus.

Perhaps not surprisingly, the topic associated with studying the disciplinarity of writing studies—what I've called "Disciplinary Formations" (T32)—is much more common in the writing studies corpus, appearing over five times as often as in other programs. (Likewise, figure 4.1 showed that the Meta-analytical/Discipliniographic method [META]—though

Table 4.3. Topics of rank 1–10, by aggregate percentage of tokens in the confirmed-RCWS corpus (across 1,684 dissertations). Topics in italics are in the top 10 for the confirmed non-RCWS corpus (N = 695) as well; topics in bold are ranked much lower in that corpus.

RCWS rank	% of RCWS corpus	Assigned Label (topic #)	% of non-RCWS corpus	Non-RCWS rank
1	6.6%	**Disciplinary Formations** (T32)	1.27%	31
2	6.1	*Scenes of Teaching* (T49)	3.33	9
3	5.2	*Rhetorics of Power, Conflict, and Politics* (T21)	5.73	2
4	4.74	*Personal Narrative and Oral History* (T26)	4.5	3
5	4.69	*Collaborative Learning* (T41)	3.22	10
6	4.3	**Institutional Supports, Barriers, Constraints** (T35)	2.09	23
7	4.02	Image, Body, Materiality (T2)	2.97	12
8	3.77	**Literacy Practices** (T28)	1.06	35
9	3.46	Rhetorical Frameworks (T33)	3.07	11
10	3.05	*Reading Rhetoricians, Interpreting Philosophy* (T48)	4.36	5

still uncommon overall—is significantly more common in the RCWS corpus than the non-RCWS, an exception among aggregable methods.)

"Literacy Practices" (T28), a top-ten topic in the RCWS corpus both by aggregated tokens and by its frequency as a top-rated topic within dissertations, is one of the bottom-ten topics in the non-RCWS corpus. In chapter 2, based on what else it clusters with, I established that this topic is not only about observing literate practices in the real world, but also about defining and redefining *literacy* itself; in that sense, it is part of a theory-focused cluster, along with "Disciplinary Formations" in the sense of defining and redefining *disciplinarity*. In both cases, the thing being studied is in part the way we study things, and in that sense, the characteristic theoretical move is toward the meta, even when dialectic and not empirical meta-analysis is the primary method being used. That both these topics are especially distinctive between the two subcorpora corroborates the generally more theory-oriented posture in RCWS as opposed to cognate disciplines.

Vieira et al. (2020) elaborate on the distinctive understandings of *literacy* and *literacies* as they are used by researchers in the field. "While literacy is commonly understood as a set of skills" involving reading and writing as straightforward actions (36), they clarify that thanks to "grounded studies of literacy practices in particular settings," those who focus on literacy recognize that "it is almost never *on its own*. It is always tied up in complex agendas, personal histories, technological changes, shifting winds of power, individual bodies" (37). As a result, they go on to say, literacy as RCWS scholars interpret it is never neutral; it acts on people, shaping possibilities, influencing what can be learned and what is emphasized, by whom and for whom. This ramification of literacy, from discrete to networked and from objective to politically implicated, also illustrates what I mean when I say that RCWS has a theory-oriented posture: It's not that concrete exhibits aren't observed, because they very much are, but rather that what is seen is rarely seen only as itself; surface meanings are conjoined with reflections, a palimpsest of what's behind and what's beneath, and how those things align or harmonize or jar. In the kind of theory I have in mind, objects of study lead away from themselves, becoming mirrors or lenses recursively rewriting the worldview of the author.

Even within more concrete topic clusters, such as the one I've labeled "Teaching and Administration," comparing the focal points across the RCWS and non-RCWS corpora suggests that composition-rhetoric in this time period has tended more toward systemic analysis and other fields toward more individuated analyses. Consider the third major topic that, per table 4.6, is ranked high in the RCWS list but low outside of it: Institutional Supports, Barriers, Constraints (T35). As I noted in chapter 2, this topic is among the more administrative/WPA-focused in the model; top titles address "instructor working conditions and student learning conditions," "the impact of WPAs' leadership at two-year colleges," and comparative studies of writing programs across regions, institutional types, or time. It shares the Teaching and Administration cluster with one of the topics common across both corpora, Scenes of Teaching (T49), along with two that were in the top list for the non-RCWS corpus but relatively low-ranked within RCWS: Writing Process (T18) and K12 Writing Pedagogy (T42). Taken together, these differential emphases suggest that, when other fields are thinking about what *sets* the scene for teaching and writing in schools, they are more likely to be thinking about classrooms and writers than about larger curricular, institutional, or staffing structures, while for compositionists the reverse would be true.

The two corpora's different emphases within this topic cluster also point to the institutional position of composition/rhetoric relative to other fields. While the areas researched by the field extend far beyond first-year college composition, the FYC requirement at many colleges and universities nevertheless means that composition faculty (and, indeed, many graduate students, sometimes even more so) are entwined within a large bureaucratic structure of many course sections. Drawing on both survey data and a review of the scholarly literature, Anthony Edgington and Stacy Hartlage Taylor (2007) documented the ways that administrative service is commonly expected to be all but required of rhet/comp faculty at some point in their careers—and thus of interest to grad students as well (Edgington and Taylor 2007, 150, 154–56). As one of their survey respondents put it, "Teaching, research and scholarship, and administration triangulate productively in my mind, and I believe it's important to help build, shape, and structure the environments in which teaching and research take place" (qtd. in Edgington and Taylor 2007, 157). Notice the movement of the frame of reference here: a step back from teaching and research to the environments where they take place, and from the environments to the forces and people that "build, shape, and structure" them. This comment encapsulates the move toward meta that I'm arguing underlies the group of topics most indicative of RCWS as compared to non-RCWS dissertations on language, rhetoric, and composition.

WHAT HOLDS UP, AND WHAT FALLS THROUGH?

In chapter 2, I proposed that a good way of thinking about what carries across dissertations, programs, and thus the discipline is to examine the "reach" of topic clusters: how many individual documents devote at least X% of their words (for some value of X) to groups of topics that are similar to each other and distinct from others. Examining the RCWS corpus, I established that two topic clusters—Theoretical Orientations, which includes the meta-move topics discussed above, and Applied Composition, which combines teaching and administration with technical writing, genre analysis, and a few other topics—both reach the great majority of dissertations in the field (see tables 2.8 and 2.10). I interpret this finding to signify that these clusters therefore represent common touchstones that unite the various factions of the discipline. But I have to acknowledge a more skeptical interpretation: that these topics are so broad as to be hard *not* to include, and that, therefore, they don't represent anything distinctive about rhetoric, composition, and writing studies as a discipline. To test this hypothesis, I conducted the same analysis on the non-RCWS corpus;[6] the results are in table 4.4.

As the rightmost column of table 4.4 shows, no cluster achieves the same universality in the non-RCWS corpus as in the RCWS corpus, as measured by the portion of dissertations including a discernable presence of those topics (treated cumulatively). At a 5% criterion, the cluster that reaches the greatest number of non-RCWS dissertations, "Theoretical Orientations," peaks at around 77%—a significantly lower proportion than the 90% of RCWS dissertations, for the same cluster. At 87% of dissertations, the "Applied Composition" cluster is also significantly more common across RCWS than any topic cluster is for the non-RCWS corpus.

But then, we shouldn't really expect a common throughline in the non-RCWS corpus, as that very name suggests. In the case of confirmed-RCWS dissertations, we can reasonably assume there's a single discipline at work and try to determine what that means. The other corpus, however, is "other": an amalgamation of several disciplines, including communication, education, linguistics, psychology, and so on. Thus it makes sense that we don't see a near-universal thread but instead a more even division among a range of topics: even the lowest-ranked cluster ("Popular Entertainment") still reaches more than 15% of the non-RCWS corpus at the 5% criterion level; and in all topic clusters except for the top two, the non-RCWS corpus includes a greater proportion of dissertations at the 50% criterion level—that is, dissertations with more than half the words attributed to those topics—than the RCWS corpus for the same cluster. This is just what you'd expect from an admixture of disciplines, each focused on different specific aspects of the shared general subject matter.

By that same token, however, the fact that we *do* see near-universal reference to the top two clusters in RCWS reaffirms the intuition that these dissertations have a discipline in common. If RCWS were merely an umbrella for separate subdisciplines—if it had splintered entirely as North ("Death" 197) and Connors (18) feared it might—we would see a topic distribution more like the one for non-RCWS. In other words, the inconsistency of "non-RCWS" gives us reason to believe that the consistency of "RCWS" is signal, and not noise.

PREPARING A FACE TO MEET THE FACES THAT WE MEET

In conclusion, I'd like to consider how rhetoric and composition/writing studies, as a discipline, "presents" to colleagues in other disciplines. In other words, what will those colleagues expect a compositionist to be an expert in, given their own likely experiences of people who study writing

Table 4.4. Comparing topic cluster reach across datasets shows more common ground in the RCWS corpus. Cell values in column "X% reach" give the percentage of dissertations (N = 695 for the non-RCWS corpus, 1,684 for the RCWS corpus) for which the topics in the given cluster cumulatively account for at least X% of the words in that document. For a list of topics included in each cluster, see chapter 2. Data in italics correspond to values in tables 2.8 and 2.10.

Assigned cluster label	Corpus	% of aggregated corpus	50% reach	22% reach	13% reach	5% reach
Applied composition	RCWS	34.86%	29.45%	58.08%	72.8%	87.17%
	Non-RCWS	30.49	28.02	43.82	51.58	67.10
Theoretical orientations	RCWS	26.10	11.94	51.13	72.92	90.44
	Non-RCWS	18.46	6.61	32.76	52.01	76.87
Public rhetorics and political writing	RCWS	9.22	1.96	13.9	23.28	45.49
	Non-RCWS	17.90	10.20	31.90	43.10	59.05
Peoples and places	RCWS	6.71	0.89	11.7	17.99	30.17
	Non-RCWS	7.57	1.72	13.65	19.83	33.33
Narrative and reflection	RCWS	6.48	0.53	6.53	14.73	40.44
	Non-RCWS	6.97	1.15	6.61	16.24	40.66
Poetics and oratory	RCWS	4.37	0.65	4.81	10.45	22.21
	Non-RCWS	4.91	1.15	6.47	11.93	20.83
Popular entertainment	RCWS	1.89	0.00	1.9	4.22	9.26
	Non-RCWS	4.03	0.72	6.18	9.63	16.24

or rhetoric? After all, as Linda Adler-Kassner (2018) has pointed out, "Writing *is* everybody's business (in some ways), and everybody believes that they can and sometimes should 'speak for writing'" (325); we can anticipate that a great number of conversations about writing and what constitutes "good writing" will (and should) include more than just RCWS scholars. Grant applications, job interviews, and collaborations across the curriculum would also put compositionists in conversation with people who value their work, but perhaps in ways subtly different than the ways compositionists themselves might value it. Understanding how writing, rhetoric, and composition are studied outside of rhetoric, composition, and writing studies should make it more possible to find common ground or navigate differences during these conversations.

The data from dissertations discussed above suggests there is a fair amount of shared focus and methodology across fields:

- Among those who complete dissertations on writing, rhetoric, and composition, regardless of whether their graduate program is affiliated with the rhetoric and composition consortium, *dialectical/ humanistic methods* are the most common: interpretive work with primarily textual sources, emphasizing individual authors' reasoning. Framed another way, this also suggests that replicable, aggregable data about writing practices is not likely to be the primary thing people associate with a focus on writing in their fields—even though it might well be the dominant language of evidence for people who don't themselves study writing, or for fields where few people do.

- *Narrative descriptions* are a commonly accepted written form in scholarship about writing and rhetoric, across the disciplines that study it; these include but are not limited to descriptions of classroom activities and other learning spaces, as well as first-person reflection.

- Both inside and outside of RCWS, questions of *power, agency, and politics* are an abiding concern associated with the study of rhetoric and discourse.

That said, there are also surprises or disjunctions we can anticipate, now that we've seen more of what's distinctive of work in rhetoric and composition/writing studies as opposed to work outside of it—including different definitions of some of those shared terms. For example:

- *Rhetorical analysis,* outside of RCWS, seems generally to mean taking an existing framework and using it as a lens to read a text or similar concrete exhibit. Inside RCWS, rhetorical analysis is more likely to involve developing new frameworks.

- Based on how the methods co-occur, we can infer that *teacher research*, outside of RCWS, often involves experimentation, such as trying new class plans and comparing measurements of student learning or engagement beforehand (pretest) and afterward (posttest)—or with that class plan (treatment) and without (control). Inside RCWS, teacher research is more likely to involve ethnographic (including autoethnographic) reflections on teaching, learning, and motivation—and/or philosophical arguments comparing the merits of competing curricular designs.

- A dissertation on *politics and rhetoric*, outside of RCWS, probably has something to do with government policies and bureaucratic lobbying, quite possibly with the words of politicians themselves. A political question likely involves who is elected or appointed, and what decisions they are able to put into legislation, to what effect. Inside RCWS, all writing is political, involving positionalities that emerge through the rhetorical framing of shifting and multiple selves and audiences. Who gets to write and see their writing circulated, to whom, is already a political question.

- *Literacy*, in RCWS, is a complex phenomenon involving negotiations of power and control, operating through nonalphabetic modes and genres in addition to the production and decoding of written words. Outside RCWS, it's not clear that discussions of literacy give much focus to these interpenetrating layers beyond the skill of reading and writing words.

I offer these interpretations of the findings above with a few important caveats. First, I want to reiterate Mueller's caution that these patterns are "not proofs, finally, but provocations": generative hypotheses that should be tested in multiple local contexts (*Network* 4). I suggest that we can take these patterns as a first set of expectations, but expectations are always probabilistic, and it's a mistake to infer from the general case to the specific. A tendency is not a prophecy.

Second, related to the first, I hope it's clear there are already known exceptions to these patterns—both for rhet/comp scholar/researcher/ teachers and for scholar/researcher/teachers in other disciplines. Of particular note with regard to teacher research are empirical efforts within RCWS to study the transfer of writing knowledge, skills, and strategies from one context to another (including into and out of academia, and into and out of writing courses such as first-year composition). Such transfer studies, which have been a particularly strong strand of research in RCWS at least since the Elon University seminar on Writing and Question of Transfer (2011–13)—for instance, Yancey (2018) cites the consistency of this line of research as evidence of an emergent disciplinary core (23–25)—often do involve some measure of experimental or discourse-analytical research, alongside clinical case studies and surveys.

Third, and stemming from the second, these patterns are not fixed for all time. My inferences are based on a distant-thin reading of dissertations in the past (2001–2015), and I do not intend for them to take on a normative force for the future, as if to say, for example, that rhetorical analysis in rhetoric and composition should (let alone must) move from the specific to the general in order to be recognizable within the field. Rather, what I'm trying to do is make visible the places where meanings can bend—to articulate these meanings as both joined and jointed, to allow for a more flexible and enunciated conversation among people who might not have realized another interpretation was (or could be) in practice. Graduates of composition/rhetoric PhD programs, already attuned to writing about writing and thinking rhetorically about rhetoric, are well situated to notice and name such disciplinary patterns.

In "The Death of Paradigm Hope," Stephen North (1997) lamented all the writing within composition about composition as a field, what he called (referencing Russell Durst's language) "composition's 'inordi-nate' self-consciousness regarding its research enterprise" (North 1997, 196). Although he rejected the idea, which he attributed to Durst, that people just aren't trying hard enough to do *the real work*, he in some ways went farther, suggesting that the reason so many people have writ-ten to ask what comprises the work of composition is that there is no "work of composition" after all: that people in the field "have found it harder and harder . . . to recognize any extant research 'us' in" the idea of a shared research enterprise (North 1997, 197). I'd like to offer another explanation: that the reflective move toward examining the framework of any given activity is itself a constitutive element of rhetoric and composition/writing studies as a discipline. By "constitutive" I don't mean that it's imperative on everyone, all the time, with nothing else involved in disciplinary work, but rather that making such a move is a distinctively "rhet comp" thing to do, across several areas of subject mat-ter. And given that such a meta-move is already available and applied to written style, to literacy, to teaching, and so on, is it really a surprise that people would apply it toward the discipline itself?

Naming differences across disciplines does come at the risk of reify-ing those differences, and if we police boundaries too assiduously we can actually make interdisciplinary collaboration harder. On the other hand, conflicting interpretations might exist in any collaboration, whether named or not, and naming them could make it easier to under-stand where partners are coming from and thus to negotiate meaning more cooperatively. As Wardle and Adler-Kassner (2020) write, "If we want learners and stakeholders to join us in our work, we must be able to clearly and explicitly explain what it is we are doing and what basic assumptions we make that are different from those made in other com-munities of practice" (31). Importantly, though, as we unearth those assumptions and discuss them, we may find that this very process begins to shift them. We must remain open to that possibility alongside the pos-sibility of reaffirming what we've previously assumed.

5

A MAP IS NOT A MANIFESTO

"Would you tell me, please, which way I ought to go from here?" "That depends a good deal on where you want to get to," said the Cat.
—Lewis Carroll, *Alice's Adventures in Wonderland*

in the end, I'm feeling
more and more
there won't be any end
—The Oh Hellos, "Glowing"

Metaphors matter. They frame the world to us and shape what we see as there, as good, as possible (Therborn [1980] 1999). I've used a lot of metaphors in this book to describe writing studies and its components: Lego pieces. Currents and waves. Ecosystems. Currency. Woven fabric. Elizabeth Wardle and Doug Downs (2018, 112) remind us, with a hat tip to Anne Ruggles Gere (1993, 4), that a *field*, in physics, is a region affected by (permeated by) a force: think of magnetism. The path of a particle moving through a field is shaped and constrained not only by its own momentum, coming in, but also by invisible pushes and pulls. There's some real appeal in that image of people as particles interacting with disciplines as fields, taking energy and direction from them while warping them in turn (as a magnetic field is shaped by the movement of electrons). In that sense, the dissertations I've tracked as they move through this field are like iron filings laid down on paper over a magnet, rendering visible in their arrangement the lines of force that had been present before, but unseeable.

But the metaphor I've come back to most often in describing this project is the map: I've been trying to orient myself, and my readers—especially any newcomers to this field of interlocking forces—within some kind of disciplinary space. I've been trying to get a sense of the lay of the land, where people have gathered, the paths that are most traveled as well as those "wanting wear" (Frost [1915] 2021).

Mapmaking is far from politically neutral; ask any member of a formerly (or presently) colonized group. I've tried to do justice to the

https://doi.org/10.7330/9781646423224.c005

complexity of what I've been labeling, but I know there will always be other valid ways of naming what we do in RCWS. The term *poetic/fictive* made sense to me based on my own reading and background, but *narrative inquiry* could have served as well, with more emphasis on story; and a label like *storying/counterstorying* would have emphasized the stakes in telling true stories, and in whose stories get told.

This book has attempted to characterize some fifteen years of disciplinary history as seen from a particular vantage point: the kinds of methods and topics taken up in doctoral dissertations, which is to say the work taken up by researchers and scholars crossing the threshold of disciplinary credentialing. I've chosen large-scale digital research methods—what might be characterized as one kind of "big data" approach—as a way of temporarily decentering my own experiences, to create the possibility of surprise as well as confirmation, and especially to facilitate reentry into the data from multiple angles. Where I've been able to find corroboration through multiple analytical lenses, I've been most confident in drawing conclusions, but it follows that further investigations, with new data, new questions, and, yes, new interpretations of what answers the data can give to those questions, will further illuminate the landscape, adding new layers and new maps. And we can then look for interesting correlations or counterpoints as we compare those maps against and alongside each other.

All maps reduce the terrain. It is perhaps cliché to say again, but the only map that completely matches the territory is the territory itself: perfectly accurate and perfectly unhelpful. In making the maps in this book, I am aware of some of what's lost; for example, I did not look through lenses of embodiment—I did not consider the effects of gender, or race, or age, or (dis)ability, because the relevant information was not included or reliably inferable from the dissertations and would require extensive additional work to determine. Still, doing so would no doubt reveal some interesting divisions among the methods or topics I've identified here, in addition to some basic demographic statistics about how well (or poorly) our discipline's PhD graduate pool matches the general population.

In focusing on doctoral dissertations, I'm also aware of leaving out a large number of contributors to our disciplinary knowledge and practice, including a great many excellent and committed teachers of composition who either never wrote a dissertation or who wrote one on something other than writing, rhetoric, composition, or literacy. I'm in no way trying to discount those members of the field; I am simply choosing one cross-cutting variable to investigate, this time. Another time, a different approach to data gathering might better represent their work and tell us, in turn, something new about how RCWS plays out in the world. I am encouraged by recent efforts in the field to gather syllabi and assignments (Bannon et al. 2019) and to learn more about instructional staffing (Gladstein and Fralix n.d.), both of which will help support future large-scale contextualizing data analyses.

And, of course, my dataset was limited to a relatively narrow slice of time, 2001–2015, that recedes further into the past even as you read this. Even if we did nothing but repeat the same analyses I have already described, we would no doubt see things change. That's not a reason to distrust or avoid performing the analysis; on the contrary, some things change gradually enough that, without a recorded measurement, we might not be sure they were changing at all. While I have so far treated the fifteen-year span of dissertations as a single, synchronic unit, the truth is that some things change even within that period.

Consider how the three topics in figure 5.1 have changed over the fifteen-year span of the dataset. Although the year-over-year changes (the local slopes of the lines) are fairly similar across these topics, in the case of Institutional Supports, Barriers, Constraints (T35, dashed line) the changes oscillate between increasing and decreasing, leaving the overall contribution to the corpus roughly constant over this time span. By contrast, for Online Circulation and Social Media (T44, dotted line), the change from 2001 to 2015 is positive year after year, leading to a strictly increasing proportion of the text coming from this topic; Disciplinary Formations (T32, solid line), the top topic in this corpus overall, shows a net decrease, so that by the year 2015 the proportions of all three topics are quite close to each other (around 4% of the tokens, or one in every twenty-five words, on average), despite starting quite far apart.

Some of these changes are easier to explain than others: social media was just getting started back in 2001, in the form of blogs and comments; then Facebook started in 2004, and Twitter in 2006, and the iPhone was introduced in 2007 and the Android platform in 2008. By 2015, the online environment was quite different—and online engagement nearly ubiquitous. It only makes sense that as discourse moved more thoroughly into networked and mobile platforms, scholarly attention to writing and circulation in these spaces would move in that direction, as well.

Other changes are harder to explain: there's no inherent reason, given the sustained interest in disciplinarity that I document in chapter 1 and the distinctive interest in meta-topics within RCWS I discuss in chapter 4, that the previous top topic, Disciplinary Formations (T32)—accounting

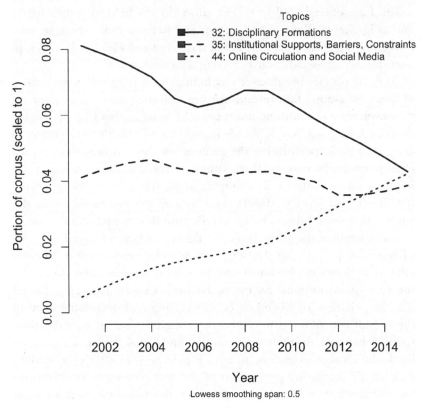

Figure 5.1. *Changes in weight of selected topics as a proportion of aggregate tokens in the confirmed-RCWS corpus over time. N = 1,684 dissertations. Scatterplot was smoothed using the LOWESS method of locally weighted polynomial regression, with a smoothing span of 50% of the data.*

for an average of roughly one in every twelve tokens in 2001's set of confirmed-RCWS dissertations—would drop so steadily. It's not as though the questions raised under that banner had been settled by 2015. And in fact, 2015 was the year in which *Naming What We Know* was released, in some ways reigniting the flame of "paradigm hope" (North 1997) and certainly triggering a lot of discussion about disciplinary knowing. So it would be interesting to repeat the analysis five years from now, and see whether that downward trajectory has continued, abated, or even reversed.

The people have not stood still, and so the landscape itself changes. Mapmakers' work is never done.

Still, while each map undeniably has a perspective, and can shape the expectations of those who use it, it does not, in itself, tell you where to go. A map is not a manifesto. Knowing what's "out there" can, but doesn't have to, change the direction you're moving in.

What it does, instead, is provide a shared reference for planning and discussion across time and among people. Even a single map suggests *multiple* possible destinations and can become a document upon which to add layers of annotation, either singly or as part of a group. It can identify crossroads not only as points of divergence but as places to come together for exchange and camaraderie. I said in chapter 2 that maps can help us find people and places with whom to stand—and to push off from. Taking a map along as we depart affords an increased possibility of returning to tell what we've found in doing so. A map is a tool for *repeated* journeys.

Nor do we have to make our travel decisions alone. Frost's solitary traveler was faced with a binary choice of roads, and expected, "knowing how way leads on to way," never to come back. But the many people who make up a discipline can, collectively, travel down multiple paths. A graduate program, for example, can diversify its research agenda internally, or instead focus its offerings around unifying themes (literacy, say, or Black rhetorics, etc.) or methods (such as archival history, classroom ethnography, and so on). It's possible some of these paths will be difficult to combine with each other in a given department, but that doesn't mean they're incompatible across the full consortium of doctoral programs. So long as we remain in communication with each other, using shared terms (or at least airing our different uses of those terms), there are many good ways forward.[1]

In their introduction to the collection *Under Construction*, Christine Farris and Chris Anson (1998) recognize that despite the impossibility of attaining a single vantage point from which to unify all our studies, such a position would, in any case, be less useful than a set of multiple positions from which to triangulate and gain perspective. In their words, "This notion that theory, research, and teaching are all practices *providing a location from which to view and critique the others* . . . offers a way out of battling binaries" (Farris and Anson 1998, 3, emphasis added). Articulating the locations of topic and method, as I have done in the previous chapters, can work to combat a problematic condition that David Smit (2011) seems to take as inevitable, that "composition studies has no means for even talking about the differences that divide the profession" (225).

Having "a way out of battling binaries" does not mean simply that we should live and let live, free from the task of mapping out the field's contours. On the contrary, it suggests that multiple maps are needed "to view and critique the others"—and, if I may flip the affect, to view and *celebrate* their different contributions—even as we recognize that any one map is insufficient.

* * * * *

The best thing about Legos is their replay value. Following the expected path of instruction straight out of the box gets you somewhere fun, but then, no matter how big or beautiful the structure you make of them, eventually the pieces come apart and remix, and you get to make something new again. Maybe a different charted path; maybe a new combination not seen before. Seeing how the builds come together and come apart, you develop new skills in Lego-ing. In letting go. In making something that won't break—or, at least, not until you're ready.

I'll come clean and say it: for all that my son and I sort the Legos when we start to build a set, when it's time to clean up, the pieces get mixed up again, with different shapes, sizes, and colors in the same bins. Neither I nor my son is *that* compulsive, and we both enjoy the generative surprises of juxtaposed blocks as much as we like seeing a planned set come together. But even then, having previously taken stock of what's available makes it easier to imagine what might work well in our more free-form creative play. It gives us a sense of what we might build *toward*, even if noticing nearby pieces (or a lack of certain pieces) raises other possibilities along the way.

Writing a dissertation, or a discipline for that matter, may not always feel like play in the sense of lighthearted recreation, but even so, both are composed by the play of ideas off of each other, and off of what the world presents to us. And both disciplines and dissertations necessarily partake of both chance juxtapositions and a sensed larger pattern. What we make of what we have will vary, and it should. But if we're making it together, let's put all our pieces on the table.

And build.

Appendix A
PRE-PROCESSING STEPS AND PARAMETERS FOR TOPIC MODELING

Files received on DVD-ROM from ProQuest Dissertations and Theses (PQDT) included pdf files with dissertation full-text and MARC-formatted metadata for 4,251 dissertations matching Subject Code 0681 (at various times labeled "Language, Rhetoric and Composition" or "Languages and Literature: Rhetoric"). Of these files, inspection of abstracts led to the removal from the dataset of 144 dissertations as false positives, consisting mostly of theology, biblical exegesis, and literary criticism as their primary or complete focus; another 385 were determined to be on the borderline. These 529 dissertations were excluded from further analyses. An additional 75 dissertations in the metadata files were found to be either missing fulltext or to have scanned pdfs of sufficiently poor quality that no useable text could be retrieved through Optical Character Recognition. Removing these led to a final training set for fulltext analysis of 3,647 dissertations in the years 2001–2015, inclusive.

All processing files are open access at https://github.com/ben miller314/dissertation-research/; locations of files relevant to text pre-processing and topic modeling are mapped in the tree below, with ~ representing the repository home. A brief text description of each function follows the tree. For full implementation details, please see the files themselves, which are not included in their entirety here because of the extensive whitespace in the code.

```
~/
 |
 `—Shell scripts and commands/
 |      |—ben_clean_and_consolidate.sh
 |
 |—r2mallet with foreach.R
 |
 `—Open Refine/
        |—clean_titles_and_abstracts.json
```

https://doi.org/10.7330/9781646423224.c006

ben_clean_and_consolidate.sh

Bash shell (command line) script to loop through fulltext pdf files. Performs two key preprocessing functions:

1. Extract text from pdfs using **pdftotext**. Export to new folder.
2. Clean extracted text for analysis
   a. Using **iconv**, convert text encoding from ISO 8859–1 (Latin-1) to UTF-8 (unicode standard)
   b. Using **sed**, attempt to delete boilerplate first page added by UMI/ProQuest; fallback to complete text if it fails
   c. Using **sed**, delete all instances of boilerplate added by UMI /ProQuest warning against reproduction
   d. Export to new folder.

r2mallet with foreach.R

R script to set parameters for MALLET topic modeling software (McCallum 2002), including tokenizer, number of iterations, stopwords, and number of topics (k). For the model discussed in this book, the key parameters were as follows:

```
optimize-interval = 20
optimize-burn-in = 50
num-iterations = 250
token-regex = "'\\p{L}+[\\p{L}\\p{Po}]*
  [-]?\\p{L}+'"
```

This regular expression corresponds to a sequence of characters that begins and ends with one or more letters (\\p{L}+), with the intervening characters consisting of some combination of variable length ([. . .]*) that includes zero or more letters (\\p{L}) or punctuation characters that are not dashes, brackets, quotes, or connectors (\\p{Po}), and at most one hyphen ([-]?). See http://www.regular-expressions .info/unicode.html for more on these character classes.

For **num-topics**, a series of values including 10, 15, 23, 30, 50, 55, 60, 100, and 150 were tested before settling on 50.

Non-round values in this list were derived from clustering the 150-topic model (see chapter 2, "From Topics to Topic Clusters") and cutting the resulting tree in ways that reflected but consolidated the hierarchy in that model. The final decision of 50 topics was based on a desire to balance the length of time required to inspect the models and label topics, on the one hand, and on the other, reaching a point of minimal change in Log-Likeliness per Token (LL/token) measurements of model fit, as output by MALLET through the --diagnostics-file option.

I used the **remove-stopwords** option to exclude a standard set of 524 high-frequency English words, such as "a," "the," "is," etc.

from the model. The full list is available at https://github.com
/mimno/Mallet/blob/master/stoplists/en.txt.

clean_titles_and_abstracts.json

"Redo" code for use with Open Refine software to process metadata. In
the two columns named, trims leading and trailing whitespace and
transforms escaped html characters into standard characters.

Open Refine was also used to consolidate equivalent author-supplied
keywords (e.g., "Burke, Kenneth" and "Kenneth Burke") and to regularize school names provided in the metadata. To facilitate matching,
school names were reconciled against the 2010 datafile for Carnegie
Classification of Institutions of Higher Education, available at https://
carnegieclassifications.iu.edu/downloads.php.

Appendix B
CALCULATING TERM FREQUENCY *
INVERSE TOPIC FREQUENCY (TF-ITF)

The software I used for topic modeling, MALLET (McCallum 2002), represents its output by listing for each topic the words (tokens) assigned to that topic with the highest probability. Some of these highly probable words, however, are not useful for distinguishing the content of a given topic from the others. To address this problem, I adapted a common statistic used in text modeling, *term frequency * inverse document frequency* (TF-IDF), for use with topics.

TF-IDF, as Wikipedia explains, is "often used as a weighting factor in searches of information retrieval, text mining, and user modeling" because "the tf-idf value [for a word] increases proportionally to the number of times [that] word appears in the document and is offset by the number of documents in the corpus that contain the word, which helps to adjust for the fact that some words appear more frequently in general." (Wikipedia Contributors 2021)

The now-traditional TF-IDF statistic is calculated for each pair of terms and documents by multiplying the *term frequency* (i.e., the number of times that term appears in that document) and the *inverse document frequency*: a logarithm of the fraction produced by dividing the total number of documents in the corpus over the number of documents containing the term. That is, IDF = log(total number of documents/ number of term-containing documents). Note that IDF is stable across all documents for a given term, while TF changes in each document, and thus the product of TF * IDF changes for each term-document pair.

To calculate an equivalent statistic for each term-*topic* pair, I begin with MALLET's `word-topic-counts-file` output: a space-delimited matrix in which each row corresponds to token (i.e., word, or term), and each column gives a key-value pair of assigned topic and the frequency with which that term was assigned to it. Because this is clearer to see than to describe, here is the start of the word-topic matrix, with column labels added for clarity:

https://doi.org/10.7330/9781646423224.c007

token_index	token	TopicRanked1	TopicRanked2	TopicRanked3 . . .	
0	em	11:13057	49:6232	33:736	. . .
1	vernacular	4:2080	19:1625	13:1611	. . .
2	rhetorics	32:7604	1:3383	31:2085	. . .
3	transgression	37:260	47:246	20:208	. . .
4	control	5:8000	20:6867	37:4924	. . .
. . .	. . .	. . .	. . .	. . .	

This indicates, for example, that of all the times the word *vernacular* appeared in the corpus, 2,080 of those were associated with topic 4; it was associated 1,625 times with topic 19; and so on. The columns continue out to the number of topics, and the rows to the number of unique tokens: for the model discussed in this book, 50 topics and 1,616,842 words. For a speed boost, I eliminated rare terms by cutting tokens for which the maximum assigned frequency was lower than 5; this reduced the total number of tokens (rows) from 1,616,842 to 254,092 and increased the median term frequency from 1 to 13, and the mean from 24.6 to 150.4. (The maximum assigned frequency was 415,883, for the token *students* in topic 48.)

Traversing this matrix one topic at a time, I constructed a topic-word table in which each row corresponds to a topic-token pair. In addition to the frequency of each pair (the term's *weight* within the topic), taken from the word-topic matrix, I added a column for the pair's probability—calculated by dividing the weight of the specific token-topic pair by the sum of weights for the term across all topics. The beginning of the topic-word table looks like this:

topic	token_ind	weight	token	probability
1	5	936	control	0.0006221948
1	6	640	york	0.0004254323
1	9	326	light	0.0002167046
1	10	692	dissertation	0.0004599987
1	11	526	submitted	0.0003496522
1	17	2171	requirements	0.0014431463
. . .	. . .	. . .	. . .	. . .

To calculate the *inverse topic frequency* (ITF) for each token, I take $\log(\text{ntopics} / .N)$, where ntopics is the number of topics (in this case, 50) and .N is the number of rows in which that token appears. The

ITF value is stable for each term across all topics, just as IDF is stable across all documents (as discussed above). The *term frequency* for each pair is the weight. (Though an exactly equivalent ordering of terms follows from using the probability instead.) And, as in TF-IDF, the final TF-ITF value for each topic-term pair is produced by multiplying term frequency by inverse topic frequency.

The keyword labels used in chapters 2 and 4 are the tokens with the 20 highest TF-ITF values for each topic. To compare TF-ITF keyword labels with those produced by probability values alone (the MALLET default), see appendix C.

For full implementation details, please see the files `tfidf_for_topics.R` and `get_topic_word_grid.R` (which the first file references) in the home directory of https://github.com/benmiller314/dissertation-research.

Appendix C
COMPLETE LIST OF TOPIC KEYS, ASSIGNED LABELS, AND RANKS

The topics below were generated by the model discussed in chapter 2, using the procedures described in appendix A and B. Numbers associated with the topics are arbitrary, but the table is sorted by these topic numbers for ease of reference while reading the main text.

Nine of the 50 topics were deemed non-content-bearing and removed from visualizations but are included here with a cluster indicated as "(non-content topics)." Topic 24, despite being one of the smallest topics (~0.6% of the corpus), seems to combine several even smaller topics; I believe this is because a handful of dissertations using these subtopics together carried more weight than they would have in a topic represented by a larger sample. Such a topic may well split in a model with a greater number of topics, but it seems to do so at the cost of some coherence in larger topics, which split first.

Topic: 1
Assigned label: Technical Communication
Cluster: Applied Composition (unstable subset)
Top 20 Keywords:
  by TF-ITF: technical communication design engineering workplace professional business team employees management information usability documents user engineers organizational document users company organizations
  by probability: communication technical information work design business professional documents engineering system project process document knowledge workplace company organization management team report
Portion of corpus:
  confirmed RCWS (N=1,684): 2.83% (rank 12)
  confirmed non-RCWS (N=696): 1.36% (rank 30)
  full training set (N=3,647): 1.98% (rank 21)

https://doi.org/10.7330/9781646423224.c008

Topic: 2

Assigned label: Image, Body, Materiality

Cluster: Theoretical Orientations

Top 20 Keywords:

by TF-ITF: visual memory images body image objects bodies art space embodied object affective experience meaning invention bodily design spatial brain materiality

by probability: visual memory body images image work space meaning experience art process material objects ways figure bodies sense text world time

Portion of corpus:

confirmed RCWS (N=1,684): 4.02% (rank 7)
confirmed non-RCWS (N=696): 2.97% (rank 12)
full training set (N=3,647): 3.37% (rank 10)

Topic: 3

Assigned label: Missing fulltext (proquest boilerplate)

Cluster: (non-content topics)

Top 20 Keywords:

by TF-ITF: permission owner prohibited reproduced copyright reproduction fo modem chip bom intern-net hat jack ml newman ju learning violeta ff zeeb

by probability: permission copyright owner reproduction prohibited reproduced fo study social language theory history learning modem process written information general view terms

Portion of corpus:

confirmed RCWS (N=1,684): 1.19% (rank 32)
confirmed non-RCWS (N=696): 1.08% (rank 35)
full training set (N=3,647): 1.21% (rank 33)

Topic: 4

Assigned label: Environment and Nature

Cluster: Peoples and Places

Top 20 Keywords:

by TF-ITF: environmental wilderness ecology animals species animal water humans natural forest land nature sustainability warming conservation ecological management environment agriculture sustainable

by probability: environmental nature natural ecological human wilderness environment land ecology world humans population animals water species conservation animal management forest state

Portion of corpus:

confirmed RCWS (N=1,684): 0.79% (rank 37)
confirmed non-RCWS (N=696): 0.98% (rank 37)
full training set (N=3,647): 0.78% (rank 40)

Topic: 5

Assigned label: Race and Ethnicity

Cluster: Peoples and Places

Top 20 Keywords:

    by TF-ITF: african black race racial white racism american identity immigrants ethnic americans language cultural immigrant racist mexican whiteness asian color immigration

    by probability: american white black race language identity african racial culture cultural social people racism americans class ethnic education whiteness immigrants color

Portion of corpus:

    confirmed RCWS (N=1,684): 2.17% (rank 19)

    confirmed non-RCWS (N=696): 1.24% (rank 33)

    full training set (N=3,647): 1.73% (rank 27)

Topic: 6

Assigned label: Testing Predictive Models

Cluster: Applied Composition (unstable subset)

Top 20 Keywords:

    by TF-ITF: scores score participants variables table test scoring results item data raters measures scale total hypothesis correlation reliability group sample variable

    by probability: study group table scores results research significant participants test score data groups total number differences model variables level effect scale

Portion of corpus:

    confirmed RCWS (N=1,684): 0.95% (rank 34)

    confirmed non-RCWS (N=696): 3.91% (rank 7)

    full training set (N=3,647): 2.78% (rank 14)

Topic: 7

Assigned label: Popular Media: Film, TV, Music

Cluster: Popular Entertainment

Top 20 Keywords:

    by TF-ITF: film films music television documentary characters narrative media performance video scene fantasy comic movie drama popular fan audience trauma story

    by probability: film narrative performance audience music popular media story culture films characters scene television character video world images fantasy documentary drama

Portion of corpus:

    confirmed RCWS (N=1,684): 1.34% (rank 27)

    confirmed non-RCWS (N=696): 2.2% (rank 21)

    full training set (N=3,647): 1.53% (rank 29)

Topic: 8

Assigned label: ProQuest boilerplate + names

Cluster: (non-content topics)

Top 20 Keywords:

by TF-ITF: ission perm ner prohibited erm ithout ced ro ep ow reproduction copyright eproduced scrapbooks machiavelli scrapbook medici itho prince arendt

by probability: ission perm copyright reproduction prohibited ro ep erm ow ithout ner ced eproduced press machiavelli scrapbooks scrapbook rush university arendt

Portion of corpus:

confirmed RCWS (N=1,684): 0.23% (rank 48)

confirmed non-RCWS (N=696): 0.27% (rank 46)

full training set (N=3,647): 0.29% (rank 49)

Topic: 9

Assigned label: Historical Public Rhetoric, esp of Women

Cluster: Public Rhetorics and Political Writing

Top 20 Keywords:

by TF-ITF: public rhetoric women sphere civic archives american movement rhetorical education nineteenth history citizenship century archival suffrage social speech publics nineteenth-century

by probability: public rhetoric american history rhetorical movement social education century university work women society civic early members sphere time historical national

Portion of corpus:

confirmed RCWS (N=1,684): 2.18% (rank 18)

confirmed non-RCWS (N=696): 2.36% (rank 19)

full training set (N=3,647): 1.92% (rank 22)

Topic: 10

Assigned label: LGBTQ and Gender Studies

Cluster: Peoples and Places

Top 20 Keywords:

by TF-ITF: gay queer sexual lesbian sex sexuality jewish marriage identity lgbt jews lesbians homosexuality heterosexual activism gender violence holocaust couples homosexual

by probability: gay identity sexual queer lesbian sex marriage sexuality jewish rights people lgbt gender activism violence jews men community coming lesbians

Portion of corpus:

confirmed RCWS (N=1,684): 0.71% (rank 38)

confirmed non-RCWS (N=696): 0.86% (rank 39)

full training set (N=3,647): 0.69% (rank 43)

Topic: 11

Assigned label: Genre and Move Analysis

Cluster: Applied Composition (unstable subset)

Top 20 Keywords:

> by TF-ITF: genre text texts genres readers textual reading visual research reader analysis citation page articles citations data features graphic introductions sources

> by probability: text genre texts analysis research genres readers reading study information textual reader move rhetorical articles specific features section page sources

Portion of corpus:

> confirmed RCWS (N=1,684): 2.83% (rank 11)
> confirmed non-RCWS (N=696): 2.48% (rank 16)
> full training set (N=3,647): 2.61% (rank 16)

Topic: 12

Assigned label: Bad OCR

Cluster: (non-content topics)

Top 20 Keywords:

> by TF-ITF: ith ent hat riting em ents hen ost om ore ould hich ork en ay im som er ber ho

> by probability: ith ent hat im riting em om en ore hich er ents hen ost ork ould ay ed ow som

Portion of corpus:

> confirmed RCWS (N=1,684): 1.21% (rank 31)
> confirmed non-RCWS (N=696): 0.49% (rank 42)
> full training set (N=3,647): 1.17% (rank 35)

Topic: 13

Assigned label: Politics, Empire, Radicalism

Cluster: Public Rhetorics and Political Writing

Top 20 Keywords:

> by TF-ITF: political politics democracy war radical violence freedom democratic critique power liberal capitalism public ibid social american revolution ideology critical ideological

> by probability: political politics university power press world york social american society war history democracy public people freedom culture critical cultural violence

Portion of corpus:

> confirmed RCWS (N=1,684): 2.48% (rank 17)
> confirmed non-RCWS (N=696): 4.36% (rank 4)
> full training set (N=3,647): 2.95% (rank 12)

Topic: 14

Assigned label: Literary Poetics

Cluster: Poetics and Oratory

Top 20 Keywords:

by TF-ITF: poetry literary poem fiction readers creative reading poet poems poets writers reader english book writing narrator poetic writer art literature

by probability: literary literature readers reading poetry reader book english text creative writers fiction poem work writing language books read art century

Portion of corpus:

confirmed RCWS (N=1,684): 2.72% (rank 13)
confirmed non-RCWS (N=696): 2.33% (rank 20)
full training set (N=3,647): 2.65% (rank 15)

Topic: 15

Assigned label: French language indicator

Cluster: (non-content topics)

Top 20 Keywords:

by TF-ITF: la de le des les dans du qui une en sur pour est par di pas cette comme che texte

by probability: de la le des les du en dans qui une est il par di sur ce pour au pas se

Portion of corpus:

confirmed RCWS (N=1,684): 0.04% (rank 50)
confirmed non-RCWS (N=696): 0.09% (rank 49)
full training set (N=3,647): 0.28% (rank 50)

Topic: 16

Assigned label: Creative Writing and Reflection

Cluster: Narrative and Reflection

Top 20 Keywords:

by TF-ITF: night water door eyes man hair car house room mother girl head sun feet death ritual woman morning back black

by probability: back man time day house eyes night long room water left face head place hand death home body life made

Portion of corpus:

confirmed RCWS (N=1,684): 1.74% (rank 23)
confirmed non-RCWS (N=696): 2.47% (rank 17)
full training set (N=3,647): 2.09% (rank 20)

Topic: 17

Assigned label: Nationalisms: Black, White, Palestinian, Israeli

Cluster: Peoples and Places

Top 20 Keywords:

by TF-ITF: black african arab africa south blacks slave negro palestinian slavery israel white americans rights islam american muslim civil israeli carter

by probability: black african american south white rights people americans civil blacks africa political arab war slavery martin southern history king negro

Portion of corpus:

confirmed RCWS (N=1,684): 0.97% (rank 33)
confirmed non-RCWS (N=696): 2.49% (rank 15)
full training set (N=3,647): 1.3% (rank 32)

Topic: 18

Assigned label: Writing Process

Cluster: Teaching and Administration

Top 20 Keywords:

by TF-ITF: writing writers essay feedback students write peer writer revision draft essays errors sentence drafts composing grammar paragraph sentences process comments

by probability: writing writers essay students process write feedback writer study written essays comments sentence ideas revision peer paper text grammar errors

Portion of corpus:

confirmed RCWS (N=1,684): 2.67% (rank 14)
confirmed non-RCWS (N=696): 4.26% (rank 6)
full training set (N=3,647): 3.65% (rank 6)

Topic: 19

Assigned label: Presidential Discourse

Cluster: Public Rhetorics and Political Writing

Top 20 Keywords:

by TF-ITF: bush president presidential war clinton reagan campaign policy presidents military public iraq political news obama u.s nuclear media speech election

by probability: war president public political american policy u.s national news bush states united campaign media presidential speech military government york clinton

Portion of corpus:

confirmed RCWS (N=1,684): 1.26% (rank 29)
confirmed non-RCWS (N=696): 6.2% (rank 1)
full training set (N=3,647): 2.83% (rank 13)

Topic: 20

Assigned label: Architecture and Place as Text

Cluster: Peoples and Places

Top 20 Keywords:

by TF-ITF: space museum visitors mexican spaces spatial memorial city memory map mexico maps park puerto exhibit architecture museums urban community public by probability: space place city spaces museum history public memory community national memorial places mexican center map visitors park people spatial urban

Portion of corpus:

confirmed RCWS (N=1,684): 1.22% (rank 30)
confirmed non-RCWS (N=696): 1.37% (rank 29)
full training set (N=3,647): 1.2% (rank 34)

Topic: 21

Assigned label: Rhetorics of Power, Conflict, and Politics

Cluster: Theoretical Orientations

Top 20 Keywords:

by TF-ITF: discourse social public community identity power discursive discourses critical cultural process conflict dialogue political agency action values communication dialogic ideological

by probability: social discourse public power community identity process cultural action critical individual analysis understanding values change people communication ways context language

Portion of corpus:

confirmed RCWS (N=1,684): 5.2% (rank 3)
confirmed non-RCWS (N=696): 5.73% (rank 2)
full training set (N=3,647): 4.99% (rank 2)

Topic: 22

Assigned label: Linguistics

Cluster: (inconsistent)

Top 20 Keywords:

by TF-ITF: metaphor linguistic metaphors utterance verb language lexical corpus clause sentence verbs clauses speech collocations speaker discourse linguistics semantic grammatical features

by probability: language metaphor discourse linguistic metaphors text speech words features speaker analysis sentence meaning utterance verb verbs corpus speakers clause word

Portion of corpus:

confirmed RCWS (N=1,684): 0.91% (rank 35)
confirmed non-RCWS (N=696): 1.41% (rank 28)
full training set (N=3,647): 1.35% (rank 30)

Topic: 23

Assigned label: Native American Rhetorics

Cluster: Peoples and Places

Top 20 Keywords:

by TF-ITF: indian indians native indigenous cherokee american tribal tribes india postcolonial sovereignty colonial land removal natives cultural colonization tribe hawaiian reservation

by probability: indian american native indians cultural people indigenous
   land culture colonial history identity cherokee tribal nation sovereignty
   government u.s white states

Portion of corpus:

   confirmed RCWS (N=1,684): 0.85% (rank 36)
   confirmed non-RCWS (N=696): 0.63% (rank 40)
   full training set (N=3,647): 0.73% (rank 41)

Topic: 24

Assigned label: East Asian Rhetorics—and video games

Cluster: (inconsistent)

Top 20 Keywords:

   by TF-ITF: chinese china japanese korean games game korea mao japan
      players translation gaming gamers player zedong hong koreans video
      beijing kong
   by probability: chinese game games china japanese translation korean
      korea japan players world mao cultural gaming video people player
      foreign play gamers

Portion of corpus:

   confirmed RCWS (N=1,684): 0.6% (rank 40)
   confirmed non-RCWS (N=696): 1% (rank 36)
   full training set (N=3,647): 0.69% (rank 44)

Topic: 25

Assigned label: Classical Rhetoric

Cluster: Poetics and Oratory

Top 20 Keywords:

   by TF-ITF: socrates cicero humor isocrates greek medieval plato roman
      orator classical aristotle speech phaedrus cf quintilian athens de an-
      cient speeches cicero's
   by probability: socrates humor speech greek cicero de roman medieval
      isocrates classical plato ancient orator art press speeches rhetoric soul
      aristotle university

Portion of corpus:

   confirmed RCWS (N=1,684): 0.66% (rank 39)
   confirmed non-RCWS (N=696): 1.09% (rank 34)
   full training set (N=3,647): 1% (rank 37)

Topic: 26

Assigned label: Personal Narrative and Oral History

Cluster: Narrative and Reflection

Top 20 Keywords:

   by TF-ITF: i'm don't it's that's school stories didn't write writing story lot
      people i've parents family life you're wanted experiences experience
   by probability: people time life story stories school it's don't experience
      personal family write i'm work writing things make good years read

Portion of corpus:

confirmed RCWS (N=1,684): 4.74% (rank 4)
confirmed non-RCWS (N=696): 4.5% (rank 3)
full training set (N=3,647): 4.72% (rank 3)

Topic: 27

Assigned label: Writing Centers

Cluster: Applied Composition (unstable subset)

Top 20 Keywords:

by TF-ITF: tutors writing tutor tutoring center centers tutorial student tutees session sessions consultants peer tutorials yeah conferences owl students um consultant

by probability: writing center tutors tutor tutoring student centers session conference sessions work tutorial questions paper students writers peer tutees conferences consultants

Portion of corpus:

confirmed RCWS (N=1,684): 1.26% (rank 28)
confirmed non-RCWS (N=696): 0.45% (rank 41)
full training set (N=3,647): 0.97% (rank 38)

Topic: 28

Assigned label: Literacy Practices

Cluster: Theoretical Orientations

Top 20 Keywords:

by TF-ITF: literacy writing students literacies community classroom literate pedagogy reading critical practices service-learning learning education freire social texts experiences school print

by probability: literacy writing students practices work community social ways critical reading education texts classroom learning print pedagogy cultural literacies experiences school

Portion of corpus:

confirmed RCWS (N=1,684): 3.77% (rank 8)
confirmed non-RCWS (N=696): 1.06% (rank 35)
full training set (N=3,647): 2.55% (rank 17)

Topic: 29

Assigned label: Writing in Law and Government

Cluster: Public Rhetorics and Political Writing

Top 20 Keywords:

by TF-ITF: court law legal supreme moral constitution justice political courts constitutional laws england liberty public judicial trial rights government parliament speech

by probability: law legal court state political moral justice case public states common rights government people constitution act authority speech men laws

Portion of corpus:

confirmed RCWS (N=1,684): 1.5% (rank 25)

confirmed non-RCWS (N=696): 2.59% (rank 14)

full training set (N=3,647): 1.87% (rank 23)

Topic: 30

Assigned label: German language indicator

Cluster: (non-contènt topics)

Top 20 Keywords:

by TF-ITF: und der das fuen combustible zu ist german die chavez sie von nicht lat hugo p.p ich den ein eine

by probability: und die der german das fuen combustible ist chavez zu von es hugo ich sie ein nicht lat p.p den

Portion of corpus:

confirmed RCWS (N=1,684): 0.34% (rank 47)

confirmed non-RCWS (N=696): 0.04% (rank 50)

full training set (N=3,647): 0.3% (rank 48)

Topic: 31

Assigned label: Labor Unions and Economic Activism

Cluster: Public Rhetorics and Political Writing

Top 20 Keywords:

by TF-ITF: workers labor economic economy farm market homeless worker union corporate appalachian welfare government capitalism industry ufw financial globalization companies economics

by probability: economic workers labor social work government state economy market working people system public states global local united class money business

Portion of corpus:

confirmed RCWS (N=1,684): 1.8% (rank 22)

confirmed non-RCWS (N=696): 2.39% (rank 18)

full training set (N=3,647): 1.82% (rank 24)

Topic: 32

Assigned label: Disciplinary Formations

Cluster: Theoretical Orientations

Top 20 Keywords:

by TF-ITF: writing composition pedagogy students teachers teaching english writers classroom disciplinary pedagogical textbooks rhetoric academic writer pedagogies discipline theory write compositionists

by probability: writing composition studies teaching work pedagogy students theory rhetoric english teachers writers academic knowledge field language process discourse scholars research

Portion of corpus:

confirmed RCWS (N=1,684): 6.6% (rank 1)

confirmed non-RCWS (N=696): 1.27% (rank 31)

full training set (N=3,647): 4.21% (rank 4)

Topic: 33

Assigned label: Rhetorical Frameworks

Cluster: Theoretical Orientations

Top 20 Keywords:

by TF-ITF: rhetoric rhetorical ethos audience argument arguments aristotle rhetor persuasion epideictic persuasive invention kairos rhetors classical pathos argumentation speech situation appeals

by probability: rhetoric rhetorical audience argument ethos arguments situation theory chapter speech persuasion communication people study understanding make persuasive important analysis audiences

Portion of corpus:

confirmed RCWS (N=1,684): 3.46% (rank 9)
confirmed non-RCWS (N=696): 3.07% (rank 11)
full training set (N=3,647): 3.05% (rank 11)

Topic: 34

Assigned label: Bad OCR

Cluster: (non-content topics)

Top 20 Keywords:

by TF-ITF: die ti ion ae en diat fth ev tt ft ag eo ol advl rm ang ia ea widi ik

by probability: die en ti ae ion ed ing ev iv diat ch fth ft ag eo rm ia tt im ce

Portion of corpus:

confirmed RCWS (N=1,684): 0.69% (rank 41)
confirmed non-RCWS (N=696): 0.21% (rank 47)
full training set (N=3,647): 0.59% (rank 46)

Topic: 35

Assigned label: Institutional Supports, Barriers, Constraints

Cluster: Teaching and Administration

Top 20 Keywords:

by TF-ITF: students faculty college writing education courses english colleges composition program teaching instructors programs student universities graduate curriculum academic higher developmental

by probability: students college education university writing faculty program english courses teaching programs composition higher academic student graduate department colleges community school

Portion of corpus:

confirmed RCWS (N=1,684): 4.3% (rank 6)
confirmed non-RCWS (N=696): 2.09% (rank 23)
full training set (N=3,647): 3.38% (rank 9)

Topic: 36

Assigned label: Bad OCR

Cluster: (non-content topics)

Top 20 Keywords:

   by TF-ITF: om fiom firom ae listserv tae hom a&ican grst munoz hke
   leam wiu four-color fbr horn tsa fae fi'om jibaro

   by probability: om fiom ae firom leam process modem hom analysis listserv tae part fo study a&ican made grst munoz questions outlaw

Portion of corpus:

   confirmed RCWS (N=1,684): 0.47% (rank 46)
   confirmed non-RCWS (N=696): 0.39% (rank 44)
   full training set (N=3,647): 0.47% (rank 47)

Topic: 37

Assigned label: Across Languages

Cluster: Applied Composition (unstable subset)

Top 20 Keywords:

   by TF-ITF: english esl language students learners spanish languages participants chinese linguistic thai learning bilingual native multilingual
   tesol proficiency efl li arabic

   by probability: english language students esl study research learning cultural languages learners participants spanish linguistic native university
   culture international academic american teaching

Portion of corpus:

   confirmed RCWS (N=1,684): 1.51% (rank 24)
   confirmed non-RCWS (N=696): 2.17% (rank 22)
   full training set (N=3,647): 1.78% (rank 26)

Topic: 38

Assigned label: Reading (through) Feminisms

Cluster: Unstable

Top 20 Keywords:

   by TF-ITF: women feminist women's woman gender female feminine
   male feminism men masculine sex gendered womens girls sexual femi-
   nists mothers patriarchal mother

   by probability: women feminist gender woman women's men female male
   power work feminism body family feminine girls social sex mother
   womens sexual

Portion of corpus:

   confirmed RCWS (N=1,684): 2.51% (rank 16)
   confirmed non-RCWS (N=696): 2.64% (rank 13)
   full training set (N=3,647): 2.28% (rank 18)

Topic: 39

Assigned label: Homiletics

Cluster: Poetics and Oratory

Top 20 Keywords:

   by TF-ITF: preaching sermon god church biblical sermons christ christian jesus bible preacher preachers religious theology scripture faith
   theological god's congregation gospel

by probability: god church christian religious preaching sermon bible faith biblical jesus sermons christ religion people preacher word paul life spiritual text

Portion of corpus:

confirmed RCWS (N=1,684): 0.99% (rank 32)
confirmed non-RCWS (N=696): 1.49% (rank 26)
full training set (N=3,647): 2.18% (rank 19)

Topic: 40

Assigned label: Scientific Discourse

Cluster: Applied Composition (unstable subset)

Top 20 Keywords:

by TF-ITF: science scientific scientists scientist nuclear research technical data doe public cells votes laboratory biology lab sciences dna physics genome mathematical

by probability: science scientific research scientists public knowledge human data evidence information work technical risk article claims report sciences scientist community lab

Portion of corpus:

confirmed RCWS (N=1,684): 1.05% (rank 31)
confirmed non-RCWS (N=696): 1.25% (rank 32)
full training set (N=3,647): 1.04% (rank 36)

Topic: 41

Assigned label: Collaborative Learning

Cluster: Applied Composition (unstable subset)

Top 20 Keywords:

by TF-ITF: participants research interview data interviews participant collaborative learning researcher qualitative study group collaboration community experiences researchers participation activity members writing

by probability: research participants study group data interview work interviews learning questions project process community time members social knowledge participant collaborative experience

Portion of corpus:

confirmed RCWS (N=1,684): 4.69% (rank 5)
confirmed non-RCWS (N=696): 3.22% (rank 10)
full training set (N=3,647): 4.16% (rank 5)

Topic: 42

Assigned label: K12 Writing Pedagogy

Cluster: Teaching and Administration

Top 20 Keywords:

by TF-ITF: students writing teachers teacher school learning student classroom teaching grade instruction education schools assessment skills educational curriculum instructional portfolio write by probability: students writing teachers school learning teacher student teaching education instruction study classroom educational grade research skills schools development assessment reading

Portion of corpus:

confirmed RCWS (N=1,684): 2.01% (rank 21)
confirmed non-RCWS (N=696): 3.55% (rank 8)
full training set (N=3,647): 3.48% (rank 7)

Topic: 43

Assigned label: Sports

Cluster: Popular Entertainment

Top 20 Keywords:

by TF-ITF: sport sports advertising food football baseball cooking ads advertisements television athletes consumer players consumers athletic detroit colbert league athletics foods

by probability: food advertising sports sport television culture media football baseball consumer ads game cooking players american consumers cultural university advertisements team

Portion of corpus:

confirmed RCWS (N=1,684): 0.55% (rank 41)
confirmed non-RCWS (N=696): 1.83% (rank 24)
full training set (N=3,647): 0.82% (rank 39)

Topic: 44

Assigned label: Online Circulation and Social Media

Cluster: Applied Composition (unstable subset)

Top 20 Keywords:

by TF-ITF: online blog blogs web internet posts facebook virtual users site media sites websites blogging digital posted website post user twitter

by probability: online web site media internet sites social users information blog community people post virtual communication blogs website content page websites

Portion of corpus:

confirmed RCWS (N=1,684): 2.01% (rank 20)
confirmed non-RCWS (N=696): 1.44% (rank 27)
full training set (N=3,647): 1.59% (rank 28)

Topic: 45

Assigned label: Digital Media Affordances

Cluster: Applied Composition (unstable subset)

Top 20 Keywords:

by TF-ITF: digital technology computers computer technologies hypertext online software electronic multimodal technological media composition writing composing selfe internet web design interface

by probability: technology digital computer computers technologies online media university web writing electronic technological composition software design access information internet hypertext multimodal

Portion of corpus:

confirmed RCWS (N=1,684): 2.65% (rank 15)
confirmed non-RCWS (N=696): 0.98% (rank 38)
full training set (N=3,647): 1.78% (rank 25)

Topic: 46

Assigned label: Medical Discourse

Cluster: Unstable

Top 20 Keywords:

by TF-ITF: medical disability patients medicine health autism illness patient clinical physicians disease care breastfeeding doctors cancer physician symptoms therapy pregnancy disabled

by probability: health medical care medicine disability patients body autism patient disease children illness people clinical child physicians birth mental treatment doctors

Portion of corpus:

confirmed RCWS (N=1,684): 1.44% (rank 26)
confirmed non-RCWS (N=696): 1.59% (rank 25)
full training set (N=3,647): 1.35% (rank 31)

Topic: 47

Assigned label: Spanish Language

Cluster: (non-content topics)

Top 20 Keywords:

by TF-ITF: en el la de del las por los una como se con es su lo este para entre esta sobr

by probability: de la en el los del se las por una como con es para su al lo este ms entre

Portion of corpus:

confirmed RCWS (N=1,684): 0.11% (rank 42)
confirmed non-RCWS (N=696): 0.12% (rank 42)
full training set (N=3,647): 0.66% (rank 45)

Topic: 48

Assigned label: Reading Rhetoricians, Interpreting Philosophy

Cluster: Theoretical Orientations

Top 20 Keywords:

by TF-ITF: burke aristotle truth plato philosophy burke's human philosophical rhetoric language kant gorgias nietzsche heidegger dialectic ethics thought dewey sophists art

by probability: human language rhetoric philosophy world burke truth nature knowledge sense terms thought form things life order theory words time work

Portion of corpus:

confirmed RCWS (N=1,684): 3.05% (rank 10)
confirmed non-RCWS (N=696): 4.36% (rank 5)
full training set (N=3,647): 3.43% (rank 8)

Topic: 49

Assigned label: Scenes of teaching

Cluster: Teaching and Administration

Top 20 Keywords:

by TF-ITF: students student class classroom writing instructors semester teacher teachers instructor assignment assignments composition teaching paper essay eng classes papers write

by probability: students class student writing classroom teacher teachers paper teaching instructors instructor assignment semester college classes work composition assignments essay write

Portion of corpus:

confirmed RCWS (N=1,684): 6.1% (rank 2)
confirmed non-RCWS (N=696): 3.33% (rank 9)
full training set (N=3,647): 5.03% (rank 1)

Topic: 50

Assigned label: Bad OCR

Cluster: (non-content topics)

Top 20 Keywords:

by TF-ITF: te tio ts ro en ra le ith rs se ir tu sh su ic stu fo ritin ta ry

by probability: te en ro se fo le tio ts ra ith la tu ta id ic er su ed rs stu

Portion of corpus:

confirmed RCWS (N=1,684): 0.62% (rank 43)
confirmed non-RCWS (N=696): 0.3% (rank 45)
full training set (N=3,647): 0.71% (rank 42)

NOTES

CHAPTER 1: DISCIPLINARY ANXIETY AND THE COMPOSITION OF COMPOSITION

1. This was not always the case. As Maureen Daly Goggin notes, in a classical college prior to the nineteenth century, "The goal . . . was not to create knowledge; that was not within the province of students or faculty. Rather the goal for faculty was to instill knowledge, moral values, and piety, and the goal for students was to demonstrate that they had attained these ends. In short, it served to construct a particular way of thinking and behaving" (4–5).

2. At the time of writing, WAC Clearinghouse maintained a list of 106 active scholarly journals that regularly (if not exclusively) publish RCWS materials, located at https://wac.colostate.edu/resources/general/journals/.

3. The term is Maureen Daly Goggin's, originally naming scholarly activity that "writes the field" (xviii), such as journal editing; Mueller extends it to encompass also the study of such activity: any meta-analyses of the discipline, in other words, albeit without the social-scientific sense of aggregating data-driven studies that was operative in Hillocks's meta-analysis.

4. My dissertation analysis code is at https://github.com/benmiller314/dissertation-research/.

5. Major exceptions include those who pursue "alt-ac" careers such as publishing, or those who teach at secondary schools or two-year colleges without doctorates as prerequisites for employment. But a doctorate is required for positions at many colleges and universities, and even in other positions many who identify with RCWS but aren't required to do so earn PhDs nevertheless.

6. Or, at least, the recent past into which the present keeps slipping.

CHAPTER 2: SO WHAT'S YOUR DISSERTATION ABOUT?

1. Kopelson (2008) cites many more, including C. Jan Swearingen, "Rhetoric and Composition as a Coherent Intellectual Discipline: A Meditation," in *Rhetoric and Composition as Intellectual Work*, ed. Gary A. Olson (Carbondale: Southern Illinois UP, 2002); Gerald Mulderig, "Is There Still a Place for Rhetorical History in Composition Studies?" in *History, Reflection, and Narrative: The Professionalization of Composition, 1963–1983*, ed. Mary Rosner, Beth Boehm, and Debra Journet (Stamford, CT: Ablex, 1999); and Stephen North's (1987) *The Making of Knowledge in Composition* and Kurt Spellmeyer's (2003) "Education for Irrelevance?," both cited in chapter 1.

2. Alberto Cairo, in a book about data visualization, argues that all models (mental or mathematical) fall on continuum between Absolutely Untrue, on the left, and Absolutely True, on the right—but that we can never fully know our model's position on that scale, nor how close we are to either end in any measurable sense.

Nevertheless, he writes, we can reliably expect "that evidence-based reasoning may move you closer to the right-most end" (Cairo). The pun on striving to be more "right" is, I suspect, intentional.

3.   That is, there are 650 dissertations in the ProQuest dataset that I could confirm were completed at those programs in the years 2006–2010, inclusive. The actual number is likely larger.

4.   See Mueller (2017), discussed in chapter 1.

5.   That is, subject code 0681; see the next section for some interpretive challenges of such subject codes and terms.

6.   "Affiliated programs" are the ninety-four programs listed on rhetmap.org's program map as of summer 2019, plus the University of Rhode Island's PhD in English (Rhetoric and Composition concentration), which was at that time the only member of the Consortium of Doctoral Programs in Rhetoric and Composition not already included on rhetmap.

Though it was easy to determine the *school* of a given dissertation, frustratingly, many of the dissertations' front matter and PQDT metadata did not indicate their *departments*—and many departments do not keep full records of alumni against which to verify. I am grateful to both the scholars and the administrators who did provide such information. A comparison of dissertations known to be from affiliated and from unaffiliated programs will be taken up in chapter four.

7.   The term "folksonomy" was coined by Thomas Vander Wal in 2004 to refer to a "user-created bottom-up categorical structure development with an emergent thesaurus," in response to the then-emergent practice of user-based tagging in sites like Flickr (for photographs) and del.icio.us (for websites) (Vander Wal). In theory, folksonomy would lead to serendipitous discovery of adjacent articles of interest that included the same tags, while democratizing the terms by which such discovery was facilitated. In the case of some large databases—including those mentioned above—this has had some measure of success, as users gravitate toward existing terms, coalescing in a relatively contained number of combinations. In others, though, and especially in smaller databases without robust synonym matching or term-suggestion engines, the selection of terms has been so varied as to be more idiosyncratic than collaborative. It is this widening spread of individual, personal terms that I refer to as "diffusion."

8.   See especially Scott Weingart's (2012) roundup of such introductions, which includes links to Matthew Jockers' (2011) "The LDA Buffet Is Now Open" and Ted Underwood's (2012) "Topic Modeling Made Just Simple Enough," as well as several rather less-simple articles by Edwin Chen (2011), David Blei (2012), David Mimno (2012; 2013), and others.

9.   The algorithm first "tokenizes" the text, counting the instances of the same words, or tokens, after stripping connective tissue and overly common "stop words" such as "a, an, and, of, the" and so on that would overwhelm and obscure the more interesting content. (For a discussion of tokenizing and other preprocessing steps, see appendix A.)

10.   "Text" here is broadly construed: these approaches could equally well describe traditional writing or images or waveforms. Ben Schmidt (2013) has used them to identify common routes taken by nineteenth-century whaling ships.

11.   Every unique word, or token, is assumed to be part of every topic, but each topic associates a different probability with any given token; words with a high probability are used to identify the topic, while many words in a given topic will have a probability at or very close to zero.

12.   Note that this has some bearing on our interpretation of top topic weights as worthy of investigation: it's not simply that we're dividing 100% of the corpus among

however many topics we put into the model. If topic sizes had been purely arbitrary, our top ten of fifty would have accounted for only around 20% of the corpus.

13. The interquartile range (IQR) is the difference in the *values* at the upper and lower quartiles. In the case of the top-ranked topic, e.g., the IQR is 0.3556–0.2252 = 0.1304, so the upper whisker shows the maximum observed value below the "fence" of (0.1304x 1.5) + 0. 3556 = 0.5512. In the present case, that maximum nonoutlier value is 0. 5502, and any top-ranked topic representing more than 55.1% of the dissertation is considered an outlier.

14. Nine topics of the fifty in the model were deemed "non-content-bearing," representing instead the presence of a non-English language or, more frequently, the garbled nonlanguage produced by faulty optical character recognition (OCR) scanning of printed pages. See appendix C.

15. Though there are some outliers at the bottom for ranks below the first, and some extremely high top-topic outliers above the levels discussed in this section, these both appear to consist solely of dissertations for which the "real" top-ranked topic was non-content-bearing, e.g., a "topic" of nonwords resulting from a poor scan of a print document. Where these took up 90–99% of the dissertation, the remaining content-bearing topics misleadingly seem to represent an extremely low proportion of the text.

16. In other words, there is less than one chance in a thousand that selecting a random sample this size would result in a similar degree of offset.

17. To be fair, selecting three values at random from forty-one topics would yield 10,660 possible combinations, so 0.9% (15/1,684) is actually a much higher concentration of attention than chance. But even so, it is difficult to get a sense of the field's overall patterns from these very small slices.

18. Writing Centers (T27), the other high-skewed top topic, is down at rank sixteen in the new measure, appearing as the top topic in thirty-nine of 1,684 dissertations, or 2.3% of the time.

19. This 13% cutoff, like the previous one at 5%, is derived from the lower hinge of the distribution for a high-ranked topic: in this case, the second-most prominent topic within a given dissertation.

20. To make this active selection of inclusive language possible, doctoral programs would do well to periodically check course offerings and other materials against the most current sets of dissertations, field wide. I say *periodically* because the kind of mapping I offer in this book is not intended to be done once and treated as true for all time; it is, rather, a snapshot. The disciplinary landscape does change over time, as I will discuss in chapter 5. What the models allow, though, is a more concrete sense of what is changing and how, grounded in a wide base of evidence.

21. This approach is influenced by Rolf Fredheim (2013).

22. The Pythagorean theorem familiar from high school math states that for a right triangle with legs of length a and b and hypotenuse of length c, $c^2 = a^2 + b^2$. Or, taking the square root of both sides, $c = \text{sqrt}(a^2 + b^2)$. More generally, the distance between point A at (x_1, y_1) and point B at (x_2, y_2) is the hypotenuse of a right triangle, whose legs are the change in x and y: $d = \text{sqrt}((x_2-x_1)^2 + (y_2-y_1)^2)$. The formula generalizes beyond the two-dimensional plane of x and y: you just keep summing the squares of differences in however many dimensions there are and take the square root of the sum. To find the distance from one topic to another, we can treat each token as a dimension, for which every topic has a unique value (even if some values are vanishingly close to zero) and sum the squares of differences in value for each token. The square root of that sum gives the distance between the pair of topics. In practice, because the values for each token are probabilities and not counts, I used a more complex variation of this approach, the Jensen-Shannon Distance. For more on the distance-measuring

software, see Drost (2018); for more on Jensen-Shannon Distance, see https://en
.wikipedia.org/wiki/Jensen%E2%80%93Shannon_divergence.

23.   Specifically, I used the agnes() function in the R package "cluster" specifying Ward's
method to minimize within-cluster variance, with variance measured as Euclidean
distance. For more on agnes, see Maechler (n.d.), "Agnes"; for more on Ward's
method, see https://en.wikipedia.org/wiki/Ward%27s_method.

24.   Color may not be available for all print editions; in that case, see the online version
of this figure.

25.   That is, this cluster splits off quite early from the rest of the topics under divisive
clustering: it separates in one of the first four divisions, and then remains stable as
other clusters further subdivide.

26.   One additional topic pairing, of topics 44 (Online Circulation and Social Media)
and 45 (Digital Media Affordances) appears in both clustering diagrams but seems
to be part of a larger grouping that joins only under agglomerative clustering, and
is discussed elsewhere.

27.   The only other cluster that moves across the major divisions in the tree in the same
way is the much smaller "Narrative and Reflection": storytelling, in other words,
including the stories we tell about the writing we ourselves have done.

28.   This raises an interesting question about the *recency* of the theoretical citations
made by dissertation-writers; a future study of citation networks would be able to
tell us whether the common theoretical references are more Gorgias or Gilyard.

CHAPTER 3: HOW DO YOU KNOW?

1.   North's assumption that teachers were the only practitioners worthy of mention
ignored other forms of practice, most notably *writing*, and his characterization
of their mode of knowledge-making as the trading of anecdotal "lore" has led to
numerous calls to either get "beyond lore" or "reclaim lore"—but "lore" has held
on as a frame of reference, for good or for ill.

2.   MKC, plus Lauer and Asher's (1988) *Composition Research*, Hayes et al.'s (1992) *Reading Empirical Research Studies*, Kirsch and Sullivan's (1992) *Methods and Methodology in
Composition Research*, and MacNealy's (1998) *Strategies for Empirical Research in Writing*.

3.   Abstracts were coded by myself and two graduate students, S.L. Nelson and Andrew
Thurman, whose time was compensated for with funding from the CCCC Emergent
Research/er Award. After an intensive training session of several days, we met
weekly throughout the three months of coding to address questions and resolve
differences. In cases of discrepancy or coder uncertainty, we strove for *interrater
agreement*, aiming to achieve consensus through discussion, rather than rely solely
on quantitative measures of *interrater reliability* among independent scores. As
Campbell et al. (2013) have argued, this approach to qualitative coding by multiple
researchers can be more appropriate in contexts where the objects under study are
especially complex or where interpretation is dependent in part on coder knowl-
edgeability. For only one dissertation were we unable to reach agreement after
discussion; that dissertation was excluded from further analysis.

4.   It feels important to add that I had some personal interest, as well: coming from an
MFA background as a poet, through a doctoral program (at CUNY) and now a faculty
position (at Pitt) in departments with large numbers of MFA writers, I was curious to
see whether and how often writers were engaging in the kinds of fictive techne valued
in creative writing programs and applying that practical knowledge to PhD work.

5.   The common impression that a final chapter on teaching must be added to sat-
isfy the "pedagogical imperative" at many schools (Kopelson 2008) may explain

the high frequency of Philosophical/Theoretical dissertations identified by my approach, and an investigation into the chapter-by-chapter proportion of this method in particular could prove quite interesting. Such a breakdown was, however, outside the scope of the present study.

6. This figure is smaller than the sum of individual tags shown in figure 3.3 (585 + 506 + 439 + 432 = 1962) because many of the documents were tagged with more than one of these methods.

7. About half of the dissertations, 846, include at least one Empirical method from either the Phenomenological or the Aggregable group; that this is lower than the reach of either group alone indicates some overlap between them, as I'll discuss later.

8. Spanning several disciplines among the authors, Juzwik et al. chose the ERIC, PsychInfo, and Linguistics and Language Behavior Abstracts databases to search, and thus their sample draws from a larger set of journals than would typically be understood as "in" RCWS. I will return to this larger interdisciplinary context for writing research in chapter 4.

9. For an introduction to dendrograms, see the discussion of figures 2.5 and 2.6.

10. Even if not likely in absolute terms, because only 2 of the 225 possible pairings occurs more than 50% of the time, and none more than 60% of the time. This lack of strong predictability reinforces my sense that the methods in the schema are meaningfully distinct, even in cases like CRIT and RHET, between which that peak value of 57% occurs.

11. Note that this finding challenges Michael Carter's (2007) characterization of writing and rhetoric as falling in the Performance metadiscipline (406): that's not where most of the energy in dissertations seems to go. This discrepancy could point to a distinction between what outcomes are expected of undergraduate vs. graduate students, with undergraduates evaluated more on production of pragmatically competent text than of new knowledge. This may, in turn, be related to the different names accorded to undergraduate majors vs. graduate programs, as Sandra Jamieson (2018) has ascertained: the former tend to emphasize "writing," while the latter emphasize "composition" and "rhetoric." It would make sense that the written artifact would hold more weight in a *writing* program, per se, while the more abstract terms at the graduate level could correspond more to the "distinct ways of knowing" that Carter (2007) associates with disciplines characterized by research from sources (Carter 2007, 406).

CHAPTER 4: BUT DOESN'T EVERYONE KNOW ABOUT WRITING?

1. A surprising number of dissertation title and signature pages state only that they were submitted in partial fulfillment of the requirements for the PhD—without naming what the PhD was *in*. I was able to track down some of these dissertators through web searches, including with the assistance of undergraduate research assistants Janetta Brundage, Michelle Hillock, Yuanton Rachel Li, and Michael Barmada, who worked to locate and reconcile CVs and alumni lists against the dissertation data from ProQuest. However, the rate of success was relatively low (and slow), and many departments did not maintain alumni listings running back to 2001 (or, in some cases, at all). Combined with the ways some composition programs are internally tracked, or not, relative to English degrees in literature, this made it difficult to pin down whether someone was in fact affiliated with the consortium program even when they could be determined to have studied at a school.

2. E.g., speech communication, communication and culture, media and communication, communication arts.

3. In practice, this can only be an approximation at most. Though I selected the time period to allow for most dissertations in the ProQuest database to come out of embargo and into circulation, the database itself is very US centric, with only a small fraction of its contents coming from other countries; and the guidance in subject tag selection is not so straightforward for graduating doctoral students that we can be 100% certain everyone in rhetoric/composition programs would be sure to select the tag I used in my search.

4. That is, TF-ITF; see appendix B.

5. For an introduction to heatmaps, see the introduction to figures 3.8 and 3.9.

6. Note that these topic clusters are based on distances within the topic-token matrix, not the topic-document matrix, and as such are stable across subcorpora within the larger corpus (N=3,647) the topic model was trained on.

CHAPTER 5: A MAP IS NOT A MANIFESTO

1. That said, there are also some traps the map suggests we would do better to avoid. It would be a mistake to be *so* focused that internal variations within a methodology come to overwhelm perceptions of similarity; and it would be equally problematic if internal unity meant that other methodological corners of the field felt entirely foreign, obscuring common interests and the possibility of corroborating (or usefully complicating) ideas from other angles.

WORKS CITED

Adler-Kassner, Linda. 2018. "Looking Outward: Disciplinarity and Dialogue in Landscapes of Practice." In *Composition, Rhetoric, and Disciplinarity*, edited by Rita Malenczyk, Susan Miller-Cochran, Elizabeth Wardle, and Kathleen Yancey, 303–30. Logan: Utah State University Press.

Adler-Kassner, Linda, and Elizabeth Wardle, eds. 2015. *Naming What We Know: Threshold Concepts of Writing Studies*. 1st edition. Logan: Utah State University Press.

Adler-Kassner, Linda, and Elizabeth Wardle, eds. 2020. *(Re)Considering What We Know: Learning Thresholds in Writing, Composition, Rhetoric, and Literacy*. 1st edition. Logan: Utah State University Press.

Bannon, Jessica, Dawn Formo, Kimberly Robinson Neary, Barbara Schneider, and Mike Palmquist. 2019. "First-Year Composition Archive." https://fyca.colostate.edu.

Bazerman, Charles. 2002. "The Case for Writing Studies as a Major Discipline." In *Rhetoric and Composition as Intellectual Work*, edited by Gary A. Olson, 32–38. Carbondale and Edwardsville: Southern Illinois University Press.

Bizup, Joseph. 2008. "BEAM: A Rhetorical Vocabulary for Teaching Research-Based Writing." *Rhetoric Review* 27 (1): 72–86. https://doi.org/10.1080/07350190701738858.

Blei, David M. 2012. "Probabilistic Topic Models." *Communications of the ACM* 55 (4): 77–84.

Blei, David M., Andrew Y. Ng, and Michael I. Jordan. 2003. "Latent Dirichlet Allocation." *The Journal of Machine Learning Research* 3: 993–1022.

Bloom, Lynn Z. 2011. "The World According to North—And Beyond: The Changing Geography of Composition Studies." In *The Changing of Knowledge in Composition: Contemporary Perspectives*, edited by Lance Massey and Richard C. Gebhardt, 28–43. Logan: Utah State University Press.

Braddock, Richard, Richard Lloyd-Jones, and Lowell Schoer. 1963. *Research in Written Composition*. Champaign, Ill.: National Council of Teachers of English.

Brown, Kate. 2008. "Breaking into the Tutor's Toolbox: An Investigation into Strategies Used in Writing Center Tutorials." University of Louisville. https://ir.library.louisville.edu/etd/159.

Brown, Stuart C., Theresa Enos, David Reamer, and Jason Thompson. 2008. "Portrait of the Profession: The 2007 Survey of Doctoral Programs in Rhetoric and Composition." *Rhetoric Review* 27 (4): 331–40.

Campbell, John L., Charles Quincy, Jordan Osserman, and Ove K. Pedersen. 2013. "Coding In-Depth Semistructured Interviews: Problems of Unitization and Intercoder Reliability and Agreement." *Sociological Methods & Research* 42 (3): 294–320. https://doi.org/10.1177/0049124113500475.

Carlo, Rosanne, and Theresa Jarnagin Enos. 2011. "Back-Tracking and Forward-Gazing: Marking the Dimensions of Graduate Core Curricula in Rhetoric and Composition." *Rhetoric Review* 30 (2): 208–27. https://doi.org/10.1080/07350198.2011.552383.

Carter, Michael. 2007. "Ways of Knowing, Doing, and Writing in the Disciplines." *College Composition and Communication* 58 (3): 385–418.

Chen, Edwin. 2011. "Introduction to Latent Dirichlet Allocation." *Edwin Chen's Blog* (blog). August 22, 2011. http://blog.echen.me/2011/08/22/introduction-to-latent-dirichlet-allocation/.

https://doi.org/10.7330/9781646423224.c009

Connors, Robert J. 1983. "Composition Studies and Science." *College English* 45 (1): 1–20. https://doi.org/10.2307/376913.

Connors, Robert J. 1997. *Composition-Rhetoric: Backgrounds, Theory, and Pedagogy.* https:// digital.library.pitt.edu/islandora/object/pitt%3A31735037493909/viewer#page/12 /mode/2up.

Cook, Devan, and Darrell Fike. 2002. "Writing Wrong: The Dissertation as Dissent." In *The Dissertation & the Discipline: Reinventing Composition Studies,* edited by Nancy Welch, Catherine Latterell, Cindy Moore, and Sheila Carter-Tod, 66–78. Portsmouth, NH: Boynton/Cook, Heinemann.

Crowley, Sharon. 2003. "Composition Is Not Rhetoric." *Enculturation* 5 (1). http://encul turation.net/5_1/crowley.html.

Diesing, Paul. 1971. *Patterns of Discovery in the Social Sciences.* Reprint. Aldine Transaction.

Dobrin, Sidney I. 2011. *Postcomposition.* 1st edition. Carbondale: Southern Illinois University Press.

Douglas, Whitney, Heidi Estrem, Kelly Myers, and Dawn Shepherd. 2018. "Shared Landscapes, Contested Borders: Locating Disciplinarity in an MA Program Revision." In *Composition, Rhetoric, and Disciplinarity,* edited by Rita Malenczyk, Susan Miller-Cochran, Elizabeth Wardle, and Kathleen Yancey, 1st edition, 225–40. Logan: Utah State University Press.

"Draft Proposal, 11 September 2013: An Open Discussion of MLA Forum Structure." 2013. Accessed May 28, 2021. https://groupsdiscussion.mla.hcommons.org/draft-proposal /#psccLsddirDRCaWS.

Driscoll, Dana Lynn, and Sherry Wynn Perdue. 2012. "Theory, Lore, and More: An Analysis of RAD Research in 'The Writing Center Journal,' 1980–2009." *The Writing Center Journal* 32 (2): 11–39.

Drost, H. G. 2018. "Philentropy: Information Theory and Distance Quantification with R." *Journal of Open Source Software* 3 (26): 765.

Edgington, Anthony, and Stacy Hartlage Taylor. 2007. "Invisible Administrators: The Possibilities and Perils of Graduate Student Administration" 31: 21.

Elbow, Peter. 1990. *What Is English?* Illustrated edition. New York, NY: Urbana, Ill: Modern Language Association.

Farris, Christine, and Chris Anson. 1998. *Under Construction: Working at the Intersections of Composition Theory, Research, and Practice.* Logan: Utah State University Press.

Fleckenstein, Kristie S., Clay Spinuzzi, Rebecca J. Rickly, and Carole Clark Papper. 2008. "The Importance of Harmony: An Ecological Metaphor for Writing Research." *College Composition and Communication* 60 (2): 388–419. https://doi.org/10.2307/20457064.

Fredheim, Rolf. 2013. "Visualising Structure in Topic Models." *Quantifying Memory* (blog). November 2013. http://quantifyingmemory.blogspot.com/2013/11/visualising -structure-in-topic-models.html.

Frost, Robert. (1915) 2021. "The Road Not Taken." Reprint, Poetry Foundation. https:// www.poetryfoundation.org/poems/44272/the-road-not-taken.

Fulkerson, Richard. 1990. "Composition Theory in the Eighties: Axiological Consensus and Paradigmatic Diversity." *College Composition and Communication* 41 (4): 409–29.

Gere, Anne Ruggles. 1993. "Introduction." In *Into the Field: Sites of Composition Studies,* edited by Anne Ruggles Gere. New York: Modern Language Association of America.

Gladstein, Jill, and Brandon Fralix. n.d. "National Census of Writing." Accessed June 11, 2021. https://writingcensus.ucsd.edu/.

Goggin, Maureen. 2000. *Authoring a Discipline: Scholarly Journals and the Post–World War II Emergence of Rhetoric and Composition.* Mahwah, NJ: Lawrence Erlbaum Associates.

Goldstone, Andrew, and Ted Underwood. 2014. "The Quiet Transformations of Literary Studies: What Thirteen Thousand Scholars Could Tell Us." *New Literary History* 45 (3): 359–84. https://doi.org/10.1353/nlh.2014.0025.

Hansen, Kristine. 2011. "Are We There Yet? The Making of a Discipline in Composition." In *The Changing of Knowledge in Composition: Contemporary Perspectives*, edited by Lance Massey and Richard C. Gebhardt, 236–63. Logan, Utah: Utah State University Press.

Harris, Joseph. 1997. *A Teaching Subject: Composition since 1966.* Prentice Hall Studies in Writing and Culture. Upper Saddle River, NJ: Prentice Hall.

Haswell, Richard H. 2005. "NCTE/CCCC's Recent War on Scholarship." *Written Communication* 22 (2): 198–223. https://doi.org/10.1177/0741088305275367.

Hayes, John R., Richard E. Young, Michele L. Matchett, Maggie McCaffrey, and Cynthia Cochran, eds. 1992. *Reading Empirical Research Studies: The Rhetoric of Research.* Hillsdale, NJ: Routledge.

Haynes, Cynthia. 2003. "Rhetoric/Slash/Composition." *Enculturation* 5 (1). http://enculturation.net/5_1/haynes.html.

Hesse, Doug. 2018. "Redefining Disciplinarity in the Current Context of Higher Education." In *Composition, Rhetoric, and Disciplinarity*, edited by Rita Malenczyk, Susan Miller-Cochran, Elizabeth Wardle, and Kathleen Yancey, 287–302. Logan: Utah State University Press.

Hesse, Doug, and Peggy O'Neill. 2020. "Writing as Practiced and Studied Beyond 'Writing Studies.' " In *(Re)Considering What We Know: Learning Thresholds in Writing, Composition, Rhetoric, and Literacy*, edited by Linda Adler-Kassner and Elizabeth Wardle, 1st edition, 76–93. Logan: Utah State University Press.

Hillocks, George. 1986. *Research on Written Composition: New Directions for Teaching.* New York, NY, and Urbana, IL: National Conference on Research in English, ERIC Clearinghouse on Reading and Communication Skills, and the National Institute of Education.

hooks, bell. 1984. *Feminist Theory: From Margin to Center.* London, UNITED KINGDOM: Taylor & Francis Group. http://ebookcentral.proquest.com/lib/pitt-ebooks/detail.action?docID=1811030.

Jamieson, Sandra. 2018. "The Major in—Composition—Writing and Rhetoric: Tracking Changes in the Evolving Discipline." In *Composition, Rhetoric, and Disciplinarity*, edited by Rita Malenczyk, Susan Miller-Cochran, Elizabeth Wardle, and Kathleen Yancey, 243–66. Logan: Utah State University Press.

Jockers, Matthew. 2011. "The LDA Buffet Is Now Open: Or, Latent Dirichlet Allocation for English Majors." September 29, 2011. http://www.matthewjockers.net/2011/09/29/the-lda-buffet-is-now-open-or-latent-dirichlet-allocation-for-english-majors/.

Johanek, Cindy. 2000. *Composing Research: A Contextualist Paradigm for Rhetoric and Composition.* Logan, Utah: Utah State University Press. https://babel.hathitrust.org/cgi/pt?id=usu.39060010190998;view=1up;seq=4.

Johnson, Nathan. 2015. "Modeling Rhetorical Disciplinarity: Factor-Mapping the Digital Network." In *Rhetoric and the Digital Humanities*, edited by Jim Ridolfo and William Hart-Davidson, 96–107. Chicago and London: University of Chicago Press.

Johnson, Robert R. 2010. "Craft Knowledge: Of Disciplinarity in Writing Studies." *College Composition and Communication* 61 (4). http://search.proquest.com.ezproxy.gc.cuny.edu/docview/501718007?accountid=7287.

Juzwik, Mary M., Svjetlana Curcic, Kimberly Wolbers, Kathleen D. Moxley, Lisa M. Dimling, and Rebecca K. Shankland. 2006. "Writing into the 21st Century: An Overview of Research on Writing, 1999 to 2004." *Written Communication* 23 (4): 451–76. https://doi.org/10.1177/0741088306291619.

Kennedy, Kristen. 2008. "The Fourth Generation." *College Composition and Communication* 59 (3): 525–37.

Kent, Thomas. 2002. "Paralogic Rhetoric: An Overview." In *Rhetoric and Composition as Intellectual Work*, edited by Gary A. Olson, 143–52. Carbondale and Edwardsville: Southern Illinois University Press.

Kirsch, Gesa, and Patricia A. Sullivan, eds. 1992. *Methods and Methodology in Composition Research*. SIU Press.

Kopelson, Karen. 2008. "Sp(l)itting Images or, Back to the Future of (Rhetoric and?) Composition." *College Composition and Communication* 59 (4): 750–80.

Kynard, Carmen. 2013. *Vernacular Insurrections: Race, Black Protest, and the New Century in Composition-Literacies Studies*. Albany, UNITED STATES: State University of New York Press. http://ebookcentral.proquest.com/lib/pitt-ebooks/detail.action?docID=3408730.

Lang, Susan, and Craig Baehr. 2012. "Data Mining: A Hybrid Methodology for Complex and Dynamic Research." *College Composition and Communication* 64 (1): 172–94.

Lauer, Janice M. 1984. "Composition Studies: Dappled Discipline." *Rhetoric Review* 3 (1): 20–29.

Lauer, Janice M., and J. William Asher. 1988. *Composition Research: Empirical Designs*. 1st edition. New York: Oxford University Press.

Li, Xiaoming, and Christine Pearson Casanave. 2008. "Introduction." In *Learning the Literacy Practices of Graduate School: Insiders' Reflections on Academic Enculturation*, edited by Christine Pearson Casanave and Xiaoming Li. Ann Arbor, MI: University of Michigan Press. https://doi.org/10.3998/mpub.231189.

Licastro, Amanda, and Benjamin Miller, eds. 2021. *Composition and Big Data*. Composition, Literacy, and Culture. Pittsburgh, PA: University of Pittsburgh Press. https://upittpress.org/books/9780822946748/.

Licona, Adela C. 2005. "Third Space Sites, Subjectivities and Discourses: Reimagining the Representational Potentials of (b)Orderlands' Rhetorics." PhD diss., Iowa State University.

Liggett, Sarah, Kerri Jordan, and Steve Price. 2011. "Mapping Knowledge-Making in Writing Center Research: A Taxonomy of Methodologies." *The Writing Center Journal* 31 (2): 50–88.

Lucas, Brad E. 2002. "Histories of Research in Composition and Rhetoric: Temporal Species and the Perils of Pedagogy." Reno, NV: University of Nevada, Reno.

MacNealy, Mary Sue. 1998. *Strategies for Empirical Research in Writing*. 1st edition. Boston: Pearson.

Maechler, Martin. n.d. "Agnes Function: R Documentation." Accessed November 20, 2020a. https://www.rdocumentation.org/packages/cluster/versions/2.1.0/topics/agnes.

Maechler, Martin. n.d. "Diana Function: R Documentation." Accessed June 1, 2020b. https://www.rdocumentation.org/packages/cluster/versions/2.1.0/topics/diana.

Maechler, Martin, Peter Rousseeuw, Anja Struyf, Mia Hubert, and Kurt Hornik. 2019. *Cluster: Cluster Analysis Basics and Extensions*.

Malaterre, Christophe, Jean-François Chartier, and Davide Pulizzotto. 2019. "What Is This Thing Called Philosophy of Science? A Computational Topic-Modeling Perspective, 1934–2015." *HOPOS: The Journal of the International Society for the History of Philosophy of Science* 9 (2): 215–49. https://doi.org/10.1086/704372.

Malenczyk, Rita, Susan Miller-Cochran, Elizabeth Wardle, and Kathleen Yancey, eds. 2018. *Composition, Rhetoric, and Disciplinarity*. Logan: Utah State University Press.

Massey, Lance, and Richard C. Gebhardt, eds. 2011. *The Changing of Knowledge in Composition: Contemporary Perspectives*. Logan: Utah State University Press.

McCallum, Andrew Kachites. 2002. "MALLET: A Machine Learning for Language Toolkit."

"Members." n.d. The Consortium of Doctoral Programs in Rhetoric and Composition. Accessed June 6, 2015. http://ccccdoctoralconsortium.org/members/.

Miller, Benjamin, and Amanda Licastro. 2021. "Introduction: Reasons to Engage Composition Through Big Data." In *Composition and Big Data*, edited by Amanda Licastro and Benjamin M. Miller, 1st edition. University of Pittsburgh Press.

Miller, Susan. 2002. "Writing Studies as a Mode of Inquiry." In *Rhetoric and Composition as Intellectual Work*, edited by Gary A. Olson, 41–54. Carbondale and Edwardsville: Southern Illinois University Press.

Mimno, David. 2012. "Computational Historiography: Data Mining in a Century of Classics Journals." *Journal on Computing and Cultural Heritage (JOCCH)* 5 (1): 3.

Mimno, David. 2013. "The Details: Training and Validating Big Models on Big Data." *Journal of Digital Humanities*. April 8, 2013. http://journalofdigitalhumanities.org/2-1/the-details-by-david-mimno/.

Moore, Cindy, and Peggy Woods. 2002. "'She Herself Is the Writing,' But the Form Doesn't Fit: The Dissertation as a Site of Becoming." In *The Dissertation & the Discipline: Reinventing Composition Studies*, edited by Nancy Welch, Catherine Latterell, Cindy Moore, and Sheila Carter-Tod, 66–78. Portsmouth, NH: Boynton/Cook, Heinemann.

Mueller, Derek. 2009. "Clouds, Graphs, and Maps: Distant Reading and Disciplinary Imagination." New York: Syracuse University.

Mueller, Derek. 2012a. "Views from a Distance: A Nephological Model of the CCCC Chairs' Addresses, 1977–2011." *Kairos: A Journal of Rhetoric, Technology, and Pedagogy* 16 (2). http://kairos.technorhetoric.net/16.2/topoi/mueller/index.html.

Mueller, Derek. 2012b. "Grasping Rhetoric and Composition by Its Long Tail: What Graphs Can Tell Us about the Field's Changing Shape." *College Composition and Communication* 64 (1): 195–223.

Mueller, Derek. 2017. *Network Sense: Methods for Visualizing a Discipline*. #writing. Colorado: WAC Clearinghouse and UP of Colorado. https://wac.colostate.edu/books/network/sense.pdf.

North, Stephen. 1987. *The Making of Knowledge in Composition: Portrait of an Emerging Field*. Upper Montclair, NJ: Boynton/Cook Publishers.

North, Stephen. 1997. "The Death of Paradigm Hope, the End of Paradigm Guilt, and the Future of (Research in) Composition." In *Composition in the Twenty-First Century: Crisis and Change*, edited by Lynn Z. Bloom, Donald A. Daiker, and Edward M. White, 194–206. Carbondale: Southern Illinois University Press.

Olson, Gary A. 2002. "The Death of Composition as an Intellectual Discipline." In *Rhetoric and Composition as Intellectual Work*, edited by Gary A. Olson, 23–31. Carbondale and Edwardsville: Southern Illinois University Press.

Pääkkönen, Juho. 2021. "Data Do Not Speak for Themselves: Interpretation and Model Selection in Unsupervised Automated Text Analysis." In *Composition and Big Data*, edited by Amanda Licastro and Benjamin M. Miller, 245–61. University of Pittsburgh Press.

Peeples, Tim, and Bill Hart-Davidson. 2012. "Remapping Professional Writing: Articulating the State of the Art and Composition Studies." In *Exploring Composition Studies: Sites, Issues, Perspectives*, edited by Kelly Ritter and Paul Kei Matsuda. Logan: Utah State University Press. http://ebookcentral.proquest.com/lib/pitt-ebooks/detail.action?docID=3442891.

Peirson, B. R. Erick, Erin Bottino, Julia L. Damerow, and Manfred D. Laubichler. 2017. "Quantitative Perspectives on Fifty Years of the Journal of the History of Biology." *Journal of the History of Biology* 50 (4): 695–751. https://doi.org/10.1007/s10739-017-9499-2.

Phelps, Louise Wetherbee, and John M. Ackerman. 2010. "Making the Case for Disciplinarity in Rhetoric, Composition, and Writing Studies: The Visibility Project." *College Composition and Communication* 62 (1): 180–215.

R Core Team. n.d. *R: A Language and Environment for Statistical Computing*. Vienna, Austria: R Foundation for Statistical Computing. http://www.R-project.org/.

Ratliff, Clancy. 2013. "Initial Foray into Topic Modeling for Rhetoric and Composition." CultureCat. February 12, 2013. http://www.culturecat.net/node/1564.

Reid, Gwendolynne, and Carolyn R. Miller. 2018. "Classification and Its Discontents: Making Peace with Blurred Boundaries, Open Categories, and Diffuse Disciplines." In *Composition, Rhetoric, and Disciplinarity*, edited by Rita Malenczyk, Susan Miller-Cochran, Elizabeth Wardle, and Kathleen Yancey. Logan: Utah State University Press.

Rickly, Rebecca J. 2012. "Review Essay: Making Sense of Making Knowledge." *College Composition and Communication* 64 (1): 224–37.

Ridolfo, Jim. n.d. "Rhet Map | PhD Program Map." Rhet Map. Accessed December 4, 2019. http://rhetmap.org/doctoral/.

Ridolfo, Jim, and William Hart-Davidson, eds. 2015. *Rhetoric and the Digital Humanities*. Chicago and London: University of Chicago Press.

RStudio Team. 2019. *RStudio: Integrated Development Environment for R*. Boston, MA: RStudio, Inc. www.rstudio.com.

Sánchez, Raúl. 2018. "Moving Knowledge Forward." *College Composition and Communication* 70 (1): 111–25.

Schmidt, Benjamin M. 2013. "Words Alone: Dismantling Topic Models in the Humanities." *Journal of Digital Humanities*. April 5, 2013. http://journalofdigitalhumanities.org/2-1/words-alone-by-benjamin-m-schmidt/.

Skeffington, Jillian K. 2011. "Situating Ourselves: The Development of Doctoral Programs in Rhetoric and Composition." *Rhetoric Review* 30 (1): 54–71. https://doi.org/10.1080/07350198.2011.530114.

Smit, David. 2011. "Stephen North's *The Making of Knowledge in Composition* and the Future of Composition Studies 'Without Paradigm Hope.'" In *The Changing of Knowledge in Composition: Contemporary Perspectives*, edited by Lance Massey and Richard C. Gebhardt, 213–35. Logan: Utah State University Press.

Smit, David W. 2004. *The End of Composition Studies*. Carbondale, IL: Southern Illinois University Press.

Spellmeyer, Kurt. 2003. "Education for Irrelevance? Or, Joining Our Colleagues in Lit Crit on the Sidelines of the Information Age." In *Composition Studies in the New Millennium: Rereading the Past, Rewriting the Future*, edited by Lynn Z. Bloom, Donald A. Daiker, and Edward M. White, 78–87. Carbondale: Southern Illinois University Press.

Steinberg, Saul, and Wikipedia contributors. 2021. "View of the World from 9th Avenue." In *Wikipedia, the Free Encyclopedia*. https://en.wikipedia.org/w/index.php?title=View_of_the_World_from_9th_Avenue&oldid=1025545375.

Taylor, Todd. 2003. "A Methodology of Our Own." In *Composition Studies in the New Millennium: Rereading the Past, Rewriting the Future*, edited by Lynn Z. Bloom, Donald A. Daiker, and Edward M. White, 142–50. Carbondale: Southern Illinois University Press.

Underwood, Ted. 2012. "Topic Modeling Made Just Simple Enough." *The Stone and the Shell* (blog). April 7, 2012. http://tedunderwood.com/2012/04/07/topic-modeling-made-just-simple-enough/.

Van Manen, Max. 1989. *Researching Lived Experience: Human Science for an Action Sensitive Pedagogy*. Routledge.

Vieira, Kate, Lauren Heap, Sandra Descourtis, Jonathan Isaac, Samitha Senanayake, Brenna Swift, Chris Castillo, Ann Meejung Kim, Kassia Krzus-Shaw, Maggie Black, Olá Oládipò, Xiaopei Yang, Patricia Ratanapraphart, Nikhil M. Tiwari, Lisa Velarde, and Gordon Blaine West. 2020. "Literacy Is a Sociohistoric Phenomenon with the Potential to Liberate and Oppress." In *(Re)Considering What We Know: Learning Thresholds in Writing, Composition, Rhetoric, and Literacy*, edited by Linda Adler-Kassner and Elizabeth Wardle, 1st edition, 36–55. Logan: Utah State University Press.

Vogler Urion, Marilyn. 2002. "Writing Selves, Establishing Academic Identity." In *The Dissertation & the Discipline: Reinventing Composition Studies*, edited by Nancy Welch, Catherine Latterell, Cindy Moore, and Sheila Carter-Tod, 1–12. Portsmouth, NH: Boynton/Cook, Heinemann.

Walls, Douglas McSweeney. 2011. "The 'Human' Network." Michigan State University. https://doi.org/10.25335/M5WT59.

Wardle, Elizabeth, Linda Adler-Kassner, Jonathan Alexander, Norbert Elliot, J. W. Hammond, Mya Poe, Jacqueline Rhodes, and Anne-Marie Womack. 2020. "Recognizing the Limits of Threshold Concept Theory." In *(Re)Considering What We Know: Learning Thresholds in Writing, Composition, Rhetoric, and Literacy,* edited by Linda Adler-Kassner and Elizabeth Wardle, 94–112. Logan: Utah State University Press.

Wardle, Elizabeth, and Doug Downs. 2018. "Understanding the Nature of Disciplinarity in Terms of Composition's Values." In *Composition, Rhetoric, and Disciplinarity,* edited by Rita Malenczyk, Susan Miller-Cochran, Elizabeth Wardle, and Kathleen Yancey, 111–33. Logan: Utah State University Press.

Weingart, Scott B. 2012. "Topic Modeling for Humanists: A Guided Tour." *The Scottbot Irregular* (blog). July 25, 2012. http://www.scottbot.net/HIAL/?p=19113.

Welch, Nancy, Catherine Latterell, Cindy Moore, and Sheila Carter-Tod, eds. 2002. *Dissertation Writing and Advising in a Postmodern Age.* Portsmouth, NH: Boynton/Cook, Heinemann.

Wesch, Michael (mwesch). 2007. "InformationR/Evolution."http://www.youtube.com/watch?v=4CV05HyAbM&feature=youtubegdataplayer.

Wikipedia Contributors. 2021. "Tf–Idf." In *Wikipedia, the Free Encyclopedia.* https://en.wikipedia.org/w/index.php?title=Tf%E2%80%93idf&oldid=1023875568.

Yancey, Kathleen Blake. 2018. "Mapping the Turn to Disciplinarity: A Historical Analysis of Composition's Trajectory and Its Current Moment." In *Composition, Rhetoric, and Disciplinarity,* edited by Rita Malenczyk, Susan Miller-Cochran, Elizabeth Wardle, and Kathleen Blake Yancey, 1st edition, 15–35. Logan: Utah State University Press.

INDEX

Page numbers followed by *f* indicate figures. Page numbers followed by *t* indicate tables.